MAKING HYBRIDS WORK

Making Hybrids Work

An Institutional Framework for Blending Online and Face-to-Face Instruction in Higher Education

JOANNA N. PAULL
Lakeland Community College

JASON ALLEN SNART
College of DuPage

National Council of Teachers of English
1111 W. Kenyon Road, Urbana, Illinois 61801-1096

Staff Editor: Bonny Graham
Manuscript Editor: Josh Rosenberg
Interior Design: Jenny Jensen Greenleaf
Cover Design: Pat Mayer
Cover Image: 2nix/iStock/Thinkstock

NCTE Stock Number: 30537; eStock Number: 30544
ISBN 978-0-8141-3053-7; eISBN 978-0-8141-3054-4

©2016 by the National Council of Teachers of English.

It is the policy of NCTE in its journals and other publications to provide a
forum for the open discussion of ideas concerning the content and the teaching of English and the language arts. Publicity accorded to any particular
point of view does not imply endorsement by the Executive Committee, the
Board of Directors, or the membership at large, except in announcements
of policy, where such endorsement is clearly specified.

Every effort has been made to provide current URLs and email addresses,
but because of the rapidly changing nature of the Web, some sites and
addresses may no longer be accessible.

Library of Congress Cataloging-in-Publication Data

Names: Paull, Joanna N., author. | Snart, Jason Allen, 1973– author.
Title: Making hybrids work : an institutional framework for blending
  online and face-to-face instruction in higher education / Joanna N.
  Paull Lakeland Community College and Jason Allen Snart College of
  DuPage.
Description: Urbana, Illinois : National Council of Teachers of English,
  [2016] | Includes bibliographical references and index.
Identifiers: LCCN 2016027931 (print) | LCCN 2016045648 (ebook) |
  ISBN 9780814130537 (pbk.) | ISBN 9780814130544 (eISBN) | ISBN
  9780814130544
Subjects: LCSH: Blended learning. | Education, Higher.
Classification: LCC LB1028.5 .P328 2016 (print) | LCC LB1028.5
  (ebook) | DDC 371.39—dc23
LC record available at https://lccn.loc.gov/2016027931

CONTENTS

FOREWORD. vii
    Matthew Russell

ACKNOWLEDGMENTS xi

INTRODUCTION 1
    Big Picture—Narrow Focus 1
    Hybrid Learning—Its Lifecycle at Your Institution as Challenge
    and Opportunity. 9
    Making Hybrids Work: An Institutional Framework. 16

1 *Defining and Advertising Hybrids at Your Institution*. 25
    The Hybrid Moment. 26
    Defining Hybrids: The Why and When 27
    Do Hybrids Already Have an Institutional History? 39
    How Hybrids Are Advertised: General Marketing. 40
    How Hybrids Are Advertised: The Registration System 46
    How Hybrids Are Advertised: Course-Level Explanations 54

2 *Developing, Supporting, and Assessing Hybrids at Your*
    Institution 58
    Field and Experiential Learning: The Original Hybrid? 59
    Developing Hybrid Curricula 63
    Supporting Hybrid Curricula. 69
    Assessing Hybrid Curricula 85

3 *Training Instructors for Hybrid Courses* 101
    Finding Leaders for Professional Development. 103
    Ongoing Training: The Inhouse Workshop. 108
    Identifying Key Areas to Cover 110
    The Faculty Training Workshop Series 112
    Continuing Support/Education/Development beyond the
    Workshop. 139
    Fit Though Few? Acknowledging Workshop Participation. 142

4 *Hybrids Across the Curriculum* 150
Fundamentals of Speech Communication—
Stephen Thompson 153
Introduction to Biochemistry—William (Gary) Roby 157
Paralegal Studies: Personal Injury, Tort, and Insurance Law—
Capper Grant 162
Biomedical Terminology—Judy Vierke 166
Principles of Sociology—Traci Sullivan 168
The Writing-Intensive Hybrid 174
   English Composition 2—Joanna N. Paull 175
   Business Writing and Correspondence—Michael W. Gos. ... 180
   Technical Writing—Sara Jameson. 182
5 *Hybrids and the Question of Technology* 187
Hybrids and Mobile Learning 188
"Technology": The Everything and the Nothing 199

CONCLUSION 206
WORKS CITED 209
INDEX 219
AUTHORS 227

Foreword

Matthew Russell
University of Texas at Austin

Open education advocate David Wiley frequently employs the following metaphor to describe how universities adopt new and emerging technological modes of teaching and learning for their institutions: it is akin to driving a jet airplane on a road. Without succumbing to a technological determinism, Wiley's metaphor reveals the classic underutilization of existing technological opportunities at universities and colleges: in the early twenty-first century, we find ourselves surrounded by marvelous opportunities and yet we often fail to take advantage of what is available. Ironically, one might point to the overabundance of educational technologies as a cause for their underutilization. Faculty members at most educational institutions are well versed in the seeming panoply of technological options for teaching and learning from well-meaning and dutifully informed educational technologists and colleagues, returning energized from conferences touting new tools or strategies, and yet they frequently see these options and discussions come and go with the academic calendar. Carving time out of one's research agenda or increasingly demanding teaching loads to try out a new tool for teaching and learning can seem daunting enough; knowing that these tools might disappear or be replaced by others within a year or two makes the decision not to "innovate" an easy one.

If simply using a new technology-based teaching or learning tool seems difficult, then imagine successfully redesigning an entire course or curriculum for hybrid (or, frequently, online) delivery. More so than experimenting with the use of a tool to increase student engagement or achieve other more discrete outcomes, hybrid or online courses present an unavoidable allure: in the modern world of shrinking public funding and enrollments for many universities, the gilded promises of creating more hybrid or online courses and "green" programs are prolific and persuasive. As anyone who has toiled in the fields of instructional technology in higher education can tell you, the reported ease with which ideal, pedagogically sound hybrid or online courses may be created, taught, and supported does not always correspond with reality. In this version of the story, instructors work in online environments, piloting or employing tools that are engaging and intuitive on platforms that are widely available to the resident student and off-campus student alike; these students easily find these environments and begin creating with or using these readily available tools that require little guidance. While the Hippocratic dictum of "do no harm" frequently arises here, in that students ought to perform no worse in these courses, the promise of hybrid or online courses is that students in fact do perform better. For those eager to discover the truth of these promises, the breathless stream of "success stories" from peer institutions, delivered through webcasts, blog posts, and social media platforms, reinforces the ease of simply adopting these practices: if these universities can, so can we. Inspired, taking a deep breath, faculty decide to try their hand at creating hybrid or online courses or recasting areas of their curricula for hybrid or online, employing methods and practices that resemble those they have seen, heard about, or researched. In many instances, these faculty (or groups of faculty), wonderfully committed classroom teachers all, work with the best of intentions and deep knowledge of their institutions, only to inevitably discover hurdle after unexpected hurdle. Wiley's metaphor of the airplane reasserts itself: initiatives of this kind remain grounded, an expensive experiment that simply rolls down the highway.

This book is extraordinarily essential because it addresses the core issues related to developing and sustaining the real promises of hybrid learning. It is rather difficult to pinpoint the beginning of an acknowledged movement toward embracing the potential of hybrid (or blended) teaching, but one might reasonably suggest the late 1990s as a first wave, when pioneers such as the University of Central Florida, the City University of New York, and the University of Wisconsin-Milwaukee began exploring the ways in which a "hybrid" course (partially taught online, partially taught face-to-face) was more than the sum of its parts and could be subject to unique research as such. Collections like *Blended Learning: Research Perspectives* (Picciano and Dziuban), emerging from Sloan Consortium conference work and investigations, revealed that each and every early story of success could not exist without an underreported (if not unmentioned) tightly interwoven network of infrastructural, administrative, and technology support, one that has undergone radical change and committed to growth that is reflective and responsive to emerging needs. These networks of support have remained chronically underreported (if reported at all) given the exciting pedagogical potential of hybrid teaching (the oft-repeated phrase of the "best of both worlds") as well as the fact that most faculty still have no need to consider them in their routine teaching experiences: one walks into a classroom with an open door (carrying or having access to the class roster, as well as notes or slides for a lecture or discussion), assuming that the chairs, and students sitting in them, will be there, the lights will turn on, the computer podium tucked safely away to the side of the room will function, and the projection screen will lower if needed. The campus LMS (learning management system) is now available as well, waiting patiently in the wings for use. Some faculty have taken these kinds of courses as undergraduate or graduate students, with newer faculty often having experienced the first sustained wave of hybrid or online course offerings. Indeed, between the first *Blended Learning* collection in 2007 and its subsequent second volume in 2014 (Picciano, Dziuban, and Graham), one might theorize that a whole new crop of faculty has been taught and experienced a university community in which "hybrid" and "online" carried the kind of resonance we associate with those terms today. As digital tools and environments have increased in sophistication and availability during this time, the first wave of committed practitioners has exploded in size. Nevertheless, hybrid learning faces the same challenges: while the promises remain, universities need to reimagine and in fact change the way in which they are physically and technologically constructed internally without causing a radical break from what works. A literal reformation is required and the language of hybrid learning is the best possible one to adopt in implementing necessary infrastructural changes.

Why reform hybrid learning, then, if the online revolution promises so much more in terms of dissemination of learning and providing access for any student with a computer and desire to learn? Universities, as the authors of this book clearly understand, are highly complex, hybrid places already and valuable for their unique qualities: they are appealing places built upon time-honored traditions, where faculty conduct innovative, cutting-edge, and technologically driven research. In many ways, as well as in the most idealistic, even nostalgic sense, they are still places where the past meets the future in order to shape a present that is in itself increasingly (if not completely) hybridized.

Making hybrids work, then, means allowing faculty a greater say in how these infrastructural issues are shaped and sustained, bringing these seemingly banal issues to the fore, and giving them the support to learn even more about their institutions. This timely book emerges at a crucial moment and should act as an insightful guide for navigating and addressing issues that will help faculty and administrators shepherd not merely "the best of both worlds," but the best of their university's worlds, into a productive future.

Works Cited

Picciano, Anthony, and Charles Dziuban, eds. *Blended Learning: Research Perspectives*. Needham: Sloan Consortium, 2007. Print.

Picciano, Anthony, Charles Dziuban, and Charles Graham, eds. *Blended Learning: Research Perspectives*. Vol. 2. New York: Routledge, 2014. Print.

ACKNOWLEDGMENTS

The process of writing this book has been quite an adventure for us. The idea grew out of our many conversations with each other, our conference presentations together, and our interactions with colleagues from across the United States and Canada. We kept seeing and hearing how great hybrid learning *could* be, but for lack of a larger institutional framework for—even a basic institutional understanding of—what hybrid learning entailed and how it could best be fostered. We should also note how important our students have been in providing feedback—whether we asked for it or not—about their hybrid learning experiences. As community college teachers, we interact with upwards of a hundred students in any given term. That's a lot of learning experience we can tap into. From students we have heard how great hybrid learning can be . . . and how frustrating, if not managed well.

With all of those conversations we've had about hybrid teaching and learning with such a broad range of folks, though, the list of thanks here could be monumental. It would ideally include all the students, teachers, friends, administrators, and colleagues whose time and input have shaped our understanding of hybrid learning and how best it might be fostered as an institutional initiative with a vision toward sustainability guiding it right from the start. Indeed, our list of thanks could include the hundreds of people we've talked with and listened to about their hybrid teaching and learning experiences. For brevity's sake, though, we will acknowledge just a few folks in particular.

We'd like to offer a special thanks to our colleagues who were part of the Conference on College Composition and Communication (CCCC) Effective Practices in Online Writing Instruction (OWI) committee—including past chairs Beth Hewett, Scott Warnock, and Diane Martinez—and that committee's Expert Stakeholder Panel, who challenged us to think and rethink our approaches toward teaching writing fully online and in the hybrid format. It was with the help of this group that our idea for a book truly crystallized: a text not on singular hybrid course design but rather on how to create an institutional framework and professional development strategy to make hybrid curricula effective and sustainable. Kurt Austin, our book editor at NCTE, has also been invaluable in shaping the manuscript and shepherding it through the publication process.

We also want to thank those many instructors who participated in our survey (cited as Paull and Snart in the text) and who shared insights and screenshots of their hybrid courses with us for use in this book (in Chapter 4): in particular we thank Michael W. Gos, Capper Grant, Sara Jameson, Gary Roby, Traci Sullivan, Steve Thompson, and Judy Vierke. The insights these faculty provided into hybrid course development, structure, and pedagogical approaches have added both clarity and value to our book. We also extend a thanks to College of DuPage (COD) librarian Jason Ertz, who provided screenshots from his work as an embedded librarian and who also talked us through much of what it meant to work in that capacity in the context of online and hybrid classes.

Joanna Paull

I would like to thank all of the faculty, administrators and staff who have been there during my Quality Matters (QM) experiences, including the APPQMR and Peer Reviewer courses; the QM national conference (Beth Knapp, Bill Knapp); and my course QM certification (Nan Klenk, Corrie Bergeron, Jeanette Brossmann, and Litsa Varonis). Together, these colleagues and professionals introduced me to new perspectives about online education and the differentiation between fully online and hybrid instruction.

In addition to the QM experiences, I have also greatly valued my coursework through the Online Learning Consortium, or OLC (formerly Sloan-C) regarding blended learning that introduced me to many hybrid instructors from around the country. This interaction challenged me to rethink my work as a hybrid instructor.

I would like to thank my campus community of hybrid instructors who have become a group providing an opportunity to challenge, grow, and question our pedagogy. Our experiences over the course of my eight-week faculty training workshop allowed me to ask myself those tough questions about how to make great hybrid courses across the curriculum.

Outside of academia, I would like to thank my husband, John Whetstone, for being such a supportive presence in my life and my stepsons, Johnny and Nathan, for keeping me grounded, inspiring me to make them proud, while reminding me that there's more to life than academia. To my furry babies, Ruby and Willie, I thank you for the many long "talks" helping me think through some of the chapter content over our woodsy morning hikes. I love all of the members of my family so much.

Jason Snart

I would like to thank friends and colleagues at the College of DuPage. From formal committee work to informal hallway conversations, this large and diverse group has helped to shape the way I think about online and hybrid learning. I continue to be challenged to imagine how the blended learning mode can most productively exist within the framework of a complex, multifaceted institution like COD. At risk of leaving those who have been so supportive off of this list, I'd like to thank Steve Thompson, Capper Grant, Judy Vierke, and Gary Roby for sharing their courses and teaching practices with me. Brett Coup (associate dean of learning technology) and his team in our Learning Technology department have been supportive from start to finish, as have my colleagues in our Teaching and Learning Center: Judy Coates, Gina Wheatley, Tim Sweeney, and Allison Lanthrum.

Last but by no means least I want to thank my wife, Alison Greene, for her generous support, even during my whiniest moments—and writers working mid-book can have quite a few of those. Nor can I forget to say how much my daughter, Jenna, remains my inspiration. It was her birth that marked the writing and publication of my first book on hybrid learning. I write this as she finishes first grade, just embarking on an educational journey that is likely to include all manner of modes and technologies that she will have to teach me about. So to my wife and daughter: I love you both and thank you.

INTRODUCTION

Big Picture—Narrow Focus

Increasingly we see new, diverse delivery modes available to today's higher education student and teacher. The traditional face-to-face (f2f) model of classroom lecture persists, of course, though it may in fact be under fire now more than ever as new pedagogical approaches and new technologies make the traditional classroom-based lecture format seem staid and unexciting, a holdover from past educational eras whose realities just do not always hold true for us now as they might have before. At present, in addition to that traditional lecture format, there are many instructional settings that students might encounter as they pursue a certificate, program, or degree. Fully distance-based, online learning is a viable option at many schools, for example. Massive online courses are making headlines, though few yet award transferable academic credit and their potential long-term impact on learning has yet to be fully understood. Some institutions offer independent study courses, which might involve both face-to-face and online components. And with the increasing accessibility and usability of mobile technologies we see new learning modes emerge that seek to take advantage of handheld devices like smartphones and tablets. In short, higher education now finds itself trying to manage many different delivery modes and instructional alternatives, weighing their pros and cons, and often trying to separate opportunities for true innovation from the noise of media hype.

A concurrent and no doubt related reality across higher education is that many institutions are beginning to rethink how they award credit across what could be a wide variety of different instructional delivery settings. Today's student can, in some cases, earn a degree having participated in many different kinds of classes: some face-to-face, some online, some independent study, and some not a traditional "class" in any sense at all. The University of Wisconsin (UW) system, for example, started offering, as of Fall 2013, what they have called the "Flexible Option," whereby students earn credit by working in a combination of learning modes, tailored to the student's background and current life situation. Dubbed a "new, innovative way to make UW degree and certificate programs more accessible, convenient, and affordable," the UW Flex Option stresses adaptability and personalization to student needs ("University of Wisconsin Flex Option FAQs"). A variant of this approach, though one mandated by the school rather than chosen by the student, is the program offered by schools like the University of Florida whereby a student who might not otherwise gain full admission as an incoming first-year student is granted a sort of conditional acceptance with the offer to take classes for their first two years fully online before being admitted as a junior and then able to take classes on campus (see Chafin).

Further, author Seb Murray, in an article entitled "Growth of Blended Online and Campus MBA Learning Gathers Pace," has noted that "the blended learning revolution at business schools is gathering pace." Citing increasing competition among big-name business programs, like those at Harvard and Stanford, and schools with less immediate name recognition, Murray describes newly emerging degree models that include a blend of both online and face-to-face coursework. As of September 2015, for example, the Miami School of Business will launch a new degree option that includes primarily online coursework leading to a master's in business administration. But this online work will be bolstered by a week-long residency at the school's Miami, Florida, campus. Murray also cites Susan Cates, executive director of the online MBA offered by the University of North Carolina at Chapel Hill's Kenan-Flagler Business School, who asserts that "without question, blended learning is an essential adaptation for business schools" (qtd. in Murray). Anthony Macardi, a professor of finance and the executive director of graduate programs at the John F. Welch College of Business at Sacred Heart University in Connecticut, argues that the blended model, especially one that combines primarily online work with intense, though short, periods of face-to-face interaction "provides flexibility for professionals who want to experience our masters, but can't commit to onsite classes on a weekly basis" (qtd. in Murray).

We find this trend toward flexibility at the course level as well. What are sometimes called HyFlex hybrid courses, for example, are an increasingly popular instructional model that allows instructors to more closely tailor their courses to reflect individual student needs and abilities. Specifically, HyFlex is "a course design model that presents the components of hybrid learning (which combines face-to-face with online learning) in a flexible course structure that gives students the option of attending sessions in the classroom, participating online, or doing both." As such, "Students can change their mode of attendance weekly or by topic, according to need or preference. In this 'flexible hybrid' design, instructors provide course content for both participation modes and can tailor activities for each format" ("7 Things You Should Know about . . . the HyFlex Course Model"). A student who finds particular aspects of a course more challenging might opt to attend classroom meetings that week rather than working through the material online, particularly if that student feels that the opportunity for immediate, real-time interaction with an instructor will enhance her learning. In other variants of the HyFlex model, teachers may require classroom attendance for students who are struggling in the online environment; alternately, students may be specifically directed to online resources to support weaknesses that emerge from classroom work. Each student's experience with a HyFlex course, then, could be quite different from any other student's experience, though each is enrolled, at least nominally, in the same course and section. Such flexibility introduces significant instructional design challenges, not to mention the potential day-to-day demands it puts on teachers to tailor dynamic learning experiences for each individual student. But the idea of the HyFlex reinforces the degree to which instructional flexibility is becoming more and more a valued part of the educational experience.

In any case, both the HyFlex course design option and programmatic blended modes, like that offered as part of the UW Flex Option, provide good examples of what we see as an especially promising direction for higher education in the future, particularly as it tries to sort out various learning modes, their relation to one another, their pace of change, and their ultimate pedagogical efficacy: the hybrid. We see the hybrid as an instructional model that can preserve what educators already do well and what many students still claim to want as part of their education experience: real-time, face-to-face interaction with peers and professors. Yet hybrids also offer opportunities for real, sustainable curricular innovation in the form of online learning: this too is often expected by students, sometimes the very same students who also want to preserve at least some classroom face-time. As we will look to show in this book, hybrids are neither brand new to higher education, nor are they a reinvention of the wheel. They have the capacity to represent real curricular innovation, but they do require focused institutional attention and support if they are to flourish.

The hybrid model generally continues to gain greater public visibility. The 2013 New Media Consortium's *Horizon Report* has stated that "institutions that embrace face-to-face/online hybrid learning models have the potential to leverage the online skills learners have already developed" and that "hybrid models, when designed and implemented successfully, enable students to travel to campus for some activities, while using the network for others, taking advantage of the best of both environments" (NMC *Horizon Report* 2013 8).

The National Education Association's 2013 policy statement on digital learning for the twenty-first century asserts that "an environment that maximizes student learning will use a 'blended' and/or 'hybrid' model situated somewhere along a continuum" between what they dub the "extremes" of fully face-to-face and fully online instruction (National Education Association). In short, interest in hybrids is growing. And hybrids are now clearly attracting the attention of highly visible, and highly influential, organizations.

To be sure, though, in the present work we'll look to complicate the overly simplistic "best of both worlds" jingoism that sometimes surrounds hybrids. We will discuss, for example, how important it is for institutions to provide clear and transparent advertising about this learning mode to current and prospective students, since hybrids can all too easily become part of an institutional marketing campaign to attract students with promises of "flexibility" (and, perhaps implicitly, "ease") even when such advertising does a disservice to the hybrid instructional setting, to faculty teaching in it, and, most importantly, to students trying to learn in it. But certainly we do believe that hybrid learning stands to make a considerable impact in the world of higher education sooner rather than later. The depth of that impact will depend crucially on effective institutional planning and a sustained investment in ongoing professional development.

Additionally, though the literature on hybrid course design remains scant, relative to the coverage that curricular design and teaching in other instructional settings has received, it continues to grow, as evidenced by works like Jay Caulfield's excellent book, *How to Design and Teach a Hybrid Course*, Jason Snart's *Hybrid Learning: The Perils and Promise of Blending Online and Face-to-Face Instruction in Higher Education*, and Garrison and Vaughan's *Blended Learning in Higher Education*. Hybrid learning also receives attention in high-profile academic journals like *Teaching with Technology*, *Computers and Composition*, and the *Online Journal of Distance Learning Administration*.

What we feel is needed, and what this book looks to provide, however, is a comprehensive look at how hybrid curriculum development—including course design, teaching, and support—can ideally exist, *and become sustainable*, on the institutional level. We are less concerned with how to design one specific hybrid course than we are with taking the broad, campus-level view. In addition, we look to provide insight on how institutions might develop effective faculty training and professional development opportunities, again thinking beyond the design and delivery of a single course, and more toward how an entire department, division or, better yet, institution can position itself for success in the hybrid learning field.

This isn't to say, of course, that attention to detail at the course level is somehow secondary for educators—it isn't. The individual class is where the learning mode brings together students and teachers, so effective course design is crucial for student success. In fact, there are already relatively robust course-design resources for those interested in seeking them out. We feel that the University of Wisconsin-Milwaukee hybrid learning website provides useful guidance for those looking to design a hybrid class (University of Wisconsin-Milwaukee, "Hybrid Courses"). Worth noting is that UW-Milwaukee has developed a dedicated website focused just on hybrid learning. It is not rolled into some other site, as often happens. Simply put, there is a recognizable "home" for hybrid learning within the institutional website. One often finds hybrid learning resources buried within an online learning website or within some version of an "innovative teaching" site.

The UW-Milwaukee dedicated site is nicely designed, by which we mean primarily that it is not overwhelming. One problem of having an institutional hybrid learning page folded into some larger website, be it an online learning site or teaching with technology or just an umbrella "teaching and learning" or "professional development" site, is the sheer intimidation factor. We look for resources on hybrid course design, but what we find is everything from how to use clickers in the classroom, to when the next "how to master the gradebook" training is, to tips on effective group work in class: in other words, a hodgepodge of technology-related material, professional development material, and instructional support material.

If we are trying to encourage faculty to think about hybrid teaching as a significant project in curricular design, one potentially involving a good deal of self-reeducation, the last thing we need them to be doing is wading through tangentially related material on "innovative teaching" or the like. It may sound overly simplistic, but the prospect of developing and then teaching hybrid courses needs to be inviting, on all levels, including how support resources are presented on the Web.

The UW-Milwaukee site provides information for faculty and for students. Their course design material includes a section titled "Ten Questions to consider when redesigning a course for hybrid teaching and learning" (University of Wisconsin-Milwaukee, "Hybrid Courses"). We like that these have, at least on the surface, little to do with technology. In other words, question one is not "are you an expert at using the LMS," as though that were some necessary prerequisite for teaching a hybrid course. Instead, the questions are about teaching: student success, learning objectives, and general pedagogy. Question one asks, for example, "What do you want students to know when they have finished taking your hybrid course?" That is a great place to start. Truthfully—and this is why we think the question works well as an unintimidating invitation to think about the hybrid model— the answer should not vary much, if at all, regardless of delivery mode. So the student who takes Math 101 online, face-to-face, or in the hybrid format should, ideally, leave the class having learned the same basic skills and having met (ideally) the same course objectives . . . objectives, we should point out, having to do with math, not technology use.

The UW-Milwaukee Hybrid Learning site also advertises its inhouse faculty development workshop on hybrid teaching. (The professional development workshop is something we cover in detail later in the book.) Of particular value for this workshop is that it is offered in the hybrid mode. So, as the UW-Milwaukee website notes, the workshop "involves several face-to-face workshops interspersed and integrated with online learning activities. As a result, faculty directly experience a hybrid course as students would, and are exposed to good examples of hybrid course design and teaching practices" (University of Wisconsin-Milwaukee, "Hybrid Courses").

Another excellent professional resource, geared primarily to course-level design fundamentals, is the BlendKit workshop offered by the University of Central Florida ("Blended Learning Toolkit"). The Blended Learning Toolkit offers material for "Building Your Course" as well as model courses, design and delivery principles, along with other curricular design resources. These are openly available to any who visit the site. The University of Central Florida also offers its BlendKit material in the form of a MOOC (a massive, open, online course). The MOOC is free, unless you want your final portfolio to be evaluated so you can earn a certificate, in the form of a digital badge. (See our "Digital Badges" section in Chapter 3 for more on this.)

Yet another example of a strong hybrid learning Web presence is provided by Oregon State University's (OSU) Hybrid Initiative. Their online hybrid learning hub provides instructors with a variety of materials to enable them to begin designing and then to teach a hybrid course on their campus (Oregon State University).

One section of the website provides a video explaining their "Hybrid Initiative," a list of helpful resources about hybrid development, and the potential components of hybrid courses that will aid in student success. In another section, instructors can review some helpful templates for developing a hybrid, including an extensive list of helpful materials for instructors like planning charts, syllabus checklists, and approaches for developing a course schedule. Also provided is a set of narrated PowerPoints, videos, and course shells about effective hybrid course characteristics. Ultimately, the OSU Hybrid Initiative website is a valuable tool for instructors.

In short, there are a number of well-developed resources focused primarily on course-level specifics. We would just as soon direct interested readers to these resources than try to duplicate them here. What we are much more concerned with, though, is that for all the effort that has been devoted to curricular design support, we have noticed a glaring absence of guidance for institutions that want to develop, and sustain, a vibrant hybrid curricula. We feel that without the broader focus and institutional planning that we argue for here, even the best-designed classes are liable to exist in a vacuum within an institution. How will what works in one particular course be communicated to others teaching in the hybrid mode? And to be realistic, how will that well-designed course come into being if there is no institutional support in the form of faculty training and development in place? Furthermore, how will that great hybrid course be nurtured if there is not an institutional vision and framework there to support it? How will students even know it exists? In the end, how can an institution leverage great *individual* hybrid course design and teaching if there are no mechanisms in place to do so?

Having asserted that we'll be taking a broad, institution-level view for our work, though, we will be relatively narrowly focused on the type of "hybrid" instructional setting we will be discussing. We will not explore the HyFlex model in further detail, for example. Nor will we consider in detail blended programs that involve a mix of courses that are entirely either online or face-to-face. Our focus will be on the hybrid course, like first-year composition, for example, that combines face-to-face, onsite classroom instruction with distance-based, online learning in one unified learning experience.

So the present work takes a broad, institution-level view for making hybrids effective, though our focus remains on one fairly particular type of hybrid. And with the jingoism aside, we do see this hybrid model as a particularly promising instructional mode for the future.

Hybrid Learning—Its Lifecycle at Your Institution as Challenge and Opportunity

Truthfully, no matter how far into its lifecycle either hybrid or online instruction is at any given institution, that institution can increase the effectiveness of its hybrid curricular development and professional support by addressing some of the fundamental questions and challenges posed throughout this work.

But our sense is that most institutions in higher education have a history of online curricular development and course delivery that stretches much further back than does the history of hybrid curricular development and delivery, where such histories exist at all of course. So it is useful to consider these instructional setting lifecycles, even in general terms, because doing so can throw into sharp relief why early planning efforts—though potentially challenging—can prove so beneficial in the long run, for it is precisely this early institutional planning phase that was missing as online curricula developed at so many schools.

What the trajectory of online learning shows us, at least as it exists for many institutions today, is what we might be able to do differently, early on, so that hybrid learning develops along an alternate, and more positive, trajectory.

We recognize, though, that some institutions have neither a history of hybrid *nor* online learning. Other institutions have a history of nothing but online learning. And still others have experienced a history of online learning that *did* include an early period of concentrated, cross-institution planning and coordination, though we imagine that this is by far the minority. So the lifecycle picture we paint is, admittedly, a broad one, and not applicable to every single institution across higher education, but we think it is instructive nonetheless.

Speaking in those broad terms, many institutions might find in their own history of online learning a lack of early planning. Acknowledging the considerable resources it requires to play institutional catch-up might provide exactly the impetus that is needed to undertake the sometimes challenging task of building a framework for hybrid learning success across an institution early on. Institutions may even benefit from taking a pause in the curricular development race in order to solidify such a framework.

So the basic question of why even bother with all the planning we suggest here, and why invest the time and effort in working through the challenges we discuss, is, we think, largely answered when we look at online learning. Without early investment in planning for sustainable effectiveness, institutions are just asking for headaches down the road.

Hybrid learning, as one learning mode among others that are available in higher education, is today in a situation much like the one that online learning found itself in around the late 1990s and the early 2000s. For many institutions, online learning began when a few colleagues across a campus, maybe one or two from different departments, began investigating what it would mean to incorporate an online component into their courses. The "learning management system" in these cases often amounted to a series of Web resources that an individual professor might develop and manage for his or her own specific purposes. There was nothing to say that the platform or digital tools that one professor used would be the same as those used by any other professor.

Often, it was then these individuals who became, by default, online leaders on campus, or at the very least the so-called "technology people" in their given departments. And great teaching certainly occurred. But at least in its earliest phases at many schools, teaching with technology was not something that happened within a broad institutional framework or shared vision. It was not systematically supported. There were few, if any, resources devoted to supporting online students, beyond of course the individual teaching faculty member him- or herself. And there may have been few systems in place to enable supportive, collaborative discussion among teaching faculty across disciplines, outside of informal hallway conversations. We were struck, for example, by a comment we received in our 2014 survey on hybrid learning, in which a respondent noted that "[w]e don't have an official 'hybrid' programs [*sic*] on the books, but many of us teach courses marked "hybrid" through our registrar, meaning they meet f2f part of the time and online part of the time" (Paull and Snart). This describes what, for many institutions, marked the early phases of online teaching. And it is precisely at this somewhat scattered moment that the institution as a whole can take stock of its hybrid offerings and work to develop a plan moving forward.

But from early, often fragmented, beginnings in online teaching, things changed. Teaching with technology, as a practice undertaken by a few faculty distributed randomly across a campus, began to coalesce into "online learning," which was teaching with technology but with wider institutional visibility (though not necessarily institutional support). A 2011 Sloan-C (now called the Online Learning Consortium) publication notes that over its years of producing reports on online learning, from 2002 to the present, the number of chief academic officers who identify online learning as a key component of institutional long-range planning has grown steadily. In fact, only about 10 percent of institutions report that online learning is *not* now critical to long-term strategy: and this 10 percent is an all-time low (Allen and Seaman 4). The increasing degree to which online learning figures into institutional planning suggests how it *now* enjoys significant visibility at the institutional level on many campuses, despite what might have been relatively humble and unorganized beginnings.

What evolved from those early, individual, largely faculty-driven efforts with technology, broadly speaking, may have looked different at various institutions, of course, but the general shape of online learning as it has developed as a force in higher education is relatively uniform. As institutions realized that offering courses online was important for students but also a significant piece of their financial, or strategic, planning, they raced to offer as many courses as they could in hopes of garnering market share before new competitors appeared on the scene. Operating on the first-mover principle, many institutions looked to capture at least part of the online-education market not necessarily by being one of the *best* in the field but by being one of the first.

Thus, from what might have been relatively humble, even casual, beginnings, we've seen a boom in online education: more courses, taught by more faculty, both full- and part-time, offered in more variable formats, all under the auspices of serving students by providing diverse course offerings, but lost in that framing can be other imperatives that connect online course enrollment and delivery just with an institution's financial situation.

What many institutions face today is an online curriculum that is not particularly well monitored or managed, or at least that did not emerge from an early phase of concerted institutional planning and preparation. So now, at any given institution that features a significant online curriculum, there are probably some good online courses but often far more that are not up to current standards and thus serving neither students nor faculty very well. There are probably also good online teachers, though often there are few established venues for them to collaborate and to share successes and challenges related specifically to their work online. Instructional design and teaching evaluations for online courses may also be ineffective and, where the two are not separated, unable to distinguish between problems of design and problems of instruction.

Further, various online teachers may have vastly different professional training and, in fact, very different ideas about what an online course should be and how it should be taught. Administrators now tasked with managing online programs and professional support systems may have little to no experience actually designing, teaching, or taking online courses. And faculty and administrators may have decidedly different ideas about how best to serve students using the online platform.

Certainly not *all* of these problems exist at every institution of higher education. But our experience leads us to believe that many of these problems can be found, sometimes in fairly acute form, at schools that have some of their curriculum online. Among the various issues related to online learning that confront institutions, evaluation seems to be a particularly sticky problem. Some schools still use course and instructor evaluation tools that were designed for the traditional, f2f classroom teaching and learning situation. One instructor has even commented to us, off the record: "Essentially, my institution scans the [student survey] forms into an electronic form and the questions are identical to the f2f sections of the course. It's bizarre" (Anonymous, email correspondence). We have heard of cases of online students being asked to answer course evaluation questions about an online instructor's "punctuality." Or online students are asked about instructor availability both "inside" and "outside" of class.

One notable result of lax planning efforts to support online curricular growth are the poor success, retention, and completion rates for online learning, which are cited with great regularity, particularly by those who are skeptical of online learning to begin with. One study from the Community College Research Consortium at Columbia University notes that "students who took a given course online had estimated withdrawal rates that were 10 to 15 percentage points higher than students who took the course face-to-face" (Xu and Jaggars).

And summarizing findings from studies that tracked tens of thousands of students from the Virginia and Washington State community college systems, Jaggars writes that "regardless of academic subject or course, demographics, or academic background, the same student performs more poorly in a fully-online course than in a face-to-face course" (Jaggars).

Of course, relatively lower success or retention rates for online courses are not singularly the product of poor institutional planning early in the development of an online curriculum. And we should also pause here to note that the problem of student retention and success in the online format is complicated. Poor student success is not necessarily the result of problems with a particular course or teacher, per se. Often, poor student success has as much to do with why students opt for the online setting to begin with. How often, for example, does the student who would never consider taking a particular course in the f2f mode, because he or she does not have time to devote to it, choose the online setting rather than not take the class at all? As many educators know, this is a withdrawal or failure just waiting to happen, and obviously skews the online success numbers in a negative direction, seemingly regardless of what we might do once that student is in a course.

So we cannot control student decision making, even bad decision making, in any absolute sense. And yet this situation is maybe not so far removed from the problem of institutional planning, even though it seems rather student-specific. For example, what effect would better academic advising, or even mandatory learner preparedness certification make in this case? What if a student who planned to take an online course, even though he or she has no time in the day (or night) to devote to coursework, had to consult with an academic advisor as part of the registration process? Or what if some kind of online learning orientation were required that made it abundantly clear to this student that learning online would be at least as much work, if not more, as taking the class face-to-face? What if there were robust *online* support systems available that included academic tutoring?

Maybe none of this keeps the student from registering and subsequently doing poorly. But such resources might increase the likelihood that a student makes informed, and thus beneficial, decisions about what classes to take and when. And even when student registration decisions are not the best, good student support can help that student succeed postregistration. Neither a student-centered registration system nor robust student support systems emerge out of nothing, of course. When they are in place, and effective, they have likely emerged from a concerted institutional effort to develop and implement them. Thus institutional planning might have a considerable impact on student success, even in cases where an individual instructor has done everything in his or her power to support student learning online and to construct an engaging, vibrant course.

But untangling the problem of online retention is not really the point at issue. In fact, what we want to note is precisely how hard it seems to be to address the apparent success-gap between online and f2f courses. There are so many variables at work that the problem often seems intractable.

Regardless, a significant contributing factor is online learning's institutional history, assuming that that history mirrors what is described above: some early years of little or no broad institutional vision, followed by boom years where administrative desires to have everything online yesterday propelled both teachers and teaching online with little or no professional oversight, training, or continuing development, and now a present of trying to get the horses back in the barn.

This is *not* the future we would like to see for hybrid learning.

What we are arguing, in fact, is that the hybrid mode seems particularly promising precisely because of its relatively youthful existence in higher education. We may even be seeing growth in online learning finally plateau (see Parry). Such a plateau may open the door for interest in other delivery formats. To put it even more bluntly, maybe now is the right time for institutional resources to be directed at a variety of learning formats where previously it seems that at most institutions online curriculum development always received the lion's share of money and attention.

Institutions that find themselves in the early stages of designing and offering hybrid classes, while challenged to create a shared institutional framework, might nonetheless be ideally situated to implement effective principles and practices since they are not expending valuable energy trying to corral an existing curriculum back into some system of professional oversight. Nor are they trying to retrofit courses with effective instructional and pedagogical practices that otherwise emerged from a series of curriculum-building years that featured little quality control.

Thinking about hybrid learning now, in its relatively early history as a learning mode across most of higher education, is especially important because it is at this point that schools need to begin working toward a shared institutional vision for what hybrid learning can and will be. If there is something that is missing in the history of online learning, as it exists for so many institutions today, it is an early phase of institutional planning. Not just financial or strategic planning . . . but pedagogic planning.

Such planning can be challenging and often resource intensive. But the investment is well worth the effort. This book provides strategies for institutional planning so that hybrid teaching and learning can be both effective and sustainable, and so that challenges read, at least in part, as opportunities for successful long-term curricular growth and student success.

Making Hybrids Work: An Institutional Framework

What should institutions be thinking about, and have in place, in order to increase the likely effectiveness of hybrid curricular offerings?

There are a number of answers to this question, but as we will see, most aspects of creating a solid institutional framework for successful hybrid curriculum development and delivery are interlinked. And often the development of such a framework will be challenging. This might be why too many institutions focus too heavily on getting courses up and running and available in the registration system—in whatever format—quickly, rather than laying the necessary groundwork to truly support new curricular design. Indeed our book title, *Making Hybrids Work*, is meant to suggest the more obvious sense of making hybrids effective, but also the less obvious sense of the work it takes to make those hybrids effective. Our goal is to try to suggest a plan for hybrid curricular development, but not to suggest that there is an "Easy" button to make it all happen.

As is often the case, though, with challenge comes opportunity. The fundamental opportunity that higher education institutions can capitalize on by undertaking the sometimes complicated work of establishing a sound institutional framework to support curricular development is sustainability. Yes, it is possible through various short-term incentives and institutional initiatives to create buzz around hybrid teaching and even to coax a few faculty into trying the hybrid mode out. Students might be enticed with public marketing about a "new" and "flexible" learning format. But that short-term thinking, though it could produce a good hybrid course or two and boost enrollment for a semester, will not produce an institutional framework capable of sustaining ongoing professional and curricular development. Nor will short-term efforts likely produce long-term student success or instructor satisfaction. To be sure, generating a little short-term buzz, maybe couched in the generic language of "innovation," is relatively easy: hire a guest speaker to address faculty, sponsor a workshop presented by an outside agency, post shiny fliers around campus or mount a few Web banners . . . these kinds of strategies can work to garner attention. But what, in the long run, has an institution really accomplished?

We are much more interested in having institutions create a strong framework for sustainability. This can be more challenging, but ultimately more rewarding, than short-term focus on getting more hybrid courses on the books and more students in the seats as fast as possible.

We should pause here to note just how commonsensical it may seem on the one hand to develop a framework for sustained success as a necessary precursor to relatively simple curricular growth. And yet many administrators, instructors, and support staff probably know from firsthand experience just how much pressure can be felt to "grow enrollment" or "diversify learning modes." Such mandates, formal or informal, are generally about capturing market share: how to get more students, or customers, through the physical or virtual campus doorways. Indeed, some of us know what it is like to receive enrollment reports, segmented by division or academic area across a college, and see enrollment growth (or decline) conspicuously color coded: green if enrollment is up and red if enrollment is down. Color coded for easy visual navigation? Probably not. Rather, color coded to denote that growth is good, decline requires a warning. Figure 1 shows the "Legend" that accompanied what used to be called enrollment "Scorecards" at Jason Snart's home institution.

Our grayscale image is a little less ominous than the scorecard itself, which circulated in full color. The shaded area, at the far right, which indicates enrollment decline, would appear in red when the scorecards were distributed among faculty and administration.

FTE stands for full-time equivalent (e.g., two part-time student course loads might combine to count as a single "full-time

Legend				
Number FTES Change				
≥10 FTES	4 to 9 FTES	3 to -3 FTES	-4 to -9 FTES	≤ -10 FTES
Percent FTES Change				
≥ 30%	10% to 29%	9% to -9%	-10% to -29%	≤ -30%

FIGURE 1. *A sample enrollment "scorecard."*

equivalent"). The way in which these enrollment reports were color coded was problematic enough, for many, but to even refer to them as a "scorecard" seemed fundamentally the wrong kind of analogy. It implied that each academic area was in contest with all others. And further, there were implied connotations behind a good versus a bad "score." The report was segmented by academic area and thus the message seemed all too clear when your area ended up in the cautionary amber, or worse, the emergency red, end of the "scoring" spectrum. (These scorecards are no longer circulated, by the way.)

So sure, it is easy enough to agree *in theory* that we sometimes need to put the brakes on enrollment or curricular growth, but in the everyday practice of teaching and learning, and via the often not-so-subtle cues we receive about the importance of continued growth, such clear thinking does not always produce concurrent practical institutional action.

One argument we'd like to make, and that might enable productive conversations at your institution, involves scalability. This is the framework that will often appeal to those whose job it is to actively grow enrollment and thus who are motivated to always get bigger as a way of getting better.

Scalability means that what is effective in one or two courses can be replicated across many courses. We are not arguing, of course, for strict design or instructional uniformity. Any good teacher knows that uniformity is not what produces good learning. We are suggesting rather that time invested in laying a strong foundation for building hybrid curricula, while it may slow the process of "growth" in the near future, stands to benefit an institution many times over in the long run. What long-range vision produces will, we hope, include consistently well-trained and motivated faculty who are developing quality courses that engage students and that produce meaningful, deep learning. We also know that what informs students' decisions about what classes, teachers, and delivery modes to take is word of mouth. No, this is not the only factor in students' planning decisions, but it is, in our experience, often overlooked, sometimes inadvertently though sometimes not. A few hybrid courses, designed in a rush to meet so-called demand, are less likely to provide a good experience to the students who enroll than might courses designed within a well-planned and thoughtful institutional framework. Whatever the case, though, that student experience will be communicated to friends and peers, either directly in person or via word of digital mouth (think here postings on social media and sites like ratemy-professor.com). Whatever brief enrollment growth blip that those hastily created hybrid courses enabled is unlikely to be duplicated if the experience was not good for faculty or for students.

Our suggestion is that in cases where significant institutional energy is devoted to "growth"—i.e., enrollment must be up each and every semester—even the best-intentioned arguments to slow down might not be very productive. The resulting "conversation" may be all too familiar to faculty and administrators alike: two sides seeming to speak a completely different language. We are suggesting that rather than eschewing the idea of growth entirely, we might find common ground by taking the longer view. Slowing down in the short term will produce sustainable growth in the long term. That might be a conversation that actually gets us somewhere.

Also, when it comes to thinking deeply and broadly across an institution about how to build and support a hybrid curriculum, we can not always provide single answers that will suit all learning situations. In fact, though we make the attempt to direct attention in specific ways throughout this work, we are ultimately not interested in being overly prescriptive, at least not when it comes to the true nuts and bolts of hybrid teaching. On the contrary, we feel that institutions will, by and large, have to think about how to support hybrid curriculum development and enable sustainable faculty engagement, collaboration, and communication in ways that make sense *for that institution*. We lay out a possible development roadmap in the next section, for example, but the specifics will have to emerge from individual campus realities.

Furthermore, in order that teaching remain focused on pedagogy, and not technology, we believe that teaching faculty will be best positioned to make individual choices about what might work, and what might not work, in their hybrid courses. Rarely will a one-size-fits-all approach produce effective results since institutions can be so different, and even those that share characteristics in common may have different visions for how hybrid learning will fit into a long-range plan.

We truly believe, however, that successful hybrid course design and teaching need to happen in the context of a shared institutional vision for what hybrid learning is, who needs to be involved, its goals, and how it will be administered on campus. This overarching assertion applies to all kinds of institutional situations.

An Institutional Roadmap

The following relatively simple visual flowchart represents what a process for sustainable institutional change might look like, as opposed to change that unfolds haphazardly and is as likely as not to lose momentum before ever becoming a recognized feature of the college or university.

We have modified Figure 2 from presentation materials developed by Una Daly and Kate Hess. Daly is the director of curriculum design and college outreach for the Open Education Consortium, an international community of organizations and institutions that promotes open education, including the adoption of open educational resources (like free, open textbooks, for example). Hess is library coordinator and a faculty member at Kirkwood College, a two-year college in Iowa. Their work does not address hybrid or blended learning directly, but in their efforts to champion the adoption of open educational resources by various institutions— institutions often hesitant about, and even resistant to, potentially disruptive instructional tools—they have ample experience thinking about major institutional change.

As such, the roadmap they offer, which represents a process for facilitating large-scale change, seems equally well suited to our purposes here. We have adapted their materials, but the fundamental idea remains: to facilitate what can be a challenging, even seemingly overwhelming process, by mapping out discrete steps that involve intentional planning and implementation phases, with an iterative phase of review and assessment.

We like this basic roadmap for a number of reasons. First, as Figure 2 shows, we start with an initial phase of needs assessment. We like this question of need in particular because it encourages

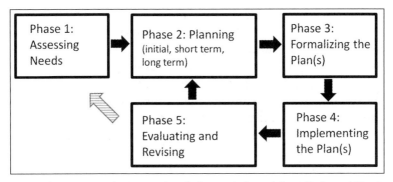

FIGURE 2. *A process for institutional change (adapted from Daly and Hess).*

an institution to take one step backwards, rather than rushing to move forward, by asking whether change is really needed at all. Or, to put it more productively, what problems are we looking to solve, what systems are we looking to improve, what are we looking to do better, by undertaking institutional change? We like starting from a place that does not just presuppose that institutional change is always, de facto, a good or necessary thing. Is change motivated by identifiable needs, as this initial needs assessment phase might indicate, or is change motivated by some perceived need to keep up with the academic Joneses? It is during this phase that we'd like to see concerted efforts at fact-finding from a broad range of constituents, be they faculty, administration, students, support staff, the community at large . . . whatever makes sense for your particular institutional situation.

We hope that an initial phase of assessing institutional needs will in fact streamline later phases, which will reflect exactly how and why developing hybrid curricula makes institutional sense. We are also convinced that early needs assessments help to ground potentially disruptive institutional change in a meaningful framework. Big change does not have to seem to some like yet another round of pouring institutional resources into the next great overhyped panacea for higher education, whatever flavor of the month that happens to be. Institutional effort, which is always of course really people hours of work, will ideally make sense when it is framed as responding to an identified need, a real problem to be addressed.

The planning phase, Phase 2 in the figure, is potentially the messiest. But hopefully the good kind of messy. Not combative messy, but brainstorming messy. Many ideas, not necessarily fleshed out. Many questions, not necessarily answered yet. A good Phase 2 will be hard to manage, but that is intentionally so. We like an identifiable phase of generating ideas before trying to formalize plans (which will come next).

Phase 2 could also involve a lot of different individuals and groups on campus, each with different imperatives, preconceptions, and constraints. Phase 2 will probably involve the formation of at least one, though likely more than one, committee charged with taking what came of needs assessment efforts and asking more questions, brainstorming strategies, and exploring what impact developing hybrid curricula might have across the college.

Phase 2 will morph into Phase 3 at some point, as committees and working groups begin to formalize ideas from early brainstorming efforts into actionable next steps. Both Phases 2 and 3 are valuable since part of what they do, even if only as a byproduct of their primary purposes, is to encourage institutional buy-in to the idea of curricular change. This is not to suggest that in developing hybrid courses that are well represented and supported by the institution at large each and every faculty member must be pressed to teach in the blended format. We would never advocate for that. But if hybrids are to become a recognized and valued piece of your institution, even those not interested in actually designing or teaching them should understand why resources are being invested in curricular change. Buy-in does not mean that everybody now does the new thing. It simply means that everybody is given the chance to have their input heard.

In fact, an important part of the early phases of institutional change is to reassure those who are *not* a direct part of that process that their work is not now somehow marginalized or obsolete. Investing in the development of hybrid learning within an institutional framework should not be perceived as a zero sum game: that is, if hybrid learning gains institutional importance, then traditional classroom teaching loses institutional importance. An inclusive Phase 2 and 3 should help to mitigate this mistaken perception.

We then find ourselves where the rubber meets the road: Phase 4—Implementation. With early planning phases having outlined clear needs and strategies to address those needs, it is time to task groups and individuals—probably far fewer than were involved in previous phases—with enacting change. This may start with professional development (a topic we cover at length later in this book). Implementation will also include marketing efforts to publicize hybrid learning within the college community and beyond, especially once well-designed courses and well-trained faculty are ready to go. Phase 4 will probably also involve an aspect of institutional change we address in greater detail below: finding your campus champions. Again, this group will include far fewer numbers than might have been asked to provide input during early planning phases. To make implementation actually happen, those with the energy and enthusiasm for hybrid learning will need to be given the opportunity to enact change. Undoubtedly, administrators with institutional leverage will have to use it. All previous planning phases have led to this moment, though, so when change happens it need not appear arbitrary, opaque, or autocratic.

Especially if institutional change is likely to be disruptive on your campus, it will be important to follow implementation closely with what Phase 5 involves: evaluation and revision. This will provide the kind of transparency that sustainable institutional change needs. Phase 5 will give stakeholders the opportunity to assess what effects change has had, both positive and negative, and will mark the chance to revise plans.

We particularly like how the flowchart brings us back to a needs assessment phase, since needs can easily change from one semester or year to another, and it will be important for an institution to revisit not just *how* it is working to develop and support hybrid learning but also, perhaps most fundamentally, *why*. We do not take this question as a foregone conclusion, though it is certainly our contention that the hybrid format has much to offer.

CHAPTER ONE

Defining and Advertising Hybrids at Your Institution

We start with the basic issue of how to define a "hybrid" course for a couple of reasons. First, it is probably one of the most important, and earliest, decisions that an institution will want to make as it creates a framework for effective and sustainable hybrid curricula. Decisions about what exactly a hybrid is will affect everything from marketing, to how hybrids are presented in a campus registration system, to individual course design. Decisions about defining hybrids will also require input early on from a diversity of constituent groups, from faculty, to administration, to IT support, to student advising.

However, despite how important it is to craft an institutionally agreed upon definition for the term *hybrid,* it seems to be one of the most commonly overlooked aspects of the process. Too many institutions have, at best, a perfunctory understanding of what the term *hybrid* means. In fact, in some cases we see contractual language about hybrids that does not align with descriptions on institutional webpages or in registration systems. And ask faculty and administrators across an institution what a "hybrid" course is and you are likely to get varying, maybe even contradictory, responses. At their peril, institutions stop thinking about what a hybrid course is after just the basic "it combines face-to-face and online learning." There should be much more to an institutional definition than this, at least if an institution is serious about supporting good hybrid curricular design and about enabling student and teacher satisfaction for those taking and teaching hybrid classes.

The Hybrid Moment

As an institution thinks about the term *hybrid* and what it will mean for those involved in designing, delivering, and supporting curricula, it might also reflect on how the word *hybrid* already has a visible cultural existence beyond the walls of academe. Keep in mind the kind of baggage—good and bad—that the term *hybrid* might carry with it. We are consistently amazed at how, historically and culturally as we make our way through the second decade of the twenty-first century, we seem to be living in a hybrid moment (see Snart, *Hybrid Learning: The Perils and Promise of Blending Online and Face-to-Face Instruction in Higher Education*, Chapter 4). The *hybrid moment* is our term to recognize the popular visibility and discursive flexibility that all things "hybrid" seem to have. There are hybrid cars, of course, which are becoming more and more common. But you can also find hybrid shoes (Keen Footwear). There are hybrid data storage solutions, like that offered by Nirvanix, which, so they claim, "combines the scalability, ease-of-management and compelling economics of the public cloud with the security and control of private cloud storage" ("Oracle and Nirvanix"). Then you could always give hybrid sushi a try, a product from AFC Franchise Corporation that claims to be "our newest concept. It features traditional recipes with a modern twist!" (AFC Franchise Corporation).

The term *hybrid* is attached to each of these products perhaps to describe their mixed-ness on some literal level, but of course the term is primarily used as a selling point to communicate positive valuation. And it is the positive connotation suggested by the term *hybrid* that is becoming more and more prevalent in popular culture. The word *hybrid* is like the word *natural*: it connotes a whole range of ideas, but almost without exception, the idea of hybridity is meant to suggest a best-of-both-worlds scenario. In many ways hybridity is becoming a modern re-inscription, and reversal, of long held cultural biases toward purity.

The seeming ubiquity of "the hybrid" as a cultural phenomenon may in fact contribute to the idea of hybridity becoming commonplace in education as well. Indeed, the positive baggage attached to hybridity as we encounter it in the form of hybrid cars (and sushi) may accompany it into the world of education. In other words, the idea of a "hybrid" course may be an easier sell if the target audience is already primed with notions of what hybridity means and what the term is meant to connote. In any case, even those unfamiliar with the term *hybrid* as it applies narrowly to one kind of instructional model in higher education may already have ideas about what a "hybrid" is and should do more generally speaking. Which brings us to our first important question.

Defining Hybrids: The Why and When

What we are looking for as we consider definitions for hybrid learning, in both broad and narrow terms, is a place to start building hybrid course offerings that are united by shared pedagogical goals and that are also supported by an institutional framework that will include professional development and support, not to mention opportunities for faculty communication and collaboration across disciplines.

In some cases, institutional stakeholders—from support staff, to faculty, to administration—might already have what they feel are common sense assumptions about hybrids. But those assumptions will not necessarily be shared by all involved. What is common sense from one perspective will not be so from another. Nor will these common sense assumptions hold up if, or when, faculty get more and more creative about how they want to design and deliver hybrid courses.

It will be the job of an institution as a whole, through committees or working groups devoted to developing effective hybrid learning (per our roadmap shown earlier), to arrive at a shared definition of what constitutes a "hybrid" class. Whatever that definition becomes, it needs to be clear but flexible. This might seem like a tricky mix, but we will try to suggest some guidelines.

First, clarity: a good definition should identify a minimum and maximum for how online and f2f learning time can be apportioned, as in "a hybrid course includes at least 50 percent face-to-face instruction," or something along those lines. Of course, if the definition is too narrow, you are likely to run into immediate scheduling problems. Take this example: "A hybrid course combines 50 percent face-to-face instruction with 50 percent online instruction." This is compact and seems clear, but what about a Monday/Wednesday/Friday course that drops the Friday meeting for online work? It is hard to take those thirds and divide them in half. Would the Wednesday class just meet for twenty-five minutes? It can be done, of course, but probably at the expense of good pedagogy.

Definitions of hybrid courses commonly include from 50 to 70 percent seat-time, though one respondent to an online survey we conducted asking faculty and administrators about their experience with hybrid courses indicated that their hybrids could have anywhere between 50 percent and 80 percent of their coursework online.

Institutions should decide on the specifics, but a clear range should be established—thus the flexible part of an ideal, clear institutional definition. The range should not be so wide that it allows for a course that is almost entirely face-to-face, with just a small fraction of the course online. This will likely feel to students like an entirely face-to-face course with a couple of ancillary online activities. The online work is likely to occur so infrequently that it may become challenging for students to remember not to come to class. Further, such an imbalance between the online and face-to-face instructional settings is unlikely to take advantage of the true integration of learning modes that characterizes the best hybrid courses.

A course that meets almost entirely online, with only a few face-to-face meeting opportunities throughout a term, is likely to present challenges for students as well. Those face-to-face meetings might feel randomly distributed and thus come as a surprise for students (who then forget to show up). Such a course is likely to attract the student who needs the flexibility of the online instructional setting and who is thus unable, or uninterested, in showing up on campus just a few times over the course of a semester.

Certainly courses that feature just a few face-to-face meetings throughout a term, or courses that involve some limited level of online work can be effective. But they should not be advertised as "hybrid." When the split between the learning modes is too heavily weighted in favor of one instructional setting over another, students will invariably feel that the work in one setting—the one that is featured in a course—is more important than work in the other instructional setting. Ideally, in the hybrid situation, students need to feel that each instructional setting is equally important, that the multiple learning modes are truly integrated, and ultimately that they are participating in one, unified course.

Also, if the definition is left too open-ended then you may end up with courses that share very little in common in terms of how they manage learning time, though they are all grouped together as "hybrid." So if a "hybrid" is any course that retains at least 50 percent seat-time, you could have one class that meets 50 percent of the time online and another that only meets online occasionally, maybe once or twice a semester. We do not believe that there is a perfect range for what defines a hybrid course; that decision should be made locally, taking into account the particulars of a campus and its learning community. What matters is that serious time is invested in making these institution-specific decisions and that the arrived-at definition be shared among all stakeholders. Equally important is that the local rationale for why a definition of what constitutes a hybrid exists the way it does be transparent.

At risk of being overly prescriptive, we offer the suggestion that there be a set of different types of hybrid models that instructors could choose to work in. But each of the options would have very clear guidelines about how learning time is apportioned. So an institution could preserve some degree of choice for those teaching hybrids, but students could know that a certain kind of hybrid will always have a set amount of face-to-face and online learning time. Each hybrid option could balance instructional time differently: an option A might meet 75 percent online; option B might balance instructional time 50-50; and option C might meet 75 percent face-to-face. Again, such a system would preserve at least some degree of flexibility, while not being so open ended as to result in courses, all called "hybrids," that actually work very differently.

Furthermore, institutions will want to think carefully, and come to decisions about not just how instructional time is divided in a hybrid, but about how instructional time in a particular setting, either online or face-to-face, can be chunked. How much of just one instructional setting can occur before a shift to the other instructional setting happens?

Consider that even the most straightforward assumptions about how time will be divided in the hybrid format can quickly lead to challenging complications. Take this example: an English class that would, in the fully classroom-based model, meet on Tuesdays and Thursdays, meets instead, in its hybrid format, face-to-face on Tuesday but not Thursday. In place of the Thursday meeting, there is a weekly online learning component. So the time is split between online and f2f 50-50. Seems tidy enough. Let us further assume that the 50 percent split is contractually mandated, so the faculty member in this hypothetical example is conforming to the letter and to the spirit of the law.

But after a few semesters of having taught her hybrid by dividing time on a weekly basis, our faculty member begins to wonder if her students would not be better served by a different arrangement of instructional time. Maybe she has noticed that in dividing her class time on a weekly basis, some students lose connection with in-depth class projects, like research essays or individual portfolios that require extended time to develop. Class meetings seem actually to be pulling students away from their work, not directing them toward it. In short, it is clear that what the students need is not more seat-time in the classroom, but rather more individualized, or flexible time to focus on their particular projects.

So this instructor considers sound pedagogy for her discipline related to supporting students in their learning and decides to meet f2f with students for a series of weeks: one, two, maybe three or four. This extended period of classroom instruction might include a combination of lecture, discussion, group work, and the like. Regardless of what is happening in the classroom, the instructional time for an extended period is fully face-to-face. Maybe this helps to alleviate the problem that some instructors in the hybrid mode experience: in meeting just once every week, students do not get immersed in the material as they need to be. Instead, each weekly meeting feels dominated by review. Students are not so easily able to see a bigger picture that an instructor is trying to present.

Back to our example: after a few weeks of meeting entirely f2f, students are at a point when they would benefit, not from more seat-time in a room together for fifty or seventy-five minutes, but from the affordances provided by the online setting: time for reflection, time to review material, freedom to pursue individual research, and the flexibility to develop their own projects, whatever those might be. Students can collaborate together in small groups, managing their time based on the group's needs. Further, it is during this phase of a hybrid course that adaptive learning might be most beneficial, since adaptive learning systems can respond to individual student needs by tailoring content to each unique learner's situation. Regardless of exactly what activities students are engaged in, learning moves online for an extended period. Once the semester is over, students will have divided their time evenly between face-to-face and online learning, but this division will not have occurred on a weekly basis. Note that our imagined instructor has maintained the prescribed 50 percent face-to-face/online split time by balancing extended periods of classroom instructional time with extended periods of online instructional time. She still adheres to the letter of the contractual law, but how many of her colleagues, or her administrative supervisors, might now feel she is testing the spirit of that contractual law?

Needless to say, creative management of learning time in the hybrid format should always be supported by sound pedagogical practice. Teachers, as experts in their disciplines, will be best able to assess how learning time can be most effectively managed.

But we imagine that many stakeholders across an institution, maybe those outside of specific teaching disciplines, will understand that a 50 percent hybrid split means de facto that instructional time will be split weekly. This will likely be "common sense" for many on the administrative side of things. Even administrators who are in support of creative division of time may feel stymied by scheduling systems that do not allow for much flexibility. Precious classroom space may seem to sit unused while a class goes online, for example, and that can be a challenging situation to explain, depending on one's position in the administrative hierarchy at a college.

Some instructors may even have the sense that administrators, and fellow faculty members who are skeptical of anything but traditional classroom learning, perceive online teaching to be somehow easier than f2f teaching. As such, any efforts to divide instructional time in the hybrid format on something other than a weekly basis could be misunderstood. In the worst case, it might look to an outsider like the faculty member is trying to produce an easier teaching schedule, rather than tailoring instruction in ways that actually make sense for students. We firmly believe that where misperceptions of this kind occur, and ultimately where mistrust is the modus operandi for faculty-administrator relations, very little in the way of creative pedagogy will occur, even at a time in higher education when it should be most valued and welcomed.

Furthermore, open discussion about basic issues of how the hybrid format will be defined at the institutional level, where that definition is both clear but flexible, will be invaluable in getting support staff, faculty, and administrators on the same page and speaking the same language with each other. In fact, the development of creative hybrid instructional opportunities for students that can truly be leveraged at the institutional level might fundamentally depend on defining the term "hybrid" and its application to the curriculum.

So let us return to our hypothetical instructor. After a few semesters teaching a particular course in the hybrid format, she decides to divide the instructional time in a new way: her class will meet face-to-face every Tuesday and Thursday for the first half of a semester. The final half of the semester, they will move entirely online.

That is about as far removed from a weekly division of learning time as you can get. What might happen at your institution for this faculty member, or the administrator to whom she reports and who will thus need to support her instructional decision up the administrative chain? Will the decision to spend the first eight weeks of the sixteen-week semester fully face-to-face and then the last eight weeks online fly? If not, why not? Is language that might prohibit such curricular design already in existence? What precedent for approving or denying such a course design proposal exists? And what reason(s) could be given to this faculty member if her proposal is denied? We would of course like this hypothetical proposal to receive the green light, but at the very least there should be some level of transparency about what blended delivery strategies can, or cannot, occur.

We know from experience, though, that one very real institutional hurdle to innovative hybrid delivery models can be a rigid campus scheduling system, especially at institutions where classroom space is at a premium and peak instructional times can see almost 100 percent classroom resource usage. But in cases where real curricular innovation is at odds with what an institutional scheduling system can manage, or has managed in the past, we hope that good faith, creative thinking on the part of faculty and administration alike can find ways to make the scheduling system responsive to curricular design and not the other way around. There is, of course, no one recipe for how to make this happen, except that all parties involved—those tasked with teaching students and those tasked with making efficient use of classroom space—can come together to assess possible institutional precedents for so-called alternative delivery models, or, where no such precedents exist, can evaluate what institutional imperatives should be driving scheduling decisions: limitations to an IT system or student learning.

But this is precisely why clearly defined terms—at the institutional level—are so important, and also why involvement from multiple stakeholders is a must. Our feeling is, again, that definitions should be institution-specific, reflecting the many variables at play that are unique in their combination to each campus. Thus, if or when stakeholders came together to talk about a hybrid course that meets entirely face-to-face for half a semester and then entirely online, or one that spent some weeks online and some face-to-face, everybody at the table can be speaking a common language and one that has the endorsement of the institution as a whole.

When it comes to blending online and face-to-face instructional time in creative ways, consideration should include the student body itself and of course the particular type of class being offered: Would, for example, a group of at-risk students in a developmental course be able to succeed without regular f2f meeting time? Would working with those students fully online for an extended period be potentially beneficial before meeting in person? These are questions best left to actual practitioners in their local contexts.

Another important set of questions to address when strategizing effective online/f2f blends surround basic questions of access. Beyond literal, and federally mandated, requirements for institutions to accommodate those with physical impairments, for example, accessibility is also about affording learners in one modality (like online) the same support structures that are afforded learners in others modalities (like face-to-face). So are there campus resources in place to support online learners *as online learners*? While good online courses will provide ample support for students who are learners in that discipline, will those students also have access to library resources, IT and tutoring help, and other special needs accommodation support *online*? Such resources need to be available online, otherwise any institution's body of online students are only truly online within their respective courses. If those students require support beyond what the individual course provides and that support is not readily available online, then one of two things happens: (1) those online learners come to campus, so they are not truly online students anymore; or, worse, (2) those students do not get the support they need and thus operate at a serious disadvantage.

It may seem like we are arguing for an unnecessarily narrow and inflexible definition for hybrid learning, given that some learners will probably benefit from regular f2f interaction with an instructor and with each other. But this is not the case. In fact, we would rather see as much flexibility as possible built into institutional definitions of hybrid learning such that courses can be configured to best serve student needs.

What we firmly believe must not inform decisions about how to define hybrid across an institution are administrative concerns over resource management, sometimes coyly called "efficiency." In other words, we feel that the *worst* place to start when it comes to discussion about defining hybrids is to think in terms of maximizing classroom space and/or minimizing campus congestion. Yes, it will always be someone's job to worry about such things, but the place to start discussion concerning hybrid learning is absolutely not how an institution can fit two classes into one classroom.

In her "WPA's Guide to the Hybrid Writing Classroom" blog, author Meagan Kittle Autry explains, somewhat problematically in our view, that:

> Logistically, hybrid courses also reduce student seat time within a physical classroom, which makes them a draw for fast-growing universities whose capital funds and building cannot keep up with demands in enrollment. For example, schools with a 4 credit hour, 4 day/week First Year Writing course could save half of their classroom space by instituting hybrid courses that meet face-to-face 50% of the time and online 50% of the time. This would allow a program to offer two classes for every time slot in each physical classroom instead of just one. Or, programs with a 3 credit hour, 3 day/week First Year Writing course could save as much or as little space as needed by implementing some classes that are held once per week face-to-face and twice per week online, while keeping some entirely face-to-face classes. Administrators who need to quickly create 15 additional courses in a fall semester could do so, at least space-wise, by shifting the format of some of the courses.

In this efficiency maximization model, the same classroom, which would otherwise accommodate just one of these two classes in the fully f2f format, can be used to house two courses.

Presumably an institution would then somehow multiply this across many sections to see significant returns on efficiency. Twice as many classes, no new buildings.

But again, we caution against this kind of approach as the basis for talking about hybrids. True, notions of such efficiencies might become part of the discussion, but only at a much later point, and only if they emerge more or less naturally from the pedagogical choices that instructors have made.

Why not talk efficiency right up front?

Consider just for a moment what the efficiency approach would entail: first and foremost, instructors would not have the ability to design courses as they deem most pedagogically beneficial for their students, since maximizing classroom space (as in the preceding example) would *require* that hybrids be constructed in a certain way. Not only would instructors be limited to a strict weekly 50-50 split of instructional time, but they would also have to defer to central scheduling about *which* day would be f2f and which would be online.

Are faculty at your institution likely to agree to a situation where so much curricular and pedagogical control is given away? Our guess is, no. And thus our belief that discussion about how to define hybrids that *begin* in terms of institutional aims for efficiency and resource maximization will not be productive.

So where should such discussion begin?

As we have indicated, it needs to begin with representatives from as many campus constituencies as possible: faculty, administration from a variety of levels, IT, support staff from the library, and counseling and advising staff. These are relatively obvious voices to have at the table. But what about student leaders? They may have valuable experience from the perspective that seems to be so often ignored: the actual student learner. Perhaps community members might have input. And board members and trustees should be informed so that policymaking at that level, if or when it does occur relative to hybrid learning, is undertaken from an informed position.

Institutions will benefit from an early stage of exploratory fact-finding, perhaps as part of the needs assessment phase we discuss above, before discussion moves to more narrowly focused committees or working groups. In other words, what do students, faculty, community members already know—or think they know—about online or hybrid learning? What would they like to know? How might creative instructional design best suit their needs?

Early fact-finding can help to strengthen discussion about how to define hybrids across an institution once that discussion moves closer and closer to the policymaking stage. And fact-finding of this kind is clearly beneficial *before* rather than *after* policies are in place, but there is nothing to say that ongoing fact-finding would not also be valuable, especially to gauge what effect, if any, institutional policies have had on teachers, students, and support staff.

Beyond broad preliminary discussions, any subsequent thinking about how hybrids will be defined (and then advertised) across an institution should ideally stay grounded in terms of teaching pedagogy.

We have advocated away from ideas about maximizing classroom space as the place to start your institutional discussion about hybrids and toward ideas of pedagogy, but that now means that faculty will have to take up a primary role in doing the research about what kinds of instruction work best in their respective disciplines. In other words, we would like to see faculty as proactive about why an institutional definition should put pedagogy first by bringing research, and of course experiential knowledge, to the table.

So what of our hypothetical earlier example in which a particular instructor wants to divide her hybrid in creative ways. Ideally, this choice will be provided for by early institutional planning, perhaps as a result of this faculty member having had a voice in what kinds of instructional designs will be permissible for the hybrid format. Given the chance, she has ideally already made the case that in her discipline, sound pedagogy suggests that where instructors see the need to do so, students would be best served by a hybrid that does not simply split instructional time on a weekly basis.

But we also realize that such "planning" will, in many cases, actually occur *after* a number of hybrid courses have already been designed and even delivered.

If there are not already clearly defined guidelines about what hybrids can, and cannot, be, it will be incumbent on the individual instructor to put pedagogy before experimentation and certainly before the exigencies of personal scheduling. The hybrid that splits its instructional time in what many will probably perceive to be an unconventional way must be grounded in sound teaching theory.

So discussion about defining hybrids at the institutional level should:

◆ happen early, not after hybrids have been offered and delivered in a haphazard way

◆ include input from as many stakeholders as possible, particularly in its earliest phases

◆ be grounded in sound pedagogy

Having a solid foundation in place from which to grow a hybrid curriculum will hopefully yield the best results, as teachers are able to explore options that work best in their disciplines. Courses can be designed within a relatively consistent framework such that one hybrid course is not drastically different from another (e.g., one splits online and f2f time 50/50 while another splits it 10/90). But within that framework, learning time can be creatively configured such that instructors are not locked into overly simplistic divisions that do not always make sense for a unique instructional setting (e.g., all hybrid classes will combine 50 percent classroom time and 50 percent online time on a weekly basis).

One last look at our now beleaguered hypothetical colleague who is looking to reconfigure the online and f2f time in her course. She finds that with little agreed upon language in place to guide her, she is having to sell the notion of splitting learning time on anything but a weekly basis to a supervisor, keeping in mind that that supervisor will in turn have to sell the idea up the reporting chain.

We are willing to bet that our faculty member's desire to reconfigure the learning time in her hybrid will sooner or later meet with resistance in the organizational hierarchy, be it with an immediate supervisor, central scheduling (if it exists), or higher up in academic affairs. Where do this faculty member and her administrator turn for guidance when there seems to be no precedent in place?

We now look to an aspect of hybrid learning that is perhaps on the face of it outside the scope of this book, though it bears directly on the immediate discussion: hybrids often have a much deeper institutional history than many people might realize.

And faculty, support staff, and administrators should consider this deeper history, where it exists, as part of what informs discussions about hybrids in the narrower sense we cover in this book. In a very practical way, our hypothetical instructor who needs to pitch the idea of her creatively designed hybrid can benefit from this broader institutional history by showing that her hybrid design is not entirely new on campus.

Do Hybrids Already Have an Institutional History?

There's no question that developing concrete, and broadly shared, definitions about what hybrids are is an important part of making hybrids as effective as they can be. But defining hybrids does not necessarily need to be a process that begins entirely from scratch. In other words, many schools already have an institutional history of "hybrid" learning; it just doesn't happen to involve hybrid classes that mix f2f instructional time with online instructional time.

A mix that might be familiar to faculty, administration, and support staff on many campuses would combine f2f time with an experiential component, as is the case for field studies classes. Students spend some time in class, but are then out "in the field" for another significant part of a course. And note too that experiential learning, or field studies, classes are often already radical reconfigurations of learning time. This version of the hybrid will often have students traveling to other states, countries, or even continents as part of a class experience. Clearly, a field studies course that has students hiking the Appalachian Trail or going to Alaska will not divide instructional time on a weekly basis.

If your institution already has these kinds of courses in place for students, could hybrid courses (that combine f2f with online instruction) follow the same principles? If you are an instructor and you are reading this, imagine your English composition course meeting for eight weeks f2f and then moving entirely online (mirroring an experiential learning model of hybridity). We imagine that in many situations, this proposed hybrid arrangement could meet with considerable resistance, and thus require from the faculty member a great deal of justification, rather than it being widely and immediately embraced. To be sure, newer learning models and proposals for innovation will usually benefit from some level of justification, evidence that a plan has been thought through and tied to particular learning outcomes. But if proposing hybrid learning models at any given institution is perceived to entail an unreasonable burden for justification on the part of the instructor—i.e., well beyond what might be required for any other kind of instructional design or delivery proposal—then you are unlikely to see very many innovative uses of the blended format, even when those various formats might be to the benefit of students taking the classes. Another, more direct, way of framing our argument here, is that instructional delivery, in the face-to-face, hybrid, or online formats, should really not exist at the mercy of what central scheduling is willing to do.

This is where it is useful to identify "hybrids," as they may already exist at your school, though in forms other than those that combine f2f with strictly online learning. If there's institutional precedent for what you want to do, why not follow it?

We are not advocating for the kind of hybrid that splits its f2f and online time so drastically as somehow superior to other hybrid formats. In the case of an experiential type of course, the hybridity of the learning modes happens the way it does largely out of necessity. But clearly an institution that supports experiential learning believes that such a division of learning modes can work. So it might be worth tapping into that existing belief when it comes to getting creative with how f2f and online time can be arranged.

If it seems we have asked a lot of administration in terms of scheduling flexibility for hybrids, we should conclude, and reiterate, that when it comes to instructional design the grounding principle needs to be sound pedagogy, not resource-use efficiency and not individual scheduling convenience. Thus, the onus is on instructors to design hybrid classes that divide time in ways that will be *most effective for students* and then be willing and prepared to demonstrate why their choices are effective by stepping up to showcase their work for others even if formal evaluation is not mandated.

How Hybrids Are Advertised: General Marketing

For many campuses, offering hybrid courses is an institutional goal, but one that unfortunately, and unproductively, starts and ends in the classroom. We argue that an important piece of any planning discussions related to hybrid learning needs to be how hybrid courses will be advertised and publicized. So we need to take a few steps back from the start of classes on day one. We need to have a plan in place for when students are choosing and registering for those classes.

Certainly in-class and syllabus-level advertising—and explanations—by individual faculty should make it clear when a class is hybrid. We will discuss some strategies for this later on. But obviously, by the time a student gets a syllabus and sits in class, he or she has already registered. Even when students show up unaware that a class is a hybrid, or unaware of what that term actually means, most are unlikely to make drastic scheduling changes based on the news that they have registered for a hybrid course. Such changes may not even be possible for high-demand classes. On day one of the semester, students are unlikely to opt out of a hybrid class, even if the learning mode does not suit their needs or abilities, when the only option is to join the waitlist for another section of that course.

And when we talk about advertising, we are not just limiting the discussion to whatever mechanisms exist for alerting students that courses are hybrids in the registration system. We are also thinking in terms of publicizing the hybrid learning format more generally as an available option. Institutions should be careful about the language used in public advertising efforts, since many of the attractive features of online and hybrid learning can be so easily, though often unintentionally, misrepresented and then misunderstood from the student side.

So first of all: campus marketing services, whatever form that takes at your institution, should be at the table when decisions about hybrid curricular development occur. They may not have input on precisely how the term hybrid gets defined, but marketing should be informed and aware of exactly what language will be used to define and describe hybrids. In fact, while marketing expertise might not bear directly on hybrid course design, such expertise might be extremely valuable when it comes to the actual language used to describe hybrids. Effective marketing, working in concert with teaching faculty, may actually have a greater impact on student success than higher education has generally heretofore acknowledged.

In fact, marketing will be absolutely key in enabling student success in the hybrid setting, since in many cases students will come to know about hybrids from contact with general campus or community marketing materials. Having those who will be responsible for general marketing informed and part of early decision making will hopefully make future marketing that much more effective.

In many cases, before a student ever sets foot in a classroom, logs in to a learning management system, or accesses the institutional registration system, we hope that they will have had some exposure—through directed marketing—to the hybrid instructional format.

Thinking about marketing in these very general terms means acknowledging not only how "alternative" learning formats are represented within an institution, but also how such learning formats—especially online—are presented to the public. What connotations tend to accompany online learning when it is broadcast to the public via various institutional media outlets, be that a school website or a highway billboard? What assumptions might students already have about something like online learning, let alone hybrid learning?

Consider, for example, the frequency with which online learning is equated with ease. Ask your neighbor, assuming he or she is not involved directly with higher education, about online learning and you can expect fairly predictable responses: not sure how it works exactly, heard lots about it, never actually taken a class, doesn't seem to replicate the classroom environment too well, may be effective but not the same work as taking a "real" class.

But don't blame your neighbor. Too often the flexibility of some kinds of online learning is sold to students as ease. We do not necessarily see this from reputable higher education institutions, at least explicitly and within the walls of those institutions, but too often we see online learning sold as the quick way to a degree, or a job, when it features in the media outside of higher education.

Take this example from JobJournal.com: "advances in online education are dramatically reducing the cost of coursework and providing timesaving shortcuts to becoming someone with the qualifications that today's employers are desperate to find" ("Capitalize on New Skills More Quickly with New Programs in Online Education"). We are not even sure if this source can truly be called an article; it poses as an article, but reads more like advertising. And if one of our composition students used such a source in an essay we would question its trustworthiness immediately. But its bias is precisely what we are pointing to here. This, among so many hundreds of similar pieces we have run across, presents online learning as fast, easy, and the quick road to employment. That perception of online learning often finds its way to students and to the general population.

The result can be that any advertising that promotes the flexibility of a given instructional setting will read to some as implying that that instructional setting is easier than traditional onsite learning, which means that advertising about hybrids should be especially careful to use language that dispels what are likely to be common presumptions about so-called "alternative" delivery modes. We have seen that it does not seem to take much in the way of advertising before students' pre- and misconceptions about online and hybrid learning kick in. Yes, they claim to "know" that learning outside the classroom takes as much time and concentration as learning inside the classroom. But they still don't always seem to act on, or organize their schedules around, such knowledge.

Another aspect of how hybrid courses are sometimes presented on institutional webpages that can be confusing for students, though easily addressed, involves the use of what we call "transactional language." In other words, when students visit an institutional webpage they might find descriptions of hybrid learning that explain the instructional mode in terms of onsite learning time being "traded" for online learning time.

For example, the University of Wisconsin-Milwaukee Hybrid Learning website (a resource we have otherwise praised) reads: "'Hybrid' or 'Blended' are names commonly used to describe courses in which some traditional face-to-face 'seat time' has been replaced by online learning activities" (University of Wisconsin-Milwaukee, "Hybrid Courses"). Other institutional webpages use even more explicitly transactional language, as in this example: "A hybrid class trades about 50% of its traditional campus contact hours for online work" ("Definitions of Online, Hybrid, and Supplemental Courses").

Students will sometimes show up to class, knowing that they have indeed registered for a hybrid, but now thinking that instructional time has been traded in some very literal way. So if a traditional version of a course might meet Monday, Wednesday and Friday, and students in the hybrid class have been immersed in the transactional language of traded instruction time, they often show up wondering if the online portion of the course must be completed on Friday, in the fifty-minute block that would other-wise, in the fully face-to-face version of the course, be classroom time. Of course, this is not the case.

Rather, that block of learning time is integrated into a weekly plan, and it occurs online, perhaps distributed in chunks throughout the week. This is relatively simple to explain on the first day of class, but it is unfortunate that some students, even the relatively well-informed ones, come in to class still unclear about how a hybrid really works.

What we end up explaining in our classes, and what might be much preferable in terms of institutional language that describes hybrids, is that in a hybrid instructional settings are *integrated*, rather than somehow traded or transacted.

Jason Snart's home institution, the College of DuPage, pro-vides a good example of a relatively straightforward description of the hybrid mode, and it focuses on integration rather than how one learning mode replaces another: "Hybrid courses integrate 50 percent classroom instruction with 50 percent online learn-ing" (College of DuPage). Unfortunately, the statement itself is inaccurate, in that not all hybrids integrate exactly 50 percent face-to-face and online time, but at least the definition does focus productively on integration, rather than exchangeability between instructional settings.

The transactional language that often surrounds hybrids probably persists because on some level instructors *do* need to imagine roughly how much work needs to occur online so that a three-credit course remains a three-credit course whether it exists in the hybrid or fully face-to-face instructional setting. But beyond this, any sense of a hybrid as a course type that trades instructional time in one setting for another is unhelpfully misguided.

Ideally, there should be coordination among faculty, admin-istration, and support staff when it comes to the public language surrounding hybrids, whether that public language is specific to individual hybrid courses or whether it is much broader in nature. So when a poster goes up on campus advertising a group of hybrid courses, or when a piece runs in the community newsletter, what language is attached to hybrid instruction and what is the perception likely to be for the average student?

One very basic aspect of effective marketing is to be sure that those involved are aware of the institutional definition of what a hybrid is. This has implications for general marketing materials, including campus websites where students might find information about instruction and course types.

At Joanna Paull's home institution, Lakeland Community College, there are multiple joint committees that involve faculty, staff, and administration who work together on distance learning concerns like creating and publicizing the hybrid definition to the entire campus community. Committees came together and decided to provide a single, consistent definition for *all* hybrid courses at Lakeland, to send a consistent message to students and faculty about how the college understands these kinds of courses. Hybrid courses are defined on the Lakeland Community College distance learning page in this way:

> The blended (hybrid) course provides the advantages of weekly face-to-face interaction between faculty and students with the flexibility and convenience of less time in the classroom. Significant coursework and interactions between instructor, students, and classmates take place both in the classroom and online. The total amount of time required for the blended course is typically the same as with a traditional face-to-face course. The percentage of face-to-face classroom time is reduced as time devoted to online activities is increased. (Lakeland Community College, "Distance Learning")

Specifically, note that there is a required weekly face-to-face component for hybrid courses. The institution emphasizes the need for online interactions between students and students as well as students and instructors, to assure that these courses are not self-paced or face-to-face courses with very little done online beyond students submitting assignments. By sharing a common definition, college employees can be assured that they all understand the term consistently.

With a shared idea of precisely what constitutes a hybrid course and a marketing strategy that takes care to present hybrids as beneficial for the way in which they integrate multiple learning modes—rather than depending on just their "flexibility"—institutions can focus on how hybrids are represented for students in the registration system.

How Hybrids Are Advertised: The Registration System

In a 2014 survey we conducted on hybrid learning, we asked, "How well are hybrids labeled in your college registration system?" Fifty percent of our respondents chose this answer: "Our hybrid courses have 'hybrid' registration tags with limited info for students." And one respondent commented that "Students don't even notice the hybrid tag [in the course registration system] and are massively confused when they show up in a hybrid class" (Paull and Snart). Our survey represents a very small sample size—we are not claiming true statistical significance—but we imagine this frustration is widely experienced.

Clearly, of immediate practical concern for students and teachers is that the registration system provide a highly visible alert to students so that they are aware that they are signing up for a hybrid class. And beyond this basic alert, a clear definition of what a hybrid entails should be provided to students. If the registration system allows for it, students should be prompted to interact with the sign-up process such that they must, at the very least, click a kind of "I Agree" box after having been presented with a thorough explanation of what a hybrid course is likely to entail. Notice that this step presupposes that the institution has taken the time to craft a shared understanding of exactly what a hybrid course is or what variations it might take.

The registration systems at both of our home institutions note simply that a course is "Hybrid" in the course search results screen. Unfortunately, there is no elaboration about what that means exactly, though the weekly schedule is likely to attract students' attention, since where a nonhybrid course will meet for three hours every week (in a sixteen-week term), a hybrid will be listed as meeting for less than that. Unless students already understand what a hybrid course is—that reduced seat-time does not mean less work—it will just appear that a hybrid English 101 meets for fewer hours than the three listed for all other nonhybrid versions of that same course. You can imagine a student's surprise when he arrives to class to discover that not only does the class involve as much, if not more, work as the traditional f2f first-year composition course, but he now needs to be interacting with the course and his classmates online every week.

In a survey we conducted, 30 percent of respondents indicated that their registration systems did not include any labels at all for hybrid courses, while 50 percent indicated that courses are indeed labeled in the registration system. Interestingly, or unfortunately, only 10 percent of those surveyed indicated that their hybrid courses are labeled as such *and* include detailed descriptions of what hybrid courses actually are.

In some registration systems, if students click a little deeper into the course description, before proceeding to the registration process, they will find something like this as part of the Course Comments field: "Hybrid format: a blend of traditional classroom and alternative instruction." We wonder how meaningful this will be to many students, if they click that deeply at all. Really, if a registration allows for this kind of comment field, why not populate it with something to explain more fully what a hybrid is and what it will likely involve?

In fact, in an ideal situation, individual faculty could supply a description or explanation about how their particular hybrid works, so that students do not just get boilerplate language but instead can find out exactly how instructional time is managed in any given course.

Another piece of information that should be included in the course information that appears as part of the basic registration process is that a hybrid class requires students to have Internet access. This information is usually provided when students access *online* course information through the registration system, but it may be curiously absent for hybrid courses. At Joanna Paull's institution, the master schedule from which students register for courses includes a column that indicates whether a course is fully on campus, a hybrid, or fully online.

In Figure 3, course types are differentiated in two ways. First, there is a designated column assigned to platform (lecture, lab, online, or hybrid). Further, to indicate the differentiation between these learning platforms, hybrid course sections are highlighted in yellow and sections that are done entirely online are highlighted in green (represented as shades of gray in the figure here). Students may also refine their course searches to just those offerings that are hybrid or online. However, the terms themselves are not defined within the scheduling system itself. As a result, many students who enroll in hybrid sections self-report to the instructor that they chose the hybrid section because they noticed the reduced class time, thinking that they just did not have to meet as often in the classroom, not really considering the potential trade-off for lessened class time.

ITIS 1005 - Comp/Info Processing [Description / Fees]

CRN	Schedule	Seats	Days	Times	Dates	Room
11487	LECTURE	19	W	10:30 AM-12:35 PM	8/27/16-12/16/16 (F)	C1011
11488	LAB	19	W	12:45 PM-02:00 PM	8/27/16-12/16/16 (F)	C1011
11261	HYBRID	19	M	08:30 AM-09:30 AM	8/27/16-12/16/16 (F)	C1011
11262	HYBRID LAB	19	M	09:35 AM-10:10 AM	8/27/16-12/16/16 (F)	C1011
11263	HYBRID	18	T	06:00 PM-07:00 PM	8/27/16-12/16/16 (F)	C1011
11264	HYBRID LAB	18	T	07:05 PM-07:40 PM	8/27/16-12/16/16 (F)	C1011
12047	LECTURE	PERM	MTWRF		8/27/16-12/16/16 (F)	AUBURN
12048	LAB	PERM	MTWRF		8/27/16-12/16/16 (F)	AUBURN
11951	LECTURE	PERM	MTWRF		8/27/16-10/21/16 (P1)	CARDINAL
11952	LAB	PERM	MTWRF		8/27/16-10/21/16 (P1)	CARDINAL
11259	LECTURE	16	MW	01:00 PM-03:05 PM	8/27/16-10/21/16 (P1)	C1009
11260	LAB	16	MW	03:15 PM-04:30 PM	8/27/16-10/21/16 (P1)	C1009
10908	HYBRID	22	T	08:30 AM-10:35 AM	8/27/16-10/21/16 (P1)	C1011
10909	HYBRID LAB	22	T	10:45 AM-12:00 PM	8/27/16-10/21/16 (P1)	C1011
10849	HYBRID	21	T	01:00 PM-03:05 PM	8/27/16-10/21/16 (P1)	C1011
10850	HYBRID LAB	21	T	03:15 PM-04:30 PM	8/27/16-10/21/16 (P1)	C1011
10851	ONLINE	FULL	-		8/27/16-10/21/16 (P1)	ONLINE
10852	ONLINE LAB	FULL	-		8/27/16-10/21/16 (P1)	ONLINE
10853	ONLINE	18	-	-	8/27/16-10/21/16 (P1)	ONLINE
10854	ONLINE LAB	18	-	-	8/27/16-10/21/16 (P1)	ONLINE
10855	ONLINE	24	-	-	8/27/16-10/21/16 (P1)	ONLINE
10856	ONLINE LAB	24	-	-	8/27/16-10/21/16 (P1)	ONLINE
10857	ONLINE	18	-	-	8/27/16-10/21/16 (P1)	ONLINE
10858	ONLINE LAB	18	-	-	8/27/16-10/21/16 (P1)	ONLINE

FIGURE 3. *Registration screen showing instructional technology and computer science courses in different delivery formats.*

In the case of Paull's home institution, for students to gather information about how hybrid courses are defined, they need to go to the distance learning website. Students are linked to that page on the course section details page that lists location, days, and times of the class. The piecemeal way in which course information is provided is clearly unhelpful for the average student, probably concerned with registering for multiple courses and configuring an entire schedule that works, rather than following multiple, and sometimes less than intuitive, hyperlinks.

Ideally, students should be alerted not only to the fact it is a hybrid course, but they should also see a quick definition of what that course model will involve prior to enrolling. This is a matter to be discussed with the registration and admissions staff as part of the publicity and marketing that accompanies hybrids being added to the curriculum.

Sometimes marketing falls to motivated instructors, though such efforts need institutional support. For example, as part of Joanna Paull's hybrid faculty workshop series (discussed later in this text), those who conducted and those who had registered for the workshop collaborated on informational fliers/handouts that reflected how their institution defined hybrid courses, the kinds of students who would be a good match for hybrid courses (e.g., self-starters, those with strong time management skills, those who benefit from online work but also enjoy weekly face-time with instructors), and all of the hybrid courses that were being offered for the upcoming semester (see Figure 4). These fliers were then provided to registration counselors for guiding their students during scheduling sessions. Fliers were made available in faculty office suites and posted in classrooms across campus. Getting the message out about how hybrids are defined on your campus is ultimately helpful for all college employees, administrators, staff, and faculty alike, not to mention the obvious benefit for what we hope will become a well-informed student population.

In reality, faculty would be well served to investigate the registration system at their institutions—from the student-side, not just the searchable catalog side—to discover precisely what information is provided, or not provided, to students about the various learning modes that are available. If course-specific information seems nonexistent, or too scant to be of much use, every

Wish you could combine the flexibility of online coursework with the benefits of classroom interaction?

Then hybrid courses are a great fit for you!

What is a hybrid course?
- Classes meet once a week in the classroom & every week online as well.
- There is meaningful instruction & interaction both online & in the classroom.
- Requires attendance every week in the classroom & online.

Who are the most successful hybrid students?
- Independent learners
- Manage their time effectively
- Self-disciplined
- Appreciate face-to-face interaction with their instructor & their classmates
- Display confidence with current technologies
- Available for weekly interactions with teacher & classmates
- Have a keen interest in the course material

CHECK OUT THESE GREAT HYBRID COURSES OFFERED IN SPRING 2013!

ACCT 1100: INTRO TO FINANCIAL ACCOUNTING, WED. @ 6:00 p.m. – 7:50 p.m.
COUN 1100: CAREER EXPLORATION, FRI. @ 9 a.m. – 11:40 a.m., P1 (CRN 31148)
COUN 1100: CAREER EXPLORATION, FRI. @ 9 a.m. – 11:40 a.m., P2 (CRN 34351)
ENGL 1120: COMPOSITION 2, TUES. @ 11 a.m.–12:15 p.m. (CRN 34815)
ENGL 1120: COMPOSITION 2, THURS. @ 11 a.m. – 12:15 p.m. (CRN 33474)
ENGL 2225: GRAPHIC FICTION NARRATIVE, WED. @ 2 – 3 p.m. (CRN 34816)
GEOG 1550: PHYSICAL/ENVIRONMENTAL GEOGRAPHY, WED. @ 2–3:50 p.m. (CRNs 34770 & 34771)
HIMT 1200: HEALTHCARE RECORDS, MON. @3:00 –5:15 p.m. (CRN 32882 & CRN 32883)
PSYC 1500: INTRO TO PSYCHOLOGY, MON. @ 12:30 – 1:45 p.m. (CRN 33444)
PSYC 1500: INTRO TO PSYCHOLOGY, WED. @ 12:30 – 1:45 p.m. (CRN 33993)
SOCY 1150: PRINCIPLES OF SOCIOLOGY, TUES. @ 12:30–1:45 p.m. (CRN 31568)
SOCY 1150: PRINCIPLES OF SOCIOLOGY, THURS. @ 12:30–1:45 p.m. (CRN 34787)
SOCY 1150: PRINCIPLES OF SOCIOLOGY, WED. @ 5:45 – 7 p.m. (CRN 33447)
SOCY 2270: SOCIOLOGY OF AGING, MON. 11 a.m. – 12:15 p.m. (CRN 34785)

FIGURE 4. *Lakeland Community College hybrid course publicity flier.*

effort should be made to enact changes. Clearly, having students register for a class with an understanding of the basic learning mode involved is fundamental to student success.

When students arrive to class with no clear idea of what hybrid learning is, instructors then face a group of students, many of whom are not prepared for, or likely to be successful in, the blended format. Basic lack of preparedness might easily skew student success numbers, which often figure into instructor performance review. Or, students frustrated with a learning model that was not clearly explained to them may express such frustration in instructor/course feedback, which again can figure prominently in performance review. In short, the teacher can end up taking a lot of heat for a situation that originates in a registration system over which he or she has little direct control.

The irony that both authors have observed is that even where institutions have invested substantial money and energy into a professional support structure for faculty interested in designing and teaching hybrids—like a great hybrid learning website and great workshop opportunities—the student experience vis-à-vis registration can seem woefully inadequate. So while we advocate strongly for an identifiable and readily accessible digital home for hybrid learning, we do not necessarily expect that home to function as a resource for students. Or at least it is not one that most students will actively seek out on their own. If that hybrid learning website contains support material geared for students, like learning style self-assessments or video-based how-tos, then great. We assume, though, that students will likely have to be actively directed to it by instructors or as part of a student orientation program.

But is the average student who is registering for classes likely to peruse an institutional website looking for descriptions of various learning modes, let alone take the deep dive that is sometimes required to discover such content? Yes, there's always a chance, and certainly in an ideal world we would love to see students so proactive about their educational choices. But more likely, we think that students will log into a registration system and start working from there. So what language do we find about hybrids in registration systems? Truthfully, from our perspective as researchers and writers, it is often hard to tell how individual institutions represent the hybrid learning model in a registration system, precisely because to get that far one often needs to be officially registered at that institution and thus have a system username and password. What we are teasing out here, though, and what we hope institutions will take time to reflect on, is how glaring the disjunction can be between the public face of hybrid learning and what exists within the gated community of the campus registration system.

To provide one telling example, we will return to an institution that we have otherwise held up as an exemplar when it comes to providing a clear home for hybrid learning as part of an institutional web presence and when it comes to offering well-developed and useful professional development resources: the University of Central Florida (UCF). UCF (along with the University of Wisconsin-Milwaukee) represents in some ways the gold standard for faculty support for hybrid learning. But the registration system—i.e., where we believe most *students* will actually come into contact, whether they know it or not, with hybrid learning—presents some interesting challenges. We single out UCF here in part because their support for hybrid learning seems otherwise so robust, but also because it is one registration system that is fully accessible from the outside. We require no username or password to access the system.

It turns out that UCF, otherwise a leader in blended learning, offers very little through its registration system about various learning modes. For example, the course search interface (which looks as clunky and unappealing as almost all registration systems) allows users to search by "Mode of Instruction." Among the choices are "Face to Face Instruction"; "Mixed Mode/Reduced Seat Time"; "Video Str/Reduced Seat Time"; "Video Streaming"; and "World Wide Web" ("Search for Classes"). A "What's This?" link next to the Mode of Instruction drop-down menu opens a new window in which the various modes are described. "Mixed Mode/Reduced Seat Time" (presumably hybrid/blended learning) is described this way: "courses include both required classroom attendance and online instruction. Classes have substantial activity conducted over the Web, which substitutes for some classroom meetings" (Center for Distributed Learning). Digging through the course catalog and perusing open sections we can find hybrid courses that are described like this: "Substitutes WWW for some class time; requires Internet access, browser, and E-mail skills" ("Browse Course Catalog"). We have to wonder if this language gives students much to go on when it comes to making good choices for themselves in terms of delivery format.

Again, UCF hosts perhaps the premier professional development resource for institutions and faculty looking to build and support their hybrid curricula: the Blended Learning Toolkit. The Toolkit website is almost exclusively for faculty, support staff, and administrators, however. There are pictures of students but no language clearly directed at them. Support provided to the student where he or she is likely to be best served by it—as part of the registration process—is surprisingly sparse.

The language in most other registration systems is not much better. It is cryptic and hard to find, often multiple clicks or menus away from basic course information. It is, in probably too many cases, all but meaningless for those students who are registering for classes and who do not already (by word of mouth or previous experience perhaps?) know what a hybrid course is likely to entail. And of course it is, more than likely, constrained by the registration and data management systems used by a college, like Ellucian (formerly Datatel) or Campus Management, such that precisely where it would be beneficial to provide students with a clear understanding of delivery mode option, we are limited by what IT can provide.

Here is one more look at a registration system: the College of DuPage system (Jason Snart's home institution) tags hybrid courses with an HYB extension. The course search page includes a drop-down menu of course types, though unfortunately so many delivery variations are captured here, most students would have to already know what specific learning mode they want. There are, as of this writing, some twenty-seven options in the "Course Type" menu, including "Adult Fast Track," "Hybrid," "Oral Communications," and the relatively indecipherable and thus unhelpful, "Custom." There are no in situ explanations for these various course types, though if one chooses to search for hybrid courses, the system will sort by courses flagged with the HYB extension.

However, what the system currently produces is a laundry list of courses that are identified as "HYB" but that involve all different manner of modified instructional time, some including online learning but not all. For example, because there has been no institutionalized definition of what a "hybrid" is or how (or why) courses should be identified as such, any student searching specifically for hybrid classes will find everything from Accounting to Computer Information Systems to English to Welding. Only some of these might be hybrids in the sense we are using the term here: the combination of online and face-to-face instructional time. Those courses are described, if one clicks far enough into the system, as such: "Hybrid format: a blend of classroom and online course work. Internet access required." Other "hybrids" are described this way: "Media enhanced course, additional hours independent work required, PC W/CD and printer required Hybrid format: a blend of traditional classroom and alternative instruction." Or, "hybrid format—a blend of classroom and alternative format coursework. One additional hour TBA." And still further, "hybrid format: The first two weeks of the course will meet on campus. The remaining 14 weeks will be online format" ("Search for Credit Classes").

We are particularly sensitive to how lack of information about hybrids *delivered when and where most students will need it* is likely to affect already disadvantaged students. Because we both work at community colleges, we think especially of an important demographic often served by open-access institutions: first-generation college students. These are students who are the first in their family to attend college. Even if these students have moral and emotional support from home for their college endeavors (and this is not always the case), they do not necessarily enjoy the practical knowledge that a college-graduated family member might share. Thus, navigating muddy registration waters can potentially have the most dramatic negative impact on precisely those students we should be most concerned to serve well and support.

How Hybrids Are Advertised: Course-Level Explanations

Now that a student is registered in a hybrid class, an intentional part of instructional design should be to reiterate (sometimes ad nauseam) that the course is a hybrid. Figures 5 and 6 are examples from each author's composition course syllabi, highlighting for students, literally, what the hybrid course format will entail. Figure 5 offers: Bolded text. Larger font. Highlighting. And with an exclamation point. It really is that important for students to understand what they have signed up for early on.

Figure 6 is another example of syllabus-level information provided to students about the hybrid instructional setting. Admittedly, these kinds of declarations do not make for the most

---

This Course is a Hybrid!

We will meet face to face, in our classroom, for two thirds of the regular class meetings. So instead of meeting on Monday, Wednesday, AND Friday face to face, we will just be meeting face to face on Mondays and Wednesdays. The remainder of our instructional time will occur online, largely through Blackboard (bb.cod.edu).

This hybrid course is still as much work as traditional face to face to face course; in fact, this hybrid will require even MORE focus on your part to ensure that you keep pace and are successful.

What You MUST have to succeed in the hybrid format:

- dependable high speed access to the internet, from a home computer
- the ability to listen to audio and watch video on your computer
- the ability to install software on the computer you will be using

Most important for your success will be your ability to stay on task *outside of the classroom* to complete work on your own.

FIGURE 5. *Snart syllabus excerpt showing hybrid course format information.*

Understanding the Hybrid Course:

The hybrid course is a combination of the traditional three-credit bricks and mortar course with the flexibility of the online environment. Just like any other college course, you should average 3 hours outside of the classroom for each credit-hour of the course. Since this is a three-credit course, you should spend an average of nine hours reading, writing, and researching materials for this course's assignments. These hours are in addition to the 75 minutes in the physical classroom where we will meet every week of the semester (except during spring break, of course) and the time you spend engaging in discussions with your classmates in our Blackboard course site. As with any three-credit course, then, you should be prepared to spend an average of 12 hours a week on this course. For those who struggle with the writing and/or researching processes, though, you may find yourselves spending even more time on this course during some weeks of the semester. The hybrid course platform is ideal for students who enjoy the flexibility that an online course allows but also appreciate the power of physical interactions with their classmates and teacher. To be successful in a hybrid course, students need to be prepared to dedicate themselves fully to both pieces of the class every week. You will not pass this course if you choose not to attend the campus meetings and/or the online work.

FIGURE 6. *Paull syllabus excerpt showing hybrid course format information.*

welcoming first page of a syllabus, but each tries to lay out the reality of what students are getting into.

We do not want to get too narrowly focused about exactly *how* instructors explain the hybrid format to students or how syllabi or LMS (learning management system) landing pages should look. Those particular decisions are best made by individual faculty. We will just remind that it is good practice to spend class time walking students through exactly how the hybrid format works.

More usefully for our broader focus, though, will be to point out again how important it is for institutions to have effective mechanisms for cross-disciplinary discussions about hybrid teaching. This allows for those who teach hybrids to talk with each other about precisely *how* they introduce the concept in their classes and how they walk students through what is going on. Also valuable will be the opportunity for teachers to share successes and challenges when it comes to the basic issue of talking to students, who are already registered in a course and sitting there on day one, about how hybrids work.

Also important from an institutional perspective will be good coordination between those teaching hybrids—i.e., those doing the explaining on day one—and various campus support systems that students taking hybrid classes might be likely to take advantage of. Such support might include student IT, of course, but also online library and research support, not to mention online academic assistance and tutoring. Folks working in those areas should know that they might be interacting with students in hybrid courses, and it certainly helps if support personnel understand how hybrids are being talked about in the classroom to students.

Figure 7 by no means provides an exhaustive collection of the constituents who might be involved in conversations about hybrid curriculum development and support, but we hope that it does suggest the wide variety of voices that could usefully be at the table. We know that some are obvious, like faculty and administration along with information and learning technology departments. But some might not be so obvious: like input from the community or from institutional marketing, not to mention students themselves.

We also realize that these and other constituents might be involved differently, some more deeply than others, and at different times, some heavily involved in early institutional planning but less so as more hybrid courses are developed and blended offerings become a recognizable institutional reality and to some degree self-sustaining. In some cases, for example, a simple online survey can be enough to gauge interest in or familiarity with the

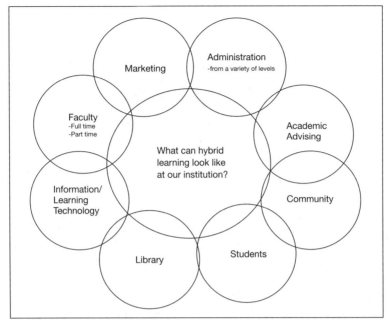

FIGURE 7. *The hybrid learning discussion: constituents at the table.*

hybrid model from the community or from students on campus. But, as our basic figure tries to show, each constituent will ideally contribute to that central question: "What can hybrid learning look like at our institution?"

CHAPTER TWO

Developing, Supporting, and Assessing Hybrids at Your Institution

This part of the book is divided into three related sections: one on developing hybrid curricula, one on supporting hybrid curricula, and one on assessing hybrid curricula. We see these as all deeply related (see Figure 8). Developing and assessing hybrid courses are iterative processes. With ongoing assessment will ideally come new ways to develop and refine courses. Instructional and student support should be available at all points.

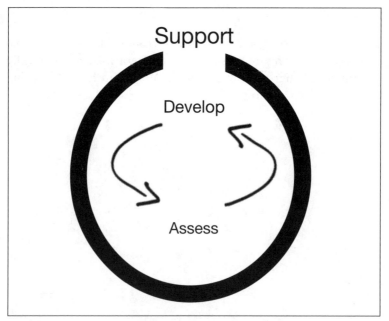

FIGURE 8. *The three essentials of hybrid curricula: develop, assess, support.*

In fact, the decision to separate these areas is as much a matter of organizational convenience as it is a reflection of our sense that they are discrete activities with easily identifiable start and end points or that any of these roles could be assigned solely to one institutional area.

Further, when it comes to developing, supporting, and assessing hybrid curricula, a useful first step—or a useful retroactive step, if your institution has already been offering hybrid courses for a while—is to take systematic stock of what models, policies, and procedures your campus already has in place that could be borrowed, and likely modified a bit, to suit the hybrid development context.

We will try to outline some of these existing precedents as they might exist at many higher education institutions.

Field and Experiential Learning: The Original Hybrid?

As we noted earlier, many colleges offer field or experiential learning opportunities. A first-year English course, for example, might spend some of its time in the classroom, but a significant portion of time out of the classroom. Sound familiar? It is basically the hybrid model, though for the majority of our discussion here that out-of-class time we've assumed to be spent specifically online: materials offered through a learning management system and students interacting with content, with an instructor, and with each other via digital tools that are, by and large, part of that learning management system. In the field and experiential model, though, that out-of-class time can range from regular field trips to local museums, libraries, natural areas, or the like. In other cases, nonclassroom time can be totally immersive: a class might travel to an out-of-state or even out-of-country location. That immersive living and learning is part of the experience of the course. Ideally, what students learn are course concepts, as they would presumably do in a traditional, fully onsite class, but they are further offered the opportunity to gain and apply knowledge in the real world. The field and experiential component teaches life skills and can often challenge students to synthesize their learning across multiple fields and to see "textbook" ideas brought to life in the world at large. The ethos driving most field and experiential programs is captured in the motto: "the world is our classroom."

Our concern here, though, is to suggest that policies and procedures in place that govern field and experiential learning might usefully be adopted and adapted to guide the development of hybrid courses (that is, hybrids in the narrow sense of online and face-to-face modes combined in a single course).

So before reinventing the wheel by developing procedures and guidelines for how a hybrid course is proposed or who might be involved in initial planning and approval, we suggest that institutions first investigate how field and experiential courses are proposed, approved, and supported. Or perhaps there is some other nontraditional delivery format on your campus whose administrative guidelines could be adapted to the development of hybrid curricula.

As has been our practice throughout this book, we are not looking to provide one model of administering hybrid courses that will fit all situations. But we would suggest that perhaps too often existing institutional models that could be at least partially mapped onto the hybrid situation are overlooked. Thus faculty, administrators, and support personnel, even those most willing to invest time and energy into developing a thriving hybrid curricula, find themselves starting from scratch when doing so is not entirely necessary. Energies are likely to flag quickly if too few people are tasked with working out all the nuances of hybrid course development, administration, and basic procedural implementation, especially if they are tasked to address all of the same obstacles that have, in fact, been confronted by others—working outside of the hybrid learning arena—but at some past time in an institution's history.

Of course there will be situations where such from-scratch work is a necessity. Perhaps there simply are no existing institutional models available to investigate and adapt. Equally possible is that there are some opening possibilities suggested by how other so-called alternative delivery modes are handled at your campus, but that beyond some surface similarities there are enough significant differences that real foundational work remains to be done.

One important aspect of handling hybrids from the administrative perspective involves, as we discuss elsewhere in this book, the basic matter of scheduling. Some institutions may have flexible enough scheduling systems and ample classroom space such that faculty can design a hybrid so that online and onsite times are not coordinated in a regular, weekly pattern.

Justifying that classroom space sitting empty, even in the interest of sound teaching practice, however, will likely be challenging, especially for those at institutions where space is at a premium. That is why most hybrids we've encountered take fairly predictable form: a fully onsite Monday/Wednesday/Friday course becomes, in its hybrid format, a Monday/Wednesday but not Friday course, with the division of online and onsite time recurring weekly. A Tuesday/Thursday or Monday/Wednesday course becomes, in its hybrid format, a one-day-a-week course.

So we are encouraging those interested in, or tasked with, developing and offering hybrid curricula, particularly where scheduling is concerned, to investigate possible existing institutional models. Is there a way in which field and experiential courses, for example, are scheduled somehow outside of a centralized scheduling system that requires courses to exist in a format that repeats weekly, as opposed to extended time either online or onsite? Can hybrid offerings take advantage of existing work-arounds that other curricular areas depend on?

Another interesting potential parallel is the way in which field and experiential courses are initially proposed and how faculty are vetted, early on, as capable of teaching in the nontraditional format. Take the case of a general education class, like first-year composition, offered in the field and experiential model. If the experiential component of the course involves a specific activity, like camping, kayaking, or mountaineering, how is a faculty member deemed able to manage the nonacademic piece? These examples involve a certain level of physical activity. And one would expect a faculty member to be well enough versed in an outdoor activity to be able to ensure the safety of his or her students. Other examples we've encountered include classes that involve craft making or walking tours: neither crafting nor giving guided tours is directly part of the academic course objectives, but each serves to bring to life those objectives. And even in these less physically demanding examples, how is it determined that the faculty member has expertise in the area of crafting, for example, so that he or she can guide students in the making of handmade crafts as a way of experiencing history?

Presumably faculty in these examples would self-select: the nonkayaker is unlikely to propose field studies involving that activity. The teacher who knows nothing of making your own apron or furniture is unlikely to introduce those activities into an experiential learning setting.

But where field and experiential learning opportunities exist at an institution, we assume that there is more than just faith in self-selection that ensures meaningful, and safe, experiential opportunities for students.

The hybrid situation is not so different, at least from an administrative perspective. Sure a faculty member hired as an English instructor can be assumed to have the background and skill set needed to teach in the discipline. But what is to say that faculty member has the technological or pedagogical know-how to design and deliver a hybrid course?

For any given field and experiential learning proposal, is there a formal mechanism in place to make sure that the basic course idea is feasible? Will students be safe? How are learning objectives met? Can the faculty member truly manage the practical demands of the motto "the world is our classroom"?

Once again, we do not seek to offer a process that has been perfected by all field and experiential offices and that can be co-opted for the purposes of developing hybrid curricula. We do, however, feel it worthwhile to investigate how these processes might already operate at an institution.

Some early fact-finding about existing institutional processes generally can pave the way for future discussions about hybrids, specifically in terms of preserving for hybrids the flexibility and openness that other so-called alternative delivery methods might enjoy.

Developing Hybrid Curricula

So who will design and then teach hybrid classes? And this is by no means a simple question. Most faculty will probably imagine that of course *they* will design their own classes. But are there any precedents—particular to your institution or not—to suggest otherwise?

Note that because the hybrid mode involves a significant online component, there might be competing precedents for how hybrid course design and development will be handled, if yours is like the many institutions that handle f2f and online course development differently. Many institutions have implemented an online pedagogy series of workshops or classes of some sort that introduce faculty new to teaching online to the characteristics of online courses with which they are likely unfamiliar. Will your institution implement a mandatory training series that teachers must pass in order to teach hybrid courses or, as an alternative, will your institution simply trust that instructors interested in teaching a hybrid course will do the necessary research to build the course and understand that pedagogy? Another consideration is whether or not these certificates for online teaching will be offered to part-time instructors as well as full-time instructors. At some institutions, decisions about part-time credentials are made by Human Resources while other institutions allow individual academic departments to review part-time instructors' transcripts and evaluate credentials, if there are any, related to teaching online and hybrid. We discuss possible approaches toward training faculty in the faculty development section of this book; it is a vital step in the process for integrating quality hybrid curriculum at your institution.

Most full-time teaching faculty, at least those teaching entirely face-to-face classes, have control over their own syllabi and course design and are hired to teach within their discipline with no further coursework required (outside of possible ongoing professional development work). Some part-time faculty will have to teach from an existing syllabus or use a preselected textbook (or choose from options) but the day-to-day operation of the classroom is still up to that instructor. In other words, once hired, faculty are assumed to be more or less classroom-ready.

The case of online course design and teaching is often radically different, however. Many faculty lose control over their ability to design their own material and choose their own textbook. Often, faculty (or even outside "content experts") are paid on a work-for-hire basis to design a course, sometimes with assistance from an instructional designer. That work-for-hire becomes the property of the institution, not the designer or faculty member, and anyone wishing to teach that class will be asked (or required) to do so by using the existing course template (sometimes called a "shell"). The freedom to design and teach to one's own strengths, as would happen in the case of teaching face-to-face, evaporates in the online environment.

Which of these precedents will dictate the handling of hybrid course design and development?

Here we will cite the effective practice that has been offered by the Conference on College Composition and Communication Committee for Effective Practice in Online Writing Instruction (OWI). In a 2013 position statement, they assert that "[o]nline writing teachers should retain reasonable control over their own content and/or techniques for conveying, teaching, and assessing their students' writing in their OWCs [online writing courses]" ("Position Statement"). The purview of this position statement includes both online and hybrid learning models, but we feel it worth making the case quite specifically for hybrid learning, since it often straddles the line between both face-to-face and online teaching.

Since individual handling of course design and delivery is, for the most part, already the norm for most instructors working in the fully face-to-face mode, we see an obvious case to be made—and we advocate strongly—for teachers retaining reasonable control over content and method when teaching in the hybrid format as well.

Beyond the basic premise of past practice, why is it better for hybrid course design, and then delivery, to remain largely in the hands of those who will do the actual teaching? In some ways, this is what we feel to be a commonsense argument about the student experience in what we hope are dynamic and engaging courses. We know, for example, that effective instructional design should use multiple content delivery tools available in an LMS. Courses (be they face-to-face supplemented with Web material, hybrid, or fully online) will not just present block after block of text to the student user. Even when this text is chunked effectively, as it should ideally be, a screen—or "course"—of nothing but text will at the very least intimidate most students and at the very worst completely confound others.

More worrisome, reliance on text alone in an LMS is unlikely to engage multiple learning styles, especially those that so many of our students are most fluent in, such as visual learning. Auditory learners too will find themselves at a severe disadvantage when content is delivered in purely textual form in an LMS.

Really, though, this is unlikely to be news to educators. How many textbooks do we see, even those most traditional in their content, tone, and formatting, that include no visual element? Most literature anthologies (those most text-centric of academic tools) tend now to include ample visual elements within their pages and also through online ancillaries. Why would we assume that pure text in an LMS would be effective, especially for engaging students who might already struggle as effective readers? Most educators probably don't assume this, and yet we've seen too many online courses that were, by and large, an instructor's syllabus, notes, and assignments seemingly cut-and-pasted from word processing documents into an LMS. (Or worse: those documents are attached to otherwise empty content items within an LMS.)

We hope you are thinking to yourself: *Do such courses exist? I've never seen one.*

If you haven't, then count yourself, and your students, lucky. But ask enough faculty, instructional designers, or IT support staff and you'll likely hear of online courses that amount to an endless webpage of text, text, and more text.

What's either changing in those once text-heavy courses, or what is informing better course design from square one, is the inclusion of multimedia elements, not just to enhance or supplement text content, but to convey with equal clarity and meaning that content. We are thinking here not just of static images, but of audio, instructor podcasts or vlogs, video, narrated slide shows—all the various ways in which instructors can be effectively present for students in the virtual environment.

Now, to bring this back to why it makes sense that instructors retain control of their content: imagine that an instructor is given a pre-made course to teach, one designed by another faculty member or a so-called content expert. Whose voice do we hear in a podcast? Whose face do we see in a video lecture? Presumably that designer and not the teaching faculty member. A guest lecture is one thing, but to consistently encounter one face and voice in an LMS, while encountering a different face and voice in the classroom, via email, or anywhere outside of the prebuilt course must be disconcerting for a student.

Turning this to the instructor side of things, we feel the argument is no less compelling. Clearly, to teach to one's strengths, regardless of delivery mode, one needs reasonable control over basic things like course design and delivery.

Further, we agree that, as Scott Warnock has asserted in regards to writing instruction, teaching is ultimately a "personality-driven endeavor" (179). This isn't to imply that teaching, whether online or face-to-face, is somehow always an impromptu, let-me-entertain-you kind of performance—and that the proverbial camera either loves you or it doesn't—but rather that students respond to an instructor's own level of passion and investment. As Adrian Furnham has suggested, what makes good teachers great is almost invariably their "enthusiasm, even passion, for their subject. They show the thrill and pleasure of acquiring skills and knowledge in a particular area. And they are able to communicate this. Indeed they cannot hide it. You can't easily fake passion—or at least not over a sustained period. All great teachers are passionate" (Furnham).

Constrained to teach what amounts to someone else's course, instructors have to work unreasonably hard to have their own personality shine through. At very least, they might feel as though they are always working *against* another personality—the original designer—lurking in the shadows. In fact, in cases where so-called master courses are created by those who will not actually teach them, often the design principle is to be as personality neutral as possible. Thus, in theory at least, the more bland and generic the template, the easier it is to farm out to as many different instructors as possible. For good or ill, it is often individual instructor quirks that students connect with, rather than with content that is abstracted and divorced from the teaching personality that presents it. So remove the quirks and you may not be left with much. Thus we argue for instructors retaining control of hybrid design, content, and delivery. Not that individual instructors work in a vacuum, of course. This entire book is an argument against that. But the scenario in which individual instructor personality is allowed to come through in the hybrid setting, just as it would in the fully face-to-face environment, makes obvious sense in terms of benefit to students and to instructors alike.

Given that most instructors will benefit from a community of support (including peers in the discipline along with learning technology experts) as they design and teach hybrids, though, the procedure for hybrid design and delivery will itself probably reflect a blend of both the f2f and online course development processes. We'd like to see the objective of this blend be retaining maximum control for the teaching faculty in order that they be able to truly "teach" a class—by bringing their own personality to bear—rather than just administering existing, static content.

What may have produced different processes for the development and then delivery of online courses were institutional concerns for creating courses that shared a unified feel. Even more important might have been the need to retain institutional control and oversight of design in a medium that teaching faculty did not necessarily have training in. The faculty member who is hired to teach f2f already has the training necessary to do the job. But this is not necessarily the case for faculty who teach online, especially those who move to online teaching only after years of teaching solely f2f. So the piece of the design and delivery puzzle that is missing, in many cases, is the training piece. Even accomplished faculty, who have enjoyed great success in the f2f environment, should not be expected to move into the online arena with no new professional development opportunities. In a similar vein, faculty should not realistically expect to forego training requirements if they wish to teach online, regardless of what success they have had as f2f teachers or how tech savvy they feel themselves to be.

The picture emerges then of a blended approach to hybrid course design and delivery. This blend is grounded in effective principles that address the primary challenges of hybrid design and teaching. First, we do not want the hybrid course design process to mirror what became the norm for so many schools in terms of their online course design process: courses were designed as works for hire, those courses became the property of the institution, and faculty wishing to teach those courses were required to use existing material with little latitude for personalization.

By the same token, though, designing and delivering hybrid courses should not happen precisely as it does in the case of most f2f teaching, wherein faculty retain great freedom in choosing texts, designing syllabi, and managing the day-to-day activities of a class *with no preparation beyond their graduate training and existing f2f experience.*

So faculty retain control over design, but they enter into the design and teaching process having been fully trained and supported specifically as *online* instructors.

What approaches might an institution take to train their instructors, then? This question is fundamental to the hybrid course development process and begs particular attention relative to adjunct and contingent teachers, since they are often (and unfortunately) less well supported and certainly less well compensated than their full-time peers. So we'd like for part-time instructors to enjoy the benefits of designing their own hybrid courses, with the support of instructional designers and learning technology experts of course. But encouraging, or requiring, adjuncts to attend professional development sessions that will hopefully prepare them for hybrid course design and teaching can be challenging, in large part because adjuncts are generally paid per course they teach. Thus, attending a workshop session is, for most part-timers, an unpaid, voluntary exercise.

It is first important to recognize just how dependent many schools are on part-time teachers. Often, adjuncts are teaching upwards of 75 percent of courses in some disciplines.

So how might an institution motivate adjuncts to attend professional development sessions? How can an institution take into consideration the hectic, often divided schedules that are the norm for many adjuncts, many of whom teach at multiple colleges, potentially commuting to multiple campuses on any given day? The simple, though rather generic, answer is that professional development opportunities provided to adjuncts need to be made meaningful. That is, an adjunct's investment of time and effort should yield skills that are as widely applicable as possible, so the time spent in an afternoon professional development session actually bolsters a contingent faculty member's resume across his or her professional endeavors, not just at the one institution offering that particular workshop.

Elsewhere we talk about using digital badges to acknowledge the work that teachers put into attending and participating in professional development opportunities. Perhaps even more formally, an institution could provide a certificate—recognizably valuable inside of that specific institution but also at other institutions as well—to recognize those who have completed an entire series of workshops or training sessions. Once a system of certification is in place, an institution might require it as a prerequisite for those who wish to teach online or in the hybrid format. And the adjunct who teaches at multiple institutions may in fact use that certification credential for more—or better—teaching assignments elsewhere.

In short, making professional development meaningful to adjuncts often means having them walk away with more than just a few pieces of technical knowledge (like what menu items are hiding within what chevrons). In an ideal world, adjuncts would be compensated directly for attending professional development sessions. We realize that this can be challenging for many institutions, but professional development is part of the work of teaching and should be treated as such.

Supporting Hybrid Curricula

We want to emphasize that new classroom realities for many students (what tools they are asked to use and what learning modes they have available to them) should mean a new support system reality for those students as well. Consider for example a student who takes a first-year writing course, the ubiquitous English 101, even in the fully face-to-face mode. Not online. Not in the hybrid format. Nothing so-called *alternative* about it. These days that student will likely be doing an appreciable amount of his or her work online, whether in the form of research, and sharing that research via collaborative class tools, or producing essays or other written work, and sharing that with others via a learning management system or other digital tools. In fact, many first-year writing students will be producing more than traditional, text-based essays. They are likely to be building a range of multimodal, and collaborative, projects, which depend on the Web for their creation.

As such, student support systems like IT help, library resources, or academic assistance need to be accessible online at almost *every* institution, even those that do not necessarily offer entirely online classes. Many students taking fully face-to-face classes are potentially, for part of their academic work, for all intents and purposes, online students. They are engaging with materials online, they depend on a learning management system, they are conducting research online, and they are writing online. They are not just using a word processor. They are using digital, collaborative tools to create and share their work.

A 2015 Educause report sums this new student support reality up nicely: supporting students now means "providing user support in the new normal—mobile, online education, cloud, and BYOD [bring your own device] environments" (Grajek et al. 12). Even where on-campus student support systems might be robust, running smoothly, have a long institutional history, and are otherwise thriving and serving students well, are they reflecting this "new normal"?

The 2015 Educause report, titled "Inflection Point," outlines tech-related issues that Educause feels will most likely impact higher education in the near future. As the author notes, "The pace of change seems not to be slowing but, rather, is increasing and is happening on many fronts." The titular "inflection point" is, according to the report authors, happening now, as technologies and trends that have otherwise been the purview of so-called early adopters, or tech-leaders, are "cascading into the mainstream" (Grajek et al. 11).

Technology now presents realizable solutions to identifiable campus or institutional problems. For early adopters (whether on the individual or institutional level), technology was often— maybe too often—a solution in search of that problem. The "Inflection Point" authors propose that because of advances in personal computing power (in the form of the smartphone, for example) along with infrastructure advances in the areas of improved Internet connection speed and bandwidth, institutions are more and more likely to see technology as truly a solution to a problem, not that solution in search of a problem to solve. Take attempts to increase student success rates, for example: improving student success rates such as class and college retention and grades has long been a challenge for many institutions and remains a seemingly intractable problem no matter how many committees we form, orientation sessions we offer, or college success classes we teach. With increasingly more state funding formulas relying on retention rates, colleges are under pressure to increase those student success and retention numbers. We are not suggesting that technology can, in fact, solve the problem of student success (if it is even the kind of problem that can ever be definitively solved). But what we (following the "Inflection Point" authors) recognize is that more and more institutions are turning to technology as perhaps the go-to resource when it comes to those long intractable problems.

What does this technology look like and what forms does it come in? As the "Inflection Point" authors suggest, these technologies have become the new higher education buzzwords: "Mobile-Cloud-Big Data-Business Value-Agile-Transformation-Social-Analytics-Online Learning" (Grajek et al. 12). Institutionally, it might take the form of learning management system analytics used strategically to identify trends that could predict student success (or lack thereof).

In their article "Beyond Retention: Using Targeted Analytics to Improve Student Success," authors Loralyn Taylor and Virginia McAleese describe how Paul Smith's College, which serves a small but high-need student population, recognized problems with their existing systems for identifying students who need academic help and timely intervention. As Taylor and McAleese explain, the small nonprofit college developed a "new Comprehensive Student Support Program using technology including data intelligence and analytics, for more efficient and effective student success interventions." The results "demonstrate that even smaller colleges with minimal institutional research capabilities can use technology to increase their analytic capability" (Taylor and McAleese).

The Paul Smith's College case provides a good example of how technology provided a means by which to re-imagine how the college used data to identify a student who might need academic help and then to intervene before that student withdrew or fell so far behind that there was no catching up. As Taylor and McAleese make clear in their article, using data and analytics in this new way meant significant institutional changes: the college purchased new software systems, for example, and support staff and faculty had to be made aware of how the new student alert and intervention systems would work. With new technologies came new institutional procedures and support systems for those using the technology.

Even if many students—even those in f2f courses—already use a learning management system or digital tools, institutional support systems need to change to reflect changing classroom realities: the "new normal" that Grajek and her "Inflection Point" coauthors identify.

What might student support look like if we acknowledge that potentially all students are, to some degree, online learners?

Academic Counseling and Advising

Here we'd like to extend our previous discussion of the role that counseling and advising can play relative to hybrids, particularly in regard to ongoing student support. Advisors and counselors, in their crucial role linking students to classes and programs, need to be well represented in early institutional conversations about hybrid development, as we mentioned earlier. Academic advisors may have valuable insight on what students need, or what they think they need, in terms of curricular choices. Are students consistently showing up in an advising office actively asking for greater flexibility in their scheduling choices? Perhaps advisors will recognize how often the choice to go online (or hybrid) is really a plan-b option when students simply cannot make a fully face-to-face schedule of classes work. Academic advisors may have important insight on whether or not students are proactively seeking curricular alternatives, or simply ending up in these learning environments because nothing else will work.

The implications for the likely student body showing up in any given hybrid or online course are profound. In one case, hybrid curricular development could occur with a specific student population in mind: those showing up to advising asking for alternatives to the traditional fully face-to-face model. Marketing can be developed with this target audience in mind. Materials can be prepared for advising use designed specifically for the student who seems fully aware of the demands of non-f2f learning. The alternative, though, and probably more the rule than the exception, is that hybrid and online delivery ends up being the fallback plan for many students. This would seem to invite a very different kind of marketing material (one that stressed the basic nature of the hybrid design and what kind of student might do well). So too might individual courses look different, especially in the early days or weeks, as ample time will have to be devoted to basic explanations about the hybrid model. Expectations for face-to-face and online participation will have to be made abundantly clear, and likely reiterated well into a course in an effort to keep students on track. So too might instructors find themselves in the role of IT troubleshooter, especially in cases where students are taking classes in the hybrid mode more because they happen to fit the schedule than because those students have any affinity with technology (or even dependable access to it and a quiet place to work online).

Academic advisor and counselor input early on may also shape the kinds of technology that instructors are willing to use in any given class. Again, a highly motivated and informed student population coming into hybrid courses may truly benefit from the use of digital tools that exist outside the institutional LMS and/or those with a steeper learning curve than some of the LMS basics. That potentially less aware or motivated student population, however, may not respond well or benefit from technologies that require them to sign up for an account, work outside the LMS, or navigate applications for which there are not well-established support materials. A discussion board in an LMS is not necessarily "easy" to use for all students, but it requires less of the user than might a non-LMS digital tool (another account, username, and password to remember, an unfamiliar interface—the barriers to success multiply quickly). At least, though, most LMS providers will have ample support materials, in the form of quick how-to videos, for example, for standard LMS features, and many institutions have produced such how-to resources inhouse as well.

The work of counseling and advising vis-à-vis the hybrid curriculum needs to be ongoing, and if hybrids become, per the "Inflection Point" authors cited earlier, part of the institutional new normal, academic advising and counseling services will have to reflect that change.

So what does academic advising look like at your institution? In the best cases, students can access these services at multiple venues, like a central hub along with satellite centers, or advising can be available as part of individual academic or disciplinary units. In either case, advising serves students best when it is highly visible and accessible. Many institutions do this very well, at least for students who can visit the advising office in person.

Online academic advising is less the norm, however, even on campuses that provide excellent in-person academic advising support for students. In fact, institutions that primarily serve students in person might do well to turn to primarily online institutions to discover what effective online advising might look like. Take Georgia Perimeter College-Online (GPC), for example, the third-largest college in the Georgia state system, serving some nine thousand students, all online.

As Sharriette Finley and Jeanna Chapman of GPC report in their article, "Actively Including Online Students in the College Experience," "to better serve our growing online population, it has been necessary for us to develop and maintain consistent, high-quality student services with a specific focus on online academic advising." Part of their advising mission is to afford the online student an advising experience equivalent in quality and depth to what a typical face-to-face student might receive. A simple tool like email connects advisors to students; beyond just the digital tool itself, though, the institution makes it a priority to respond to students "in one business day or less" (Finley and Chapman). Further, Finley and Chapman describe GPC's use of virtual classroom software to deliver real-time, but at-a-distance, workshops whose topics are probably familiar to most advisors even if the delivery mode is not: time management, stress management, and study skills.

As Finley and Chapman assert, "Accessibility to [advising] resources is essential." We'd like to reiterate this point, but where GPC has devoted concentrated energy to developing online advising resources *for online students,* our call is to have institutions that are not necessarily serving a primarily, or exclusively, online student population pay equal attention to making advising resources available online, particularly as part of institutional efforts to develop online and hybrid curricula.

Such online advising might include common tools like email, but accompanied by widely held understanding that email communication needs to be timely. In addition, numerous synchronous meeting tools are available to make online advising sessions—real-time but at-a-distance—a practical addition to an institution's advising services. In a presentation about online advising, Laura Pasquini and Clay Schwenn outline some of the tools they use to enable online advising. Among these are Skype, Twitter, and Google Docs.

Additionally, making important student planning and academic documents accessible online can support effective virtual advising so that both advisors and students have secure access to individual student records. Connecting in real time is one thing, but that needs to be supported with access to relevant records and student planning tools as well.

In a 2011 article entitled "Implications for Use of Technology in Advising 2011 National Survey" Laura Pasquini asserts that "[p]rofessional and faculty advisors need to consider the ramifications of their current technological systems and communication strategies to consider if they are meeting the needs of today's learner."

We could not agree more, though this might be a tall order. Efforts to assess whether or not resources like academic advising are meeting student needs should ideally happen as part of curricular innovation and development. In other words, if students are going online, support systems need to go there too. The Global Community for Academic Advising (NACADA) works to support effective online advising via its Technology in Advising Commission and website. The commission's purpose is to "help academic advisors, faculty advisors, and advising administrators understand the impact of using technologies in advising"

(NACADA). NACADA might be a good place to start for many institutions looking to find out about how best to support students using technology today.

Library and Research Support

It is vital to the success of hybrid students and instructors that the campus library provides online support that is sensitive to the needs of online learners, especially as those needs might be different from students who are otherwise on campus most days of the week. Many campus libraries provide, for example, online database access and video tutorials to help students with using library research resources, but something like database access from offsite will generally require that students log in to verify that they are, indeed, part of the institution that has paid for access to a research resource like a database. What online mechanisms are in place to support those students who have difficulty logging in? Can library cards be renewed, updated, or reactivated as easily for distance learners as for onsite students?

Another important way in which libraries can support distance learners—whether those students are in fully online or in hybrid classes—is to make sure that the same kinds of face-to-face drop-in sessions that are offered on campus (like how to research effectively, how to use citation systems, or what the fundamentals of digital literacy look like) are also offered online, ideally not as prerecorded sessions that limit or entirely exclude opportunities for student interaction, but as real-time, virtual sessions during which students can raise a digital hand to ask questions. If students are asked to engage in college-level research projects and have opted to take a hybrid course that by definition includes less time present on campus, they need to know that they are not getting shortchanged on library support. At root this is the foundational issue of equal access to learning resources for all students. As Corbett and Brown have noted, "[B]y providing effective educational opportunities beyond its campus boundaries. . . . [a]s well as providing a complete array of library services to distant students, [an] institution shows that it understands its responsibility to distant students and that they are being proactive in meeting their unique needs."

If a campus is forward thinking in its efforts to serve students whose primary mode of accessing school support systems will be from off campus, an institution might provide the option of an embedded librarian in their courses. An embedded librarian is one who is assigned to a particular course section. He or she will integrate instructional videos and assignments into modules of the course and provide additional research assistance for that course: but all of this will happen virtually. In some cases, embedded librarians can facilitate virtual research sessions for their particular assigned classes (as we show below). These sessions are not external to a course section but an integrated component, often facilitated through a learning management system in such a way that students are first logging in to their course to participate in a virtual research session. They will learn from the embedded librarian with the rest of their usual classmates. Corbett and Brown, following Hoffman, write that "As students interact with the embedded librarian they become aware of the resources available to them and feel more comfortable using them for research purposes." This more personalized approach to connecting students who are working online to campus resources tends to provide those students not just with basic valuable information that can help them perform better in classes, but with a sense that the institution is aware of what modes students are learning in and adapting support systems thoughtfully.

The embedded librarian can be particularly popular in courses whose very foundation requires research, such as the second-semester English Composition course, often dedicated to research writing. An embedded librarian creates an additional level of support for students who get to know this librarian and feel they can turn to someone specific—an actual person, not just a website FAQ—when in need of help beyond that provided by the course instructor.

Joanna Paull has had the experience of an embedded librarian. The notion of an embedded librarian in the hybrid or online class in particular is an opportunity for students to have a direct connection to a specific librarian on the physical college campus who becomes a liaison, coinstructor, and research mentor of sorts. The extent to which a course might embed that librarian could vary quite a bit, but Paull's experience included librarian-constructed videos about library-focused techniques and approaches for researching.

For example, the librarian might provide search strategies for preparing for library database-focused searches, identifying the differences between those database search requirements versus those of an Internet search engine like Google, including Boolean operators versus natural language auto-added "ands" in a Google search. He or she might also wish to include video tutorials about the most commonly used database searches like Academic Search Complete. Once the students are given the background instruction on using the library resources, the embedded librarian assigns students library activities, discussions and/or worksheets, giving them the opportunity to apply that knowledge to their research experiences for the course. In addition, an embedded librarian often moderates discussion forums for research-focused questions.

The embedded librarian is a different experience from having the course instructor providing library orientation, assignments, and question and answer sessions with students. Specifically, embedded librarians bring their extensive knowledge to the table, knowledge that is regularly updated with new databases, search strategies, and layered understandings of the different ways that these search systems work. While some instructors may feel comfortable with such a thing, if the course objectives include research-based items (e.g., English Composition 2, which is often research-based writing), most courses only require a research project but without direct library instruction/aid. With the embedded librarian, though, students are likely to have a more positive, critical, and elevated research process and, ultimately, produce higher-level projects for their instructors.

The embedded librarian might be part of a course for the entire semester or, if the students are only working on a project for a short period of time during a course, this librarian may be brought in during that piece of the semester only. Figure 9 shows what an embedded librarian might look like in a learning management system. Figures 10 and 11 show further screenshots from a real-time, though virtual, library session facilitated in Adobe

Connect. The embedded librarian takes students through a slide presentation and wraps the session up. The variety of enthusiastic responses from students in the chat window include "thank you for everything!"; "thank you so much!!"; and "thank you for your help!"

Greetings! From your friendly neighborhood librarian.

Posted on: Thursday, January 30, 2014 9:57:51 AM CST

Hello everyone!

I just wanted to say hello and introduce myself. My job as a librarian is to teach people how to research for themselves, and in

turn, learn for themselves, much like your college professors are here to do. The librarian profession has made many turns, but we are very much here to help you. This is our primary responsibility. For years, librarians safeguarded the knowledge in physical libraries and archives helping people access that collection of knowledge. Today, we still do this a little, but our job now is helping people navigate the tidal wave of information thrown at them both in physical form (books) and electronic form.

This is why I am here - to help you find quality sources for your research, not just the first thing that comes up. I look forward to hearing from all of you. Remember, 3 million hits in Google is cute, but useless. It is unlikely you even look at all of the first page, did you? Quantity and quality are rarely the same thing. When seeking sources and deciding whether to use it as a supporting source, remember to ask yourself, "Who created this and why should I care?" and "Do I want to base my professional/academic reputation on this?"

Don't ever be afraid to ask questions.

I look forward to working with all of you,

Jason Ertz
Associate Professor / Reference Librarian

FIGURE **9.** *Embedded librarian greeting on LMS announcement page.*

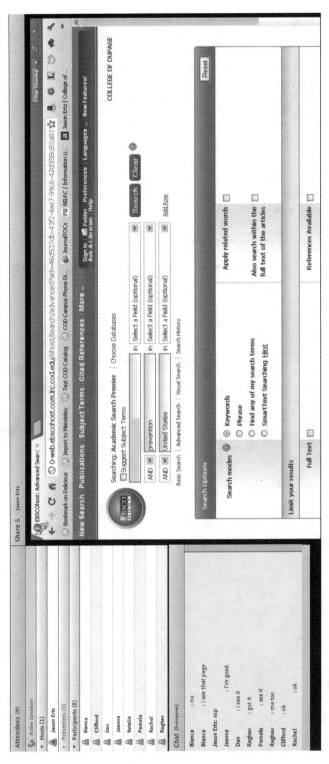

FIGURE 10. *Virtual synchronous research session in Adobe Connect.*

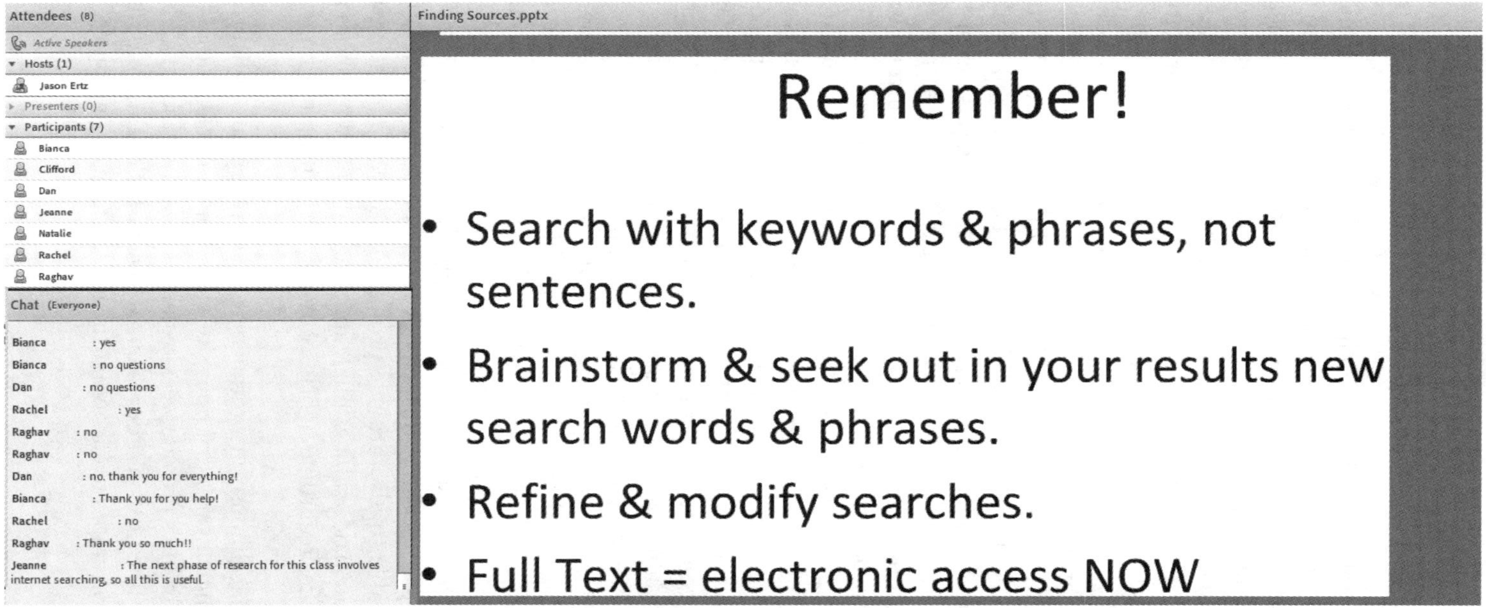

FIGURE 11. *Embedded librarian showing PowerPoint slides in Adobe Connect.*

Learner and Teacher Support

Students taking courses in digital, distance-based environments require access to academic support services that are offered in that same digital, distance-based format. This support should include access to important, though too often underused, academic resources like tutoring services. In fact, many fully onsite students can benefit from academic support—be it for writing or math or other disciplines—that is accessible remotely.

Many institutions provide a means for engaging in online tutoring or writing assistance from their campus academic support or tutoring centers via Skype, Adobe Connect, Writing-Central/WC Online, or Google Hangouts, for example. Others may offer students access to paid online tutoring services instead of support offered by the institution itself. Among some of the popular subscription-based tutoring services are Smarthinking (a Pearson product) and Tutor.com; this latter promises that "our online tutors are ready to help you 24/7" (Tutor.com). Whatever option an institution provides to support its students, it is vital for student success to have academic support services provided online, distance-based. Offering hybrid or fully online classes without concomitant academic support services, provided in the same modality as those courses, risks marginalizing students who are challenged to access solely on-campus resources.

In addition to supporting students in their work as hybrid learners, institutions will need to consider how to support their hybrid teachers as well. As is true of any successful curriculum development, implementation of a hybrid curriculum requires introduction of and continuous offerings for faculty development. For some institutions, this may occur inhouse only while others may be able to also provide professional development through local, state, regional, national, and international workshops and conferences regarding hybrid course development and improvement.

If done inhouse, institutions should be prepared to offer training through a variety of points of view. For example, both of our home campuses provide weekly courses regarding the capabilities of the online LMS in order to encourage knowledge development and opportunities to encourage faculty learning communities. The content of the sessions might include implementation of active learning activities, such as wikis and online discussion forum construction, or address approaches for creating accessible course environments, for example.

Specializing the course topics allows faculty to select those topics about which they are least versed or perhaps newly interested in incorporating into their course. Instructional design team members might also consider inviting faculty well versed in any one particular session focus to share their experiences using that feature in their classrooms. This could create a more collaborative environment for the faculty in the session and also allow the instructional designers to more fully understand the benefits and challenges with that aspect of the LMS.

But as with the support services for students we discussed earlier, which we argue need to be available online if that is the mode that students are doing coursework in, so too should faculty training and professional development be offered in a variety of formats, not limited just to onsite, fully face-to-face venues.

So informational training sessions could be offered on a variety of days and times for faculty, but they could also include options to attend remotely (via Adobe Connect or other Web-conferencing software, for example). Some sessions could be offered exclusively in the online, or webinar, format. Webinars can be recorded and made available for viewing even after they have taken place. In fact, by recording and cataloging recorded professional development sessions, institutions can quickly develop a useful repository of archived videos that faculty—or other interested parties—can tap into.

Such a repository might even be made searchable if each recorded session is tagged with relevant keywords (like "gradebook," "participation," or "discussion"). True, viewers of those recorded sessions will lose the ability to interact with a session facilitator or other participants, but at least the presented information is made available to those who are not able to attend on-campus sessions or webinars that occur on a given day and time.

It is also a good idea for institutions to introduce, and encourage ongoing participation in, a peer mentoring community of hybrid instructors, administrators, and support staff. Again, a good deal of collegial interaction may happen face-to-face, but equally beneficial will be an identifiable virtual space for such interaction as well. For example, enrolling all faculty who teach hybrid courses into a course site within the LMS allows for those faculty to pose questions and suggest answers and to share experiences with teaching hybrid courses. Equally welcome to such a virtual collaborative space should be administrators and institutional support staff whose roles on campus are connected to hybrid learning.

We particularly like the idea of institutions developing a virtual space where faculty can show off what they are finding to be especially effective practices relative to their hybrid teaching, be it a course module, or an example of how they have effectively integrated classroom work with online work to achieve a given course objective. Without a virtual home for this kind of interaction and ongoing discussion, faculty can easily feel isolated, unaware of what other courses are being offered in the hybrid format or who might be teaching them.

In addition to ongoing workshops and course offerings for faculty, institutions should also provide opportunities for faculty to access one-on-one support with IT experts who might be able to address targeted technical questions about an LMS feature or other institutionally supported digital tools.

Such IT support is likely best provided online, though should not be limited to an email-based help desk system. While asynchronous help via email is probably the primary go-to for many teachers, real-time, though distance-based, support is especially helpful when it comes to technical questions, particularly when offered via a platform that allows for screensharing, like Google Hangouts or JoinMe. It is often much easier to actually *show* an IT help staff member what is happening in your gradebook or wiki or whatever tech-tool is misbehaving than to describe in words that same problem. And with the synchronous help session, an IT expert can potentially walk a faculty member through a number of troubleshooting possibilities in real time, rather than the two having to trade numerous emails back and forth.

As we have argued for the importance of making sure that student support systems—from academic advising, to library resources, to tutoring—be made accessible to students in online, distance-based formats, so too is it important to support hybrid curricula by offering support systems to faculty in a diverse array of formats, including online and fully face-to-face modalities.

Assessing Hybrid Curricula

We'd like to look here at methods for assessing individual hybrid courses, including aspects of instruction and of instructional design, in addition to considering hybrid curricula more generally, from a broader, programmatic perspective. While it is certainly crucial to be offering effective hybrid courses, it is also important from the institutional perspective to be strategic about what hybrid courses are available to students. With no broader perspective, a college or university can end up with great hybrid courses . . . but all in English, or chemistry, or wherever there might have been a groundswell of faculty interest in building those courses. We would like to see more institutions giving students not just one or two good hybrid courses, but rather a path forward through multiple courses, leading to a certificate or degree, that is primarily, if not fully in the hybrid mode.

We'd also like to think about assessing hybrid courses in terms of learning objectives, with a particular emphasis away from what are often overly simplistic letter-grade analyses: that is, in a given course, how many students earned As, Cs, Fs, or Ws. As Michael Horn, cofounder and executive director of education at the nonprofit Clayton Christensen Institute for Disruptive Innovation, has argued, "Success metrics [for blended learning] could range from whether students were proficient on a state test to whether all students attained mastery of a set of knowledge and skills to whether we were looking to boost engagement and intrinsic motivation."

As a learning mode that involves online instruction, the hybrid model lends itself readily to what are sometimes called twenty-first-century learning outcomes. These are the kinds of learning objectives that reflect the degree to which today's students are working collaboratively but often at a distance, sometimes even in fully face-to-face classes. Such objectives are not always well articulated in academic outcomes documents or curricular guides, unless those have been recently and thoughtfully updated. But while a skill like working with a group to create a document using a collaborative tool like Google Docs does not necessarily figure as a formalized learning outcome for many classes, that skill is nonetheless of growing importance in the workplace. The Partnership for 21st Century Learning argues that "applied skills such as teamwork, critical thinking, and communication are essential for success at work" ("Most Young People"). And a National Association of Colleges and Employers (NACE) survey conducted in 2014 indicates that the skills most valued by employers included critical thinking/problem solving—nothing new to those in higher education—but also teamwork, a skill with particular relevance in the digital age, when so much collaboration is afforded by our digital devices and platforms (see Adams, "The College Degrees and Skills Employers Most Want in 2015"; "Job Outlook 2015").

So while assessment of hybrid curricula certainly needs to account for fairly traditional learning outcomes, like creative and critical thinking, not to mention whatever course-specific goals have been identified by an instructor, program, or institution, we hope that assessing hybrid courses will also attend to outcomes with particular relevance to the blended nature of the learning mode. The online component of hybrid courses lends itself so readily to the twenty-first-century outcomes that are being identified by employers and advocacy groups like The Partnership for 21st Century Learning as valuable beyond college, it would be a missed opportunity not to include these in assessment processes.

Furthermore, like any other course platform, the hybrid format requires assessment for ongoing improvement. Institutions have any number of ways to implement assessments both within the department or program and institution-wide.

Like most classes, hybrid courses will require course evaluations conducted by the students. Some institutions continue to use the same student course evaluations as they use for campus instruction, which provide limited insight into the unique elements of the hybrid course structure like the online versus f2f interactions, the fluidity of course discussions from one platform to the next, and the need to ask questions regarding online media components.

Course and teacher evaluations should ask questions targeting the nuances of instructing hybrid courses, such as the teacher's ability to create an ongoing conversation from one platform to the next, provide appropriate support for the online piece of the puzzle, and bring aspects of that online interaction back into the physical classroom meetings. While many f2f classes do include some sort of online assistant, the hybrid course requires student-to-student and student-to-teacher interaction both in the classroom and in the online course shell each week, making it noticeably different from an f2f class. Questions in the evaluations about both of these types of interactions are vital to assessing this kind of a course.

With these preferences in mind, there are many institutions that have failed to incorporate different student evaluation and/ or teacher evaluation/observation questions between platforms in an attempt to assert that all instructors should be evaluated based on the same criteria. This line of reasoning needs to stop, however. To pretend as if teaching in all platforms requires the same pedagogy will only lead to courses structured just like f2f or just like online. This domino effect could potentially lead to students treating them as if they are one or the other. Perhaps it is this mindset that may contribute slightly to the common situation wherein hybrid students attend all of the f2f *or* all of the online class meetings but fail to attend the other class meetings each week. Finally, if both teachers and students pretend as if hybrid courses are the same, and the courses' success or failure is determined by the same criteria as f2f and online courses, they will likely not grow in productive, positive ways. Questions in the student course surveys regarding their own performance in the course could help us understand the correlations between those fully participating and those absent from part of the course.

If institutions gathered a team of instructors, deans, and IT staff members to design student surveys/evaluations for the hybrid platform, what resources might they use to aid in developing said assessment for hybrid courses?

The Role of Formal Assessment Groups in Assessing Hybrid Courses

While assessment from formal organizations is not necessary for an excellent and stable hybrid curriculum, often having these kinds of insights can prove valuable during the development and master course determination stages for courses. In this section, we'd like to explore some bigger entities who might provide thoughtful assessments of hybrid courses.

One widely used assessment tool comes from Quality Matters (QM). Increasingly more institutions are adopting QM at some level, and Quality Matters' rubric annotations are expanding their coverage to include hybrid course design specifically; the tool is thus becoming especially useful for targeting aspects of hybrid instruction directly.

Quality Matters has grown since its early research stage in 2004. Specifically, "From the beginning, Quality Matters was envisioned to be more than a rubric; it was seen as a framework to facilitate inter-institutional cooperation and training for peer review of online courses." And further, "once the initial rubric was developed by the Tool Committee, the Process and Training Committees began their work in developing a replicable system of peer review for the improvement of online courses" (Shattuck). It is this system's intention to be more than just an assessment, which has helped it grow to aid in instructor development of strong online and hybrid courses. Focusing more so on the overarching structure and ease of navigation for students, this approach assesses those elements rather than the content-specific elements of the course.

The QM assessment approach is relatively closely aligned with the Illinois Online Network's QOCI (ION's Quality Online Course Initiative), which provides an open-access rubric that can be used or adapted as needed. These rubrics emphasize module-level learning objectives that match the assignments for the week and the assessment approaches for those assignments. One noticeable difference is accessibility, though, since QM only permits the general public access to the basic rubric, while those with memberships to QM can see the annotations in addition to the basic rubric. Meanwhile, though, ION's QOCI provides full access to the annotated rubric to all public readers.

QM has eight standards: Course Overview and Introduction; Learning Objectives; Assessment and Measurement; Instructional Materials; Course Activities and Learner Interaction; Course Technology; Learner Support; and Accessibility and Usability.

Meanwhile, the Illinois Online Network's QOCI (Quality Online Course Initiative) includes six areas of assessment and evaluation: Instructional Design; Communication, Interaction and Collaboration; Student Evaluation & Assessment; Learner Support & Resources; Web Design; and Course Evaluation (see Figure 12). What these assessment tools allow for is close examination of our course sites, thinking about how easily students can move through the information provided in the course; the effectiveness with which the instructors align their module-specific learning objectives with the assignments for the week; and the assessments of how students meet or fail to meet their module objectives. Both systems assess the ways that the multimedia and/or technology are both appropriate for the module as well as the ways that they contribute to the flow of the week's assigned reading. This assures that those components do not exist as pure bells and whistles but have a central pedagogical role.

Outside of these two relatively formal assessment possibilities, instructors might also consider utilizing Sloan-C (now the Online Learning Commission, OLC) or, for writing instructors, a CCCC position statement, like the 2013 "A Position Statement of Principles and Example Effective Practices for Online Writing Instruction (OWI)," which provides guidelines for these kinds of assessments without actually resulting in a score or certification of some sort. The OLC offers a Mastery Series workshop on

QUALITY MATTERS	ILLINOIS ONLINE NETWORK QOCI
Course Overview & Introduction	Instructional Design, C. Course Information
Learning Objectives	Instructional Design, B. Learning Goals/Objectives/Outcomes
Assessment and Measurement	Student Evaluations & Assessment Course Evaluation
Course Technology	Instructional Design, F. Use of Multimedia
Learner Support	Learner Support & Resources
Accessibility & Usability	Web Design

FIGURE 12. *Comparison chart between Quality Matters and Illinois Online Network QOCI.*

blended learning. Specifically, it identifies seven major learning objectives: analyze research related to blended learning design; student learning and satisfaction, and assessment; develop a blended course design plan with outcomes and objectives; analyze assessment strategies for their suitability for face-to-face or online use; develop an assessment plan for your blended course; analyze teaching methods and learning activities for use in either face-to-face or online settings; and develop a teaching unit for your blended course that includes face-to-face and online components. These types of training courses allow teachers to think through the development of their hybrid curricula alongside guides and other faculty for that mentoring and support so many of us find helpful.

Rather than trying to evaluate these various assessment tools and declare a so-called winner here, however, we believe that institutions are best served by making their own choices about what assessment and quality control instruments and processes work best within their individual contexts. In fact, while some sense of what defines "quality," and at least a basic framework that outlines course development and review processes, should be shared at the institutional level, there is nothing to say that modifications to a broader shared vision cannot usefully occur at the departmental or programmatic level, especially in cases where a college offers a wide variety of degrees or certificates. The hybrid course development and assessment process might look different in a fire science certificate program than in, say, the math department.

While quality hybrid courses in either of those cases will undoubtedly share effective fundamental aspects in common, the specifics of course design, and the processes for design, review, and revision could vary. Perhaps in one case it will make sense for all the faculty who teach in a particular program, especially if that group is relatively small, to work collaboratively on course design. Review and revision of that course might occur on a regular basis, with input from all of those faculty members. This configuration can also be beneficial in cases where a group of faculty members would like to have a single "master" course that they all teach in more or less the same way. That way, students in specialized certificate programs are getting basically the same learning experience regardless of the instructor.

But clearly in other cases there will be too many people teaching in a given program or department to work as a whole. Exactly how course design, assessment, and revision happens will need to be tailored, just as the various assessment tools and instruments will need to be evaluated, and potentially modified, to suit particular circumstances.

We, as composition teachers, for example, will often defer to discipline-specific resources, even while working in the framework of Quality Matters or other, overarching quality control systems. The CCCC Committee for Effective Practices in Online Writing Instruction provides college composition instructors of online and hybrid writing courses with some specific guidelines for how to develop and revise the strongest possible online and hybrid writing courses, for example. That committee's 2013 "A Position Statement of Principles and Effective Practices for OWI" outlines a series of effective practices that address good online teaching practice but also sound administrative and institutional practice when it comes to the teaching of writing online. For example, the position statement advocates in its first, overarching, principle that "[o]nline writing instruction [both fully online and in the hybrid formats] should be universally inclusive and accessible" ("Position Statement").

This means that learning experiences are ADA compliant, but also that we account for barriers to access beyond physical disabilities, including socioeconomic challenges. We do not build hybrid courses that assume, for example, that every student will have access to the fastest, most powerful tech devices. We should also be conscious of how income demographic is likely to predict access to a broadband Internet connection at home. An NPR report, entitled "FCC Chairman Wants to Help Low-Income Americans Afford Broadband," discusses Federal Communications Commission efforts to expand the scope of its existing Lifeline program, which otherwise subsidizes phone service for low-income households, to cover high-speed Internet access as well (Naylor). As FCC commissioner Tom Wheeler notes, "[W] hile more than 95 percent of households with incomes over $150,000 have broadband, only 48 percent of those making less than $25,000 have service at home."

Another principle outlined in the position statement that is especially important for us as online writing teachers states that "students should be prepared by the institution and their teachers for the unique technological and pedagogical components of OWI" ("Position Statement"). Again, online writing instruction as the 4Cs committee conceives it is not limited to a fully distance-based, 100 percent online class. Online writing instruction occurs in the hybrid format and may account for a significant part of what happens in an otherwise fully face-to-face writing course as well. But this particular position statement speaks to one of our primary concerns throughout this book: that when students are asked to work online, probably using features provided in an LMS, it is incumbent on teachers *and the institution at large* to provide needed orientation, troubleshooting, and ongoing support systems for those students.

And when it comes to quality course design in our particular discipline, Principle 2 from the position statement is key: "An online writing course should focus on writing and not on technology orientation or teaching students how to use learning and other technologies" ("Position Statement"). This may at first seem at odds with the aforementioned principle about teachers being at least partly responsible for preparing students for "the unique technological and pedagogical components of OWI" ("Position Statement"). The point of Principle 2 is not that instructors should expect that their students will already know how to use a tool in the LMS or know how to collaborate on a shared document and can thus forego orienting students to those tools. On the contrary, students are more than likely to need introduction (or re-introduction each semester) to how certain features work in the LMS or in online collaborative spaces. But the purpose of such technology orientation is not so that students learn the intricacies of the discussion board feature in Blackboard, or whatever tool is at hand. Rather, what they are learning is how to enable some aspect of composition—be it individual writing or, more commonly, ways to collaborate and exchange writing with peers—to meet composition course objects. In other words (as we will cover in Chapter 5), learning about and using the technology is a means to an end, not an end in and of itself.

Actually, that the principles mentioned earlier do not necessarily square with each other at first blush is at least in part why they are so valuable. Taken individually, a principle might make *prima facie* sense. But taken as a whole we often find ourselves having to work through complexities we had not at first noticed. This work is a valuable part of ensuring quality.

To support the position statement, the committee has developed an online open resource that publishes examples of effective online writing practice. Submissions are peer reviewed and those chosen for publication are made available on the Online Writing Instruction Open Resource website (OWI Open Resource). Another related resource is the Online Writing Instruction committee's 2015 collection, *Foundational Practices of Online Writing Instruction* (Hewett and DePew). Between this committee's ongoing work, the open resource it supports, and its publications about effective online writing instruction practices, we find a wealth of material that can inform assessment and quality control processes when it comes to developing online and hybrid English courses. Our broader point, though, is that while these resources speak to us as writing teachers, those in other fields will benefit from seeking out discipline-specific resources that make sense for their curricular areas. Instruments like Quality Matters and the other tools outlined earlier can provide a good institutional framework within which different curricular areas can then work to research and refine what resources work best for them.

To give a sense of how we have coordinated various course development and assessment tools that reflect both broad, effective-practice strategies, but that also include aspects specific to our work as composition teachers, in the next section we provide a course-design checklist that we have developed. We offer it not as a perfected ideal to be adopted wholesale, but rather as a potential starting place, one among many resources that those designing, teaching, and assessing hybrid courses might find useful.

Your Course Design Checklist

Truthfully, the discussion here could just as easily show up in the preceding section on course development. As we've noted, course development, support, and assessment efforts are often deeply integrated.

We include material here, though, to emphasize how important continuous improvement is for hybrid curricula to thrive. So something like a course design checklist, which encourages those building hybrid courses to carefully consider whether their courses afford students the best opportunities for success, is obviously useful from the very first stages of instructional design. But if use of some kind of effective practices guidelines ends with initial course development, curricula are too likely to stagnate. We advocate, on the other hand, for frequent use of feedback mechanisms within courses, in addition to various evaluation measures, so that teachers can actively assess their teaching and their courses and make changes. Revision and improvement is an ongoing—an in-built—part of teaching hybrid courses.

This basic design checklist reflects our own experiences designing and teaching hybrids over the past decade. We've relied heavily too, though, on existing resources (identified at the end of the checklist). In fact, we have borrowed directly from a number of established course design rubrics. Our purpose was never to reinvent the wheel.

What we'd like to highlight, in fact, is not really the checklist itself. Certainly we are not putting this one forward as necessarily a quantifiable improvement on any of the sources we've drawn from. What the checklist here represents, though, is what has emerged from a collaborative and institution-specific process. In other words, we are encouraging individual institutions to make their own decisions about what kind of design rubric makes sense for them.

The checklist we offer might be implemented at your institution as it stands. Maybe one of the design checklists we've borrowed from would make more sense for your institution. Maybe—likely—some combination of existing resources, tailored to your institution's specific needs, and workplace and contractual realities, will fit the bill. In short, we'd like to see course design expectations reflect the character of an individual institution and the students likely to be served.

Keep in mind that some, though not all, of what is below needs to occur in the online portion of a hybrid class. In many cases, it will be useful to provide materials and learning opportunities in both online and f2f modes.

1. Learner Support and Resources
   - Tips for being a successful student in a blended course
   - Quiz/questionnaire to self-assess readiness
   - Contact information for technical support or help desk
   - Orientation and/or course/LMS walk-through
   - Netiquette guidelines and expectations
   - Contact information for the instructor
   - Minimum computer hardware and software requirements
   - Sources for any required plug-ins (and links)
   - Links to appropriate campus library resources and services
   - Peer-to-peer troubleshooting help (e.g., discussion board)

2. Organization and Design
   - Syllabus is easily located and includes: course objectives; course completion requirements; expectations of students' participation
   - Clear timeline for face-to-face and in-class activities
   - Course content is organized in a logical format and chunked into manageable elements
   - Headings/subheadings are used to organize content
   - Layout of course is visually and functionally consistent
   - Language of written material is friendly and supportive
   - Learning objectives are clearly stated for each unit

3. Instructional Design and Delivery
   - Students introduce themselves online and are encouraged to respond to classmates
   - Instructor introduces himself/herself online
   - "Ice-breaker" activity or other orientation session to get acquainted online
   - Course activities clearly tied to assessment (which is connected to a learning objective)
   - Activities/assessments include opportunities to develop critical thinking and problem-solving skills
   - Collaborative opportunities are available where pedagogically relevant
   - Course includes a variety of digital media, e.g., video, audio, images

4. Integration of Face-to-Face and Online Activities

- ◆ Face-to-face and online activities are integrated (each complements the other)
- ◆ Attempt is made to constitute both online and face-to-face peer learning community
- ◆ Face-to-face and online portions of the course are treated equally (one is not "favored" over the other, intentionally or otherwise)

5. Assessment of Student Learning

- ◆ Criteria used to assess participation in online discussion groups clearly stated
- ◆ Students are not assessed solely on tests/quizzes but are provided ample opportunity to demonstrate proficiency in different ways (both formative and summative assessment opportunities)
- ◆ Meaningful and timely feedback is provided to students
- ◆ Samples of assignments illustrate instructor's expectations
- ◆ Detailed instructions and tips for completing assignments
- ◆ Due dates for all assignments
- ◆ Rubrics for all assignments identify assessment guidelines
- ◆ Course grading scale is presented clearly
- ◆ Peer review opportunities
- ◆ Students apply rubric to their own work and describe/defend their score

6. Evaluation and Student Feedback

- ◆ Student input sought at regular intervals (e.g., questionnaire, survey tools or informal open and anonymous discussion forum areas where students might express delight or discouragement with course materials as they are working through them during the semester)
- ◆ Evaluation survey at end of course

As we noted earlier in this section, the checklist material here has been adapted from a variety of sources: these include the University of Wisconsin-Milwaukee Learning Technology Center website; "Instructional Design Tips for Online Learning," produced by Joan Van Duzer at Humboldt State University; and the "Rubric for Online Instruction" designed by the California

State University, Chico, Center for Excellence in Learning and Teaching.

However, the checklist also reflects our own ideas about what good hybrid courses should entail. In some cases, you might adapt existing resources simply by reordering or regrouping individual items. And the examples provided for how an instructor or designer might meet a requirement or checklist suggestion should of course be tailored to what LMS/digital tools are available.

We think it important that institutions not feel overly tied to an existing set of course design criteria, despite the plethora of checklists you can find with a fairly simple Google search. Rather, individual contexts, not to mention the wealth of teaching experience that could be readily at hand on any given campus, should play an influential role as you develop ideas about what quality will mean, what it will look like, what it will feel like as a lived teaching and learning experience, at your specific institution.

One last note on this call for contextually sensitive assessment approaches: we recognize that in some cases, where there is not absolute policy and process consistency across all arms of a college, we run the risk of certain constituents feeling that another division has it easier or isn't required to play by the same rules as everybody else. While we cannot control for this as an individual response, which we feel would be in the minority anyway, with efforts toward transparency as to *why* it makes sense to do things in a particular way in a particular context, even if that method deviates to some degree from what happens in other departments, the group as a whole has at least the opportunity to understand why one, blanket policy or process across a college is not an ideal.

The Role of Peers and Administrators in Assessing Hybrid Courses

Peer evaluation and opportunities for observation and feedback will certainly vary from college to college, depending on a number of considerations, not least of these being basic staffing levels. For example, if peer evaluations are conducted only by full-time instructors, the full-time to adjunct instructor ratio will have an immediate impact on the amount of feedback and frequency of observation available to all instructors. And will only those faculty who teach hybrid courses be evaluating or observing others teaching hybrid courses or will evaluation or observation be open to all faculty teaching in all environments? In a similar vein, what is the faculty to administrator ratio? If an administrator is expected to observe or evaluate hybrid courses, is it feasible that he or she is able to complete those tasks given his or her schedule? Particularly large departments or divisions may find it overwhelming or even impossible to observe, evaluate, and assess each hybrid course as frequently as might otherwise be desirable.

Institutions wishing to build and sustain a thriving hybrid curriculum will need to develop a cohort of faculty (and perhaps administrators and support staff) for ongoing teaching and design evaluation. We might even refer to this cohort as responsible for undertaking observation rather than evaluation, a term that is much less loaded since it suggests that the goal of teaching and design assessment is fundamentally to report what happens, not to pass judgment. This change in an assessment cohort's charge and the rhetoric used to describe its activities can help to create an environment for growth, collegial conversation, and learning more so than if assessment becomes a summative judgment passed on any one instructor's "skill" in the hybrid format.

Early on in the hybrid curriculum and course development process, we recommend frequent review and discussion of the courses, relative to what might be needed as teachers become more confident and self-supporting. There will also be room for more significant development and revisions early on, due to the fact that building online material is significantly time consuming. Early on, before extensive content is in place or a course architecture fully framed out, revision and adjustment seems easier to undertake. Many faculty might be a little more hesitant to return to a completed hybrid course shell/plan and make significant changes to the content or structure. Further, instructors who are open to regular review and consideration of the strengthening of their courses are more likely to engage in the growth of their organic and dynamic classrooms.

If there are adjuncts involved in the hybrid curriculum, departments may wish to have a mentoring system wherein a full-time instructor is paired with the adjunct instructor. Perhaps the adjuncts will be required to use the full-time instructor's shell if instruction for hybrid sections is changing more frequently and the departments wish to have some consistency with their shells. Development of the course shells is time consuming, after all, and having adjuncts dedicating significant time to course building is unfair, unless the base pay per course increases to reflect that increased workload.

For example, Paull's full-time instructors in her English department identified some basic criteria for constructing and maintaining online and hybrid courses in that particular department, which include such requirements as instructors having an active, noticeable presence in the course not only in the physical classroom meeting each week but also in the online environment on at least three days each week; requiring student-to-student and student-to-teacher interaction each week in both environments (e.g., group work, group projects, teacher-student conferences, discussion forums, wikispaces, or teacher review of student writing assignments); implementing a clear schedule of what will be done in both environments each week; and stating which learning objectives for the course will be covered each week and, specifically, how the activities in each environment will encourage students to meet those objectives.

The review process for the adjunct instructors begins by giving each instructor's assigned full-time mentor a teaching assistant role in the adjunct's online course site, where the full-time instructor observes and comments throughout the semester in that environment while also observing in the physical classroom. Observing the assignment arcs for a hybrid week will give the mentor a much clearer picture of the quality of any given hybrid course and encourage consistently pedagogically sound hybrid courses in that department.

Beyond departmental observations and perhaps evaluations among peers, administration should also take on an important role in the formative assessment process. Not only is it vital for administrators to understand what is going on in the classrooms but, more specifically, to participate actively and vitally in the growth of the hybrid curriculum on the campus from the group up. It is likely that administrators already observe faculty's classrooms (perhaps during their nontenure years or, for those in non-tenure-track positions, each year as they sign continuing contracts). Hybrid course observations should be no different in that way. Further, administrators are more likely to continue to understand the value of hybrids if they have been in the courses themselves. Just like peer observations, administrators should welcome the opportunity to join the hybrid sections online and visit the face-to-face component as well, for at least one week of class, to be able to understand the flow of a hybrid course week. Unlike a face-to-face class observation, which likely only occurs during one day's session, a hybrid observation would be most beneficial if observation was done in both areas of the course.

Following observations done by peers or administrators, a face-to-face conversation between the two is imperative to continue a pedagogical dialogue. Again, this requires enthusiasm from all perspectives—enthusiasm for continuous improvement of hybrid curricula, including content-specific materials as well as technological ones.

Notice that our discussion here focuses on formative assessment of hybrid courses. We find that these courses, like others on campus, benefit greatly from formative assessments, allowing each other glimpses into our courses during the semester/session. As courses are ever-changing and organic things, summative assessment does not play a direct role in their growth. Rather than examining a course as a single thing, we see the value in observations as most useful in assessing hybrid courses.

The role of peers and administrators in assessing hybrid courses is a crucial one for the success of hybrid curricula on campuses. As we have noted already, there may be some obstacles along the way from many different directions. Reminding ourselves what we teach, why we teach it, and how we can become better at teaching it, will keep hybrid courses on the radar for everyone at the departmental, programmatic, and institutional levels.

CHAPTER THREE

Training Instructors for
Hybrid Courses

In the first two chapters, we explored the institutional components that factor into developing and sustaining a hybrid/
blended curriculum on the college campus. Once these institutional elements have been established on campus, the big question
arises: How do we prepare instructors and support staff for the
courses themselves? In this chapter, we will tackle many of these
difficult challenges and questions, and we will explore the moving
parts that contribute to preparing for and executing a training
workshop series for a college campus.

Some questions present themselves right from the start: Who
will need to be involved? How will you identify the knowledgeable and enthusiastic faculty, administration, staff, and support
personnel who are able to, trained to, and willing to help in this
journey? Who will spearhead these efforts and what are some
potential pitfalls for having the wrong kind of leader at the helm?

Once the leadership and support have been put in place, the
bigger task begins of structuring, developing, recruiting, executing, and supporting the training of those faculty for teaching
hybrid courses. Absolutely key to hybrids being successfully
developed and offered at an institution will be early efforts to
provide training to all constituent groups involved, including
faculty, administration, and support staff.

We argue that early, inclusive training of this kind, and early
community building within an institution, will help to provide
a trajectory for blended and hybrid learning in which growth in
course offerings is equaled by growth in professional and administrative support.

Further, upon conclusion of a formal training workshop
series itself, stakeholders will benefit from ongoing pedagogical,

administrative, and instructional design support. As the hybrid learning landscape across higher education changes, and as things shift (we hope positively) across an individual campus, all constituent groups, not just teachers, will need a mechanism to help them update skills and knowledge. This might take the form of a cross-college advisory committee, tasked with staying abreast of broader changes. Individual committee members might act as liaisons to constituent groups on campus. Particularly helpful will also be a central locus, physical and virtual, to support ongoing conversation about hybrid learning where participants can ask questions, share successes, and communicate challenges. In the following section we address how an institution might support continuing efforts to foster a hybrid curriculum and some possible challenges that might emerge along the way. Of central importance will be the following question, one that links a formal workshop training opportunity to that sustainable hybrid learning conversation: What elements might you integrate into your training plan in order to encourage an institutional community of those teaching in the hybrid format?

Identifying a solid support system from staff and administration is certainly vital for having a thriving hybrid curriculum. Once you have that support, though, equally important is establishing and providing an ongoing forum for faculty development and training. Most current college faculty did not have training regarding hybrid course development or delivery and, as a result, may find themselves confused about how to start, perhaps attempting to get the ball rolling by copy-and-pasting existing instructional material (like lecture notes or assignment handouts) that have worked for their fully face-to-face classroom sections into online course shells rather than critically engaging in how effective hybrid pedagogy needs to imagine the ways that online and f2f learning can be integrated, speaking across those delivery mode demarcations. Other faculty may find themselves in the opposite situation if the bulk of their teaching experience has occurred online, an increasingly common reality for many teachers today. In this case, even experienced online teachers may approach the hybrid format by reworking existing material, cutting half of each week's online coursework, and doing it in the classroom for example, rather than confronting what might seem like the daunting challenge of building from the ground up.

As a result, faculty may find themselves frustrated with failing hybrid courses and thus choosing other delivery modes. Just as likely, in the absence of adequate faculty training and course design support, hybrid courses may not produce good student success and thus administrators may feel obliged to remove them from the course schedule. Our hope with this chapter, then, is to provide some ideas for establishing, framing, and implementing faculty training that can be repeated each year and serve as ongoing support for faculty, administrators, and staff as they look to build and sustain quality courses that provide for both student and teacher satisfaction.

Finding Leaders for Professional Development

Successful leaders for professional development will provide the necessary understanding about hybrid courses, course structure, and implementation. We have found, in leading hybrid workshops for faculty, administrators, and staff, that foregrounding pedagogy rather than technology has proven most successful even in cases where not all workshop participants are actively teaching. In many cases these two elements—pedagogy and technology—cannot usefully be disaggregated, but again, in our experience technology-use training that is not contextualized in terms of actual teaching seems less effective: not that basic technology training is not important, but it seems to stick better when presented in terms of how a teacher might achieve an identifiable pedagogical objective, be it large or small. So if we'd like faculty better able to use an LMS-based Web conferencing system, like Blackboard's Collaborate, we've found it most useful to present the technology in terms of the teaching challenge it addresses. We might ask, for example, how we can achieve the teaching objective of conferencing individually with each student as one step in the production of an essay or other class assignment. We could meet in person with each student, of course, but we could also take advantage of a technology tool that lets us do that conferencing a little more flexibly. The technology is a solution to a pedagogical problem, not a solution in search of a problem. Nor is it presented as just one more tool in the digital toolbox, decontextualized from the *why* of its use.

What matters for our discussion here, though, is that faculty should ideally serve as the leaders for hybrid learning professional development workshops. Yet these faculty leaders need not claim any degree of technical mastery with the LMS or any other tech system. Truthfully, most faculty with experience teaching in the hybrid format are likely to be comfortable working in an LMS, having learned from experience and having sought out professional development on their own. But they need not become the go-to IT resource on campus, supplanting existing resources. That IT support role is still best played by experts who are formally trained in areas of instructional design and technology. The last thing any institution needs as it builds a hybrid curriculum is a turf war over who teaches or manages what.

Ideally, find a faculty member or members who have had some training already in hybrid curricula (often done through off-campus professional development opportunities through online training courses and/or professional conferences). They are likely not only familiar with the elements of hybrid curricula and pedagogy but also can provide anecdotal evidence and advice regarding the struggles and successes with implementing those strategies in their own classrooms.

In a similar vein, schools should identify instructional design support staff who have experience with hybrid curricula and would be best suited for leading professional development. If your campus is working on developing a vibrant hybrid curriculum, you might find that your current instructional design team is not quite large enough to handle the increased number of faculty needing training in hybrid pedagogy or how to make that pedagogy work within the existing system. As a result, the campus may need to hire additional support staff in order to assure that all of the faculty are given sufficient technological support, and/or identify means for funding some professional development opportunities for instructional designers.

These leadership selections may be quite obvious on some campuses, while others may find it useful to put out a call for interested on-campus faculty and staff and then conduct informal interviews to identify the most qualified candidates for these positions.

In addition to the faculty facilitators for professional development opportunities, having a lead administrator is equally important. In the 2014 survey we deployed for all members of the hybrid development community on college campuses (adjunct faculty, full-time faculty, administrators, and IT support staff), 50 percent of our respondents indicated that administrative support is "very important" and another 30 percent indicated that it was "absolutely vital" to the success of a thriving hybrid college curriculum. Specifically, the administrator serves as a financial and institutional support for the effort as a whole. Campuses should be assured that there is an administrator or two who are the point people for this development opportunity, identifying and supplying financial support if needed, and willing to go to bat to support the mission. Ideally, before beginning this plan, all deans, provosts, and the president should understand the hybrid curriculum's importance to the campus's success and ongoing development. However, it may take a bit longer for some than others to fully support significant alterations to the curriculum, so we recommend you find some champions and encourage those administrators to spread the good word, so to speak, helping the rest of campus administrators to see the value. We covered similar challenges and opportunities for getting people on board earlier in this book with regard to promotion of the new curriculum. Our survey respondents indicated the importance of their administration's support for things such as stipends for course developments, providing lower course caps to make the courses more enticing, and funding instructor and faculty development grants regarding hybrid curriculum.

Can institutions stay inhouse for expertise or will they be required to seek outside help when it comes to supporting hybrid curricular development and growth?

Our argument is that, in order to create a sustainable environment to support hybrid course design, teaching, and delivery, every institution will ultimately need to have inhouse expertise. Note too that this is why we stress the need for communications networks that allow for cross-discipline conversation and collaboration among those involved in hybrids, such that expertise can in fact be shared. Siloed expertise is not particularly useful outside of that limited space.

But the assertion that expertise should be cultivated inhouse inevitably begs the question: Where does it come from in the first place if not from outside the institution? In an effort to achieve greater success with regard to hybrid curriculum development—that is, to get more courses out into the hybrid online environment—collaboration with inhouse expertise is imperative and involves many moving parts. Often, however, these parts may not connect with one another as well as we'd like. Interaction and collaboration at each stage, however, may minimize some potential problems along the way. Often we see a "top-down" directive placed on IT support and faculty to get these classes ready to go as soon as possible. Certainly all institutions have some highly qualified and eager instructional designers willing to help faculty envision and implement effective course structures to meet whatever their needs may be for their courses. Commonly, however, there is also increased hesitancy from faculty when a "movement" comes forth from the top down or from the instructional design teams. Instead, we advocate for a faculty-driven initiative, something that will garner support more easily from other faculty, but a faculty partnership with administrators at the same time, in order to gather campuswide support.

In some cases, you might have eager faculty who seek out their own resources to develop knowledge about hybrid teaching. So they become "experts" of a kind, but largely of their own volition and often at their own expense, both literal and figurative. In other cases, institutions have established or begun to set in place some kind of center for teaching and learning that is a faculty-driven component of the campus environment wherein faculty help other faculty develop and refine their teaching both online and off. Perhaps there are some foundational members for the training workshop housed in those types of locations already.

Rather than hope for this kind of do-it-yourself expertise to develop, since such development, if it happens at all, is likely to be unevenly distributed across disciplines and could involve widely varying degrees of long-term professional investment, we argue that institutions need to develop clear incentive and support systems for those "early adopters" on campus who would like to pursue training in the hybrid curriculum development and teaching areas. And we should point out explicitly that incentivizing innovative initiatives needs to happen for all involved, not just faculty.

This early set of hybrid teachers, administrators, and support staff will probably have to go beyond the institution to seek out training and other professional development opportunities. However, true institutional investment and support in these extramural efforts will, we believe, help to form a solid base of what will then become sustainable inhouse expertise.

And what do we mean by "true" institutional investment and support: this is *not* the kind of support that just gives the casual nod of approval to those interested in developing new skills, so long as that development does not interfere with "regular" campus duties. This provides little incentive for those with an already full plate of academic and administrative duties to engage in any meaningful way with professional development. Real support for such endeavors needs to come in the form of compensation for professional development costs, be they travel costs, workshop fees, or course fees.

Of even greater importance, however, and something that so many institutions seem to treat as an absolute last resort in our experience, is the opportunity for release time to those pursuing genuine professional development. Release time from academic duties provides individuals with what, in our view, they need most when it comes to learning new professional skills and expertise: not a few extra dollars added to the paycheck, but more time in the day. It is important to note that release time need not be release from all academic duties; however, a reduced teaching load or workload of some kind should not be reserved for just the rarest cases. Release time should be the norm when it comes to incentives for those seeking professional development.

Supporting administrators who themselves are tasked with supporting these kinds of initiatives means identifying as part of their regular duties the work it takes to foster and manage innovative curricular efforts. Such work cannot be expected to occur above and beyond an existing set of responsibilities. Furthermore, if administrators operate in a climate in which perceived "mistakes" are likely to be punished—that is, if experiments in scheduling or curricular design do not pan out exactly as expected and thus result in negative performance reviews—then no reasonable administrator is likely to take that risk. Supporting big, innovative moves like developing hybrids across a college needs leadership and support from the very top.

It is our belief that institutional investment of the very tangible kind and in a general climate that supports risk-taking provides real incentive for those seeking new expertise. And it also tends to attract those who are truly interested in the expertise, not those who see it as a way to make more money. Keep in mind, too, that investment and support for early efforts in truly immersive professional development (taking a full class or extensive workshop, for example) is just part of a larger strategy to develop what will become that base of inhouse expertise that can produce sustainable growth.

In our view, expertise will beget expertise when it can be provided inhouse. But inhouse expertise will not appear magically. It will take investment, commitment, and support.

Ongoing Training: The Inhouse Workshop

As is true for faculty who teach in all disciplines and across all delivery modes, *ongoing* training and professional development are integral for growth and understanding both in and outside of discipline-specific concerns. This holds true of hybrid courses in particular due to the fact that there still exists a real need for guidance, as many instructors are potentially unfamiliar with the delivery model and will not have their own experiences as students to reflect on, unless they took a hybrid course as part of undergraduate or graduate work. As noted in the NEA Education Policy Brief on Blended Learning, "Ongoing professional development for teachers is essential to ensure that teachers maintain the skills appropriate for an online environment. Additional preparation time, ongoing technological support, and collaborative planning time must be granted to teachers using technology to enrich their instruction" (NEA Education Policy and Practice Department). We are aware, though, that planning and especially funding professional development opportunities will take some creativity, given that dollars across higher education are being stretched ever thinner.

In our 2014 survey, 40 percent of our respondents indicated that their institution had "regularly scheduled faculty workshops/meetings about developing hybrid curriculum." However, 25 percent noted that they had only one or two workshops or meetings about hybrid curriculum, while 35 percent had not had a single meeting about the hybrid curriculum at all. While faculty development through workshops and/or meetings are important to the development of new curricula, it does appear that most of the institutions from which our respondents come are still struggling with that component in its early stages on their campuses. Especially challenging can be large university systems, like the City University of New York (CUNY). Rather than a comprehensive, cross-campus strategy for developing hybrid curricula, each separate campus develops and integrates its own on-campus training.

When possible, anchoring a workshop series with inhouse members can carry pedagogical weight with others on the campus. There is a certain rapport and trust with our colleagues that we do not always have for outside consultants. We suggest that you send out communication to your campus staff, faculty, and administration to attempt to garner support from within. Even if you have to ultimately consult outside experts for the series, it is vital to have inhouse buy-in to make a project like this succeed.

Upon finding support from faculty who have knowledge about hybrid instruction to share and from faculty who want to learn more about the pedagogical foundations of teaching in the hybrid structure, you will also need to gather administrative support. This kind of support may come from one specific dean, a campus grant, an external grant, professional development money, or perhaps out of a center for teaching and learning or learning technologies division on your campus. As each institution is structured differently, both logistically and financially, it is best to begin with those you know you can get "on board" and then build your groups' support numbers exponentially from there.

The biggest component for this type of work is time. If people will volunteer their time for the good of the cause, it is possible that there will be no additional expense beyond the coffee necessary to work through the hours of workshop sessions. Providing a united front from a variety of internal campus constituents will aid in making this workshop series an institutional effort, rather than something originating from just one of these many perspectives. We recommend working with as many interested parties as possible to encourage more faculty interest and support for the workshop training.

Identifying Key Areas to Cover

Once you have identified the appropriate leaders, we recommend the faculty and instructional design staff gather to discuss their visions for the professional development workshop series. What does hybrid pedagogy look like? How does it differ from face-to-face classes? How is it like or unlike online pedagogy? In what ways might faculty be able to bring their skill sets from one or both of these pedagogies into the hybrid course platform? These questions need to be addressed in a focused workshop series for faculty. With all of that said, however, be prepared for some potential resistance to faculty development regarding hybrid curricula as there will likely be some faculty who believe that their training, knowledge, and experience teaching in the traditional classroom directly translates into the hybrid environment, thereby rendering the development moot. It is imperative that those leading this development experience emphasize that the faculty training is to enhance and aid in their understanding of how to translate traditional pedagogy into hybrid pedagogy, not to imply that they have no knowledge base from which to pool their resources.

Some institutions may wish to set up some kind of incentive for completing the workshop such as points toward a certificate of some sort. There are some institutions that actually require completion of the workshop training prior to being permitted to actually teach the hybrid course, which is something worth considering, especially for those teaching in community colleges with a large contingency of adjunct teachers with such a fluctuation in who might teach those sections. Others might find that simply asking instructors to volunteer to take the workshop, if they choose to do so, should suffice. Many will likely find that they will begin with one approach but, as time goes on, the incentives to complete the series might need to change or require small adjustments.

When considering the key areas to cover in the workshop, it is important to situate the workshop in what you consider the key principles of hybrid instruction and learning. What is it that is unique to hybrid instruction that will help faculty be the most successful instructor and help the students learn as effectively as possible? Keep in mind that you are working with experienced faculty who are familiar with pedagogy and instruction techniques as a whole, which makes this much easier.

When selecting key areas to cover, some institutions find themselves focusing primarily on instructional design components, for the face-to-face and for the online components. Others find themselves designing workshop training primarily for the online pieces, focusing on the Quality Matters standards. For example, the University of Wisconsin-Milwaukee established their faculty development workshop series, deemed the "Hybrid Course Project," which they have since revised in a number of ways, based on their own experiences as well as their observations of other faculty development on campuses they have visited. Specifically, their website outlining said faculty development course states that

> [t]he UW-Milwaukee hybrid faculty development model includes presentations by trainers, demonstrations by faculty of their hybrid courses, group discussions by participants, face-to-face breakouts for small group work, course redesign assignments both face-to-face and online, and facilitator and peer feedback on assignments. (University of Wisconsin-Milwaukee, "Hybrid Courses: Faculty Development")

By combining all of these approaches, they have found that faculty are provided with the most successful variety of learning experiences.

Regardless, it is important to begin by defining hybrid courses at your institution. From there, it can prove helpful to then translate active learning into the hybrid environment. After discussing active learning strategies for hybrid environments, workshops would benefit from addressing the role of instructional design for the online components that complement the hybrid structure. Finally, the workshop series may end by addressing various methods for assessing hybrid students. Again, by translating pedagogical elements from face-to-face with which they are likely to have familiarity, the workshop will allow them to feel empowered rather than overwhelmed by new information.

The Faculty Training Workshop Series

In the following section we will provide details of two different faculty training workshops, each done by one of the authors of this book. Specifically, Paull designed a faculty workshop training titled "Going Hybrid: A Faculty Workshop Series" and Snart designed a faculty workshop training session titled "Learning Hybrid: Hybrid Learning." This section includes suggestions for preparing for such a workshop, some notes from our workshop experiences, and also some ideas that came about after our having offered the workshops a number of times, as we considered ways to continuously improve upon our efforts.

Training: Technological Components

Prior to beginning the workshop for faculty interested in teaching hybrid courses, it is important to consider the capabilities and limitations of your institution's technology. Do all of your faculty have to use a particular platform (e.g., Blackboard, Canvas, or D2L)? If so, what kinds of technology are compatible for integration and use?

What kinds of technology are user friendly? Teaching at a community college can sometimes present literacy limitations when it comes to technology as well. What technology will allow the teaching and learning to come to the forefront rather than the anxiety of downloads, plug-ins, and compatibility issues? With the ever-changing technology out there from programs to apps, there are teachers and students who often feel they are being left in a cloud of dust, unable to forage through the pedagogical road before them. What technology needs to be addressed versus saved for another time; encouraged or discouraged; or, potentially, will lead to platform nightmares if used at all?

Once these overarching questions are addressed, selecting a campus location that provides access to these technologies in an interactive and accessible way will also be quite useful. Do you have classrooms with projectors for showing your desktops? Are SMART Boards or PolyVision boards available to enhance the interactive experience? One instructor utilized a Steelcase LearnLab classroom for her workshop series with faculty, to encourage faculty group discussions and community-building. The philosophy behind the LearnLab is that by having the speaker/ teacher in a central position in the room, using a computer on a tall-top table, surrounded by whiteboards on all four walls and students situated so they can all see at least one of the three projection screens without moving their chairs, the "front of the classroom" is removed. This can help to increase discussion and smooth transitions in and out of group work.

No matter which location you choose for your workshop, though, it is important to present the workshop in a space that is conducive to learning, interactivity, and the technology with which they will be working. At the same time, be cautious about having them enter a space that might be overwhelming or infusing more technology than their courses require. For example, teachers who have never taught hybrid or online prior to the workshop might find it intimidating to see many screens running different kinds of multimedia presentations at the same time. Instead, try to set a comfortable scene for learning.

There are many possible structures for these workshops/ training sessions. Some may prefer to focus on the pedagogical discussions exclusively while others might add in a hands-on component in which the faculty members apply the pedagogy they are learning in live workshops where they build their courses and have assignments related to each of the discussion topics for that session. Would the faculty at a particular campus flourish in an active workshop session? Would they prefer one-on-one consultations done after the discussions? These are decisions that should be made in conjunction with your instructional designers and with consideration to their time capabilities and preferences as well. Some schools may have limited staff in these areas, who would be unable to do individual consultations with each member of a workshop/training. However, other campuses have a booming instructional design team and would prefer having that focused discussion with each faculty member.

For pedagogical reasons, we recommend structuring the training workshop as a hybrid course. Both of us conduct faculty workshops that are in the hybrid structure, featuring a weekly blend of face-to-face and online interaction. Since hybrid/blended learning requires meaningful student-student and student-teacher interaction each week in both environments, it makes sense to have the training workshop mirror the kind of class that these faculty were planning to teach, reinforcing the platform's strengths while also allowing faculty to have the experience of being enrolled in a hybrid course as students. Logistically, this kind of a structure might be challenging and retention may flounder for some campuses (e.g., campuses where instructors are teaching fifteen credit hours a semester or more). It's important to identify the needs and the realities of faculty on your particular campus to identify an approach that might work best for your faculty. At the same time, allow yourselves to be flexible with the structure, open to revising it after the first run of the workshop series. It may take multiple semesters in different approaches before you find a structure that works for retention, enthusiasm, and quality of course shells for your institution.

The screenshots in Figures 13 and 14 show the course menus for each of our two sample workshops. To fully engage faculty in that hybrid experience, the workshop facilitator might consider integrating multimedia components to keep the faculty-students involved in the online portion of the course. For example, it might behoove a facilitator to create introductory videos to help prepare

FIGURE 13. *Course menu for "Going Hybrid."*

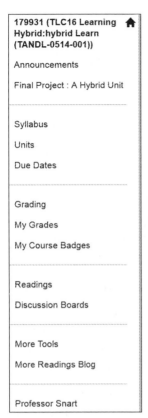

179931 (TLC16 Learning 🏠
Hybrid:hybrid Learn
(TANDL-0514-001))

Announcements

Final Project : A Hybrid Unit

Syllabus

Units

Due Dates

Grading

My Grades

My Course Badges

Readings

Discussion Boards

More Tools

More Readings Blog

Professor Snart

FIGURE 14. *Course menu for "Learning Hybrid: Hybrid Learning."*

students for what to expect. Figure 15 shows a typical workshop video announcement, posted in the LMS.

Part of what the workshop tries to do as it delivers content and assigns activities is to model effective hybrid teaching practices. For example, the workshop facilitator regularly posts video-based announcements in the LMS. These can, as pictured here, provide screencapture video that walks the viewer through pieces of the course, be it due dates or assignment information. Most participants do not actually need the refresher so much as use of screencapture technology can become an important talking point in the workshop itself.

Figures 16 and 17 show screenshots of the units that make up each of the two workshop series. The "Going Hybrid" structure covers defining hybrid learning, active learning, instructional design, and assessment.

Hybrid workshop check-in

Posted on: Tuesday, April 22, 2014 11:24:53 AM CDT

Hybrids Workshop check in

Hybrid Workshop 2014
▶
Pre-Presentation Check-In

FIGURE 15. *"Learning Hybrid: Hybrid Learning" workshop announcement in LMS.*

UNIT 1: What is Hybrid/Blended Learning?
For the first unit of our workshop, we will be discussing how we define hybrid or blended classrooms, the benefits of and challenges with this type of class set-up. What kinds of approaches work best in the bricks and mortar classroom setting versus the online? What are some common misconceptions about these approaches? How is this particular hybrid course set up for our eight weeks together?
BRICKS AND MORTAR CLASS MEETING: We will meet once during this unit on Friday, September 7, 2012 from 9 a.m. to 11 a.m. in room 201 in the Holden University Center.

UNIT 2: Creating an Active Learning Environment
During this unit of the workshop, we will discuss ways to create engagement in the hybrid classroom, asking us to consider how to develop blended group &/or collaborative assignments that span across the bricks and mortar and online classroom environments. Not only will we look at examples and discuss the pedagogical reasons for doing collaborative group work in the hybrid classroom but also you will all participate in group projects amongst yourselves and consider the types of group projects you might integrate in your own hybrid classes next semester.
BRICKS & MORTAR CLASS MEETING: We will have one campus meeting about this unit on Friday, September 14th in U-201 from 9 a.m. to 11 a.m.

UNIT 3: Instructional Design
During these two weeks, we will discuss strategies for instructional design of hybrid classes. Specifically, we will address such issues as accessibility, universal design, media components, support services and the Quality Matters rubric. You will each design a hybrid module for their upcoming hybrid course, gather feedback from each other, and present your findings to us during active discussion.
BRICKS & MORTAR CLASS MEETING: We will have one campus meeting about this unit that will be held on Friday, October 5th from 9 a.m. to 11 a.m. in U-201.

UNIT 4: Assessment
During these final two weeks of class, we will discuss approaches for assessing student work in the hybrid environment, considering different approaches, reasons for those approaches, and designs for assessing in both environments. You will engage in discussions of how you would assess this workshop as well as your own students' work in your own classrooms. What are your plans for the future with your hybrid course? Where will we go from here with our follow-up meetings about teaching hybrid courses?
BRICKS & MORTAR CLASS MEETING: We will have one campus meeting to wrap up this unit on Friday, October 19th from 9 a.m. to 11 a.m. in U-201

FIGURE 16. *Overview of "Going Hybrid" list of units.*

Another possible approach can be seen in the "Learning Hybrid: Hybrid Learning" workshop. The components there include a "Getting Started" orientation piece, followed by modules that touch on a variety of topics connected with online and hybrid course design and delivery. Both workshops conclude with a capstone project requiring workshop participants to design a hybrid course—or section of a course—and present their efforts for feedback to the workshop group.

What we'd like to point out, and what we hope the course menus suggest, is that neither workshop is focused solely on designing a hybrid course. That material is available, but it is not the only content offered in either workshop. So even as workshop

FIGURE 17. *"Learning Hybrid: Hybrid Learning" list of units.*

participants work toward their capstone presentation—which reflects ongoing discussion specific to hybrid course design—each workshop tends to touch on many broad issues that concern teaching and learning, be those related to technology or institutional policies and processes.

The "Learning Hybrid: Hybrid Learning" workshop, for example, takes an intentionally broad view of hybrid learning, with attention to aspects of online learning, the institutional culture at large, and how technology exists for us outside of higher education. Unit 3, The World of/is Online, for example, asks participants to consider both good and bad experiences they have had trying to do something online, specifically something nonacademic, like booking travel, buying electronics, or banking. Very much reflecting the broad approach we have taken in the book here, each of these workshops asks participants to think expansively about the many factors that go into creating effective hybrid learning experiences.

So too are participants asked to reflect on managing their time in what for many will be a new delivery mode. Unit 5 of "Learning Hybrid: Hybrid Learning," Staying Connected / Disconnecting, requires participants to read and respond to articles about the demands on one's time that come with teaching fully or partially online. When learning moves online, students can begin to assume that you—like the customer support offered by their favorite online retailer—will provide immediate responses, no matter what day of the week or time of day it might be. A significant part of the "Learning Hybrid: Hybrid Learning" workshop has participants thinking about what their larger professional experience will be like when or if they teach in the hybrid mode. It is potentially too easy to get so immersed in the nuts and bolts of course building—and LMS use—that these larger teacher-satisfaction questions can fall by the wayside, despite the fact that they have everything to do, not just with the effectiveness of a single hybrid course, but with the sustainability across an institution of hybrid curricula. Similar concerns are covered in the "Going Hybrid" workshop throughout each unit, as participants discuss how hybrid pedagogy is reflected in the various components of a hybrid course.

We hope our discussion of the workshops here will provide readers not with a prescriptive "how to," but rather with a sense of the wide variety of approaches and topics for a hybrids workshop. We once again reiterate our belief in designing professional development opportunities that are sensitive to the local context. What works for one institution may fall flat at another and vice versa. Whatever the specifics that emerge as an institution develops its own development opportunities though, ongoing dialogue across constituent groups can prove invaluable. Even great teachers, teaching great hybrid courses, are liable to burn out without an awareness of how hybrids exist institutionally, of what ongoing support is—or is not—available to them, and how they might need to respond to the new demands presented by an innovative teaching framework.

Training: Defining Hybrid/Blended Courses

A useful early topic for discussion in the hybrid training workshop is one we covered earlier in this book, in part because it is so fundamental: Exactly how are hybrids defined on your campus? The "Going Hybrid" workshop covers this in Unit 1 while "Learning Hybrid: Hybrid Learning" covers it in Unit 2. As we noted earlier, the definition for what constitutes a hybrid is far from static across all campuses (sometimes even on a single campus). However, hybrid workshop participants should be clear on what their own campus definition is, or, as might sometimes be the case, where confusion exists across a campus. We like the idea of having workshop participants discuss early on the challenges that defining hybrids can present. This has immediate implications for how they might design their own hybrid courses, but also points to that larger institutional picture that both of our workshops try to present.

Training: Active Learning Strategies

Both workshops unpack course design across multiple units. And one primary component of design looks at how instructors can build active learning opportunities in their hybrid courses.

A major component of any college classroom is creating an active learning experience for our students. What we mean by active learning may vary from these authors to those reading this book.

Unlike what might be labeled as "the traditional instructional approach" (albeit potentially dangerously so), aka Freire's banking concept of education in which teachers "deposit" knowledge into students' "repositories" of information, active learning asks that students take the information they are given and engage in that material through questioning, writing, and reflecting, and apply that knowledge base to new experiences in the classroom (whether physical or digital). The University of Minnesota's Center for Teaching and Learning outlined four major elements of active learning: talking and listening, reading, writing, and reflecting (University of Minnesota). To set the stage for this unit, then, it is important to configure a sequence of supportive scholarship to create a shared understanding of its definition as well as possible examples that might apply to faculty from a number of disciplines.

Often students resist active learning instructional approaches, deeming them as "not teaching" because students are at the center of the discussions, doing what looks like the most "work" in the classroom. Whether the students are engaged in pairs or in small group activities, learning in this manner solidifies understanding and engages students with each other about the assigned material.

Online, it is quite easy to lose the interactivity between students. Therefore, we feel it is crucial to integrate some work with active learning in the faculty workshop that not only speaks to ideas building for active learning in their classrooms but also a rationale for doing so. Utilizing Carrington's Padagogy Wheel 4.0, for example, participants can build course objectives first and then construct instructional plans from there, allowing teachers to see the foundation of blended learning in all pedagogy.

Instructional designers and the revised Bloom taxonomy wheel both rely on Bloom's cognitive domain: evaluation, analysis, application, comprehension, knowledge, and synthesis. By grounding the active learning discussion with models like this, faculty will see the parallels between their course objectives and applications of those objectives in the face-to-face and online aspects of their course while also seeing the alignment with their campuswide outcomes. Ultimately, this provides a broader foundation for understanding hybrid pedagogy.

For a hybrid course, then, faculty should work in the training series to identify means by which they can develop active learning that begins in one platform but carries over into the other, while also considering active learning that may exist in just one piece of the hybrid course structure for any given week. More often than not, the discussions will focus on creating active learning in the online environments, as most teachers feel quite comfortable doing this in the brick-and-mortar classes. Training workshops should provide teachers with an understanding of ways to create collaborative projects using inhouse tools like wikis, blogs, and active online discussions, as well as potential external activities like website building or collaborative video presentations.

One way to open up discussions for this phase of the workshop series is to ask the faculty participants to share active learning assignments they have already done in their classes. Doing so will get the discussion flowing by setting a foundation of familiarity with the concept. Online discussions are a great active learning activity to do within the context of hybrid courses, of course, and something that is discussed more thoroughly during this active learning unit, focusing on the elements of active learning present in such an activity. Ultimately, students are applying the concepts from the reading into the written form, analyzing its major components, drawing conclusions from that reading, and synthesizing this new knowledge with previous knowledge from our course and/or with other knowledge in their minds. When done effectively, teachers can use online discussions to build a foundation for a solid course. During this unit in particular, it is helpful to have workshop attendees review their discussion forums up to that point in the workshop series to identify the active learning going on in their discussions, picking apart and analyzing why discussions are active learning when done well.

From there, we recommend that the workshop facilitators provide a sequence of articles about active learning, relying heavily on contemporary research in addition to the traditional Bloom's taxonomy, as noted earlier, for your faculty participants to read. Once faculty have some provocative articles to inspire their conversations, invite them to engage in classroom discussions about active learning. These discussions may be tied to actual active learning assignments in small groups.

Seeing active learning in action will not necessarily be new to everyone in the workshop series; however, it is likely that there will be at least some faculty who rely heavily on lecture-based, banking-model type of class structures. Sometimes this is due to having large enrollments in their classes; other times it is the result of not fully knowing how active learning looks; and still others are convinced that they "don't have the time," dismissing active learning as childish games. It is vital to have faculty participate in thoughtful interaction to illustrate not only the logistics of how active learning appears in the classroom but also what can be learned as a result of doing it.

For example, anecdotally from those engaging in campus training courses, some of those who teach in the hard sciences like biology and chemistry may find themselves avoiding active learning strategies, feeling pressured to make sure they "get through the content" for their outside certifications and accreditations. Those sometimes panicky instructors who are at the mercy of accreditation prefer to lead the discussions to assure that their students are hearing all of the information correctly from them, and feel uncomfortable with the notion of students working through concepts among themselves. Many of them (again, not as a stereotype but rather based on personal and anecdotal experiences from others) prefer to spend their class time lecturing with PowerPoints rather than engaging students in discussions or activities. Facilitators may find that it is helpful to provide some examples to these types of instructors in the initial discussions and/or articles, though, to assure those instructors that active learning can be applied in all sorts of disciplines.

In the "Going Hybrid" workshop, faculty share their past experiences with active learning strategies or, if they do not feel they use active learning, they write about something they came across in the assigned reading that might connect to an idea that they could use to implement active learning in their future hybrid courses.

One of the instructor-students in "Going Hybrid" taught a large lecture psychology course and wrote that

> [o]ne of my favorite active learning activities targets the topic of false memories. I read a list of sleep-related words to my students (e.g., dream, slumber, cozy, etc.). I deliberately do NOT mention the word "sleep" while reading the list. Students

then do a distractor task which involves math. I then instruct my students to write down all of the words they can recall from the list which was read to them. Then, I collect data about various words from my students. Every time, a significant number of students (usually well above the majority) write the word "sleep" on their recall list. I emphasize how easily I was able to implant a false memory! Students love this activity. Some have insisted that they heard me say 'sleep' while reading the list of words. We then discuss this in the context of eyewitness testimony and how inaccurate and unreliable it can be. (Teichman)

This provides a great example for how to get a large number of students actively involved in the course material, i.e., how active learning works in the classroom. This same activity would not work online, but discussing the impact of that experiment in an online discussion would be a great way to fold one meeting into the next.

Once the workshop attendees have a handle on what active learning looks like and the rationale behind it, facilitators should design active learning projects for the participants to complete on their own. Since this is set up in the hybrid structure, we recommend that you have your participants join small groups in the online class course shell. You may, for example, have them collaborate to build an active learning lesson for anything they wish to do. This allows them not only to engage in active learning through the project but also to apply their learning by creating an active learning module.

If the training course is set up with a hands-on component wherein the participants are responsible for building their own shells, facilitators may wish to add a third component that requires participants to build an active learning sequence for their own shells after working through this active learning activity with their group members. "Going Hybrid" includes this as a unit activity. The "Learning Hybrid: Hybrid Learning" workshop, however, assigns an overarching final project that asks participants to develop a hybrid (or partial section), which would include active learning components. If assigned it is important to envision the learning arc, and having participants work through ideas with each other first will allow them to more fully comprehend the material and synthesize the reading and the discussions with this activity before ultimately applying it to their own course shells.

To make the most of the course set up as a hybrid, we suggest that the active learning assignment be constructed and worked on inside of the LMS where the course exists. While faculty may wish to ultimately bring in other technological components to their courses, we recommend sticking to the LMS for the initial training series. For example, facilitators may wish to ask participants to build their active learning module using the LMS's wiki option (or something similar), which is what was done in the "Going Hybrid" workshop.

One group in the "Going Hybrid" workshop provided this as their active learning assignment.

1. *What do you want your students to know when they have finished this assignment?* "In order to demonstrate the LCC Learning Outcome 'uses information responsibly,' the students will be able to recognize flaws in logical thinking as is evident by the presence of logical fallacies in speeches, debates, and political ads by both presidential candidates."

2. *How will you and your students know if they have achieved these learning outcomes (e.g., opportunities for self, peer, and instructor assessment)?* Students will complete a collaborative analysis of a political speech using either the LMS wiki or discussion board features. Writing/presenting an argumentative paper/speech. An option for the paper could be an argumentative or persuasive paper/speech supporting a particular candidate or position. This way they can demonstrate that as an individual they can logically support claims. This includes sifting through vague messages by all parties and making informed, well supported claims.

3. *How will you help students determine what prior knowledge and experience they have with the assessment activity?* First, students will self-check by taking an online quiz on the LMS. Then, students will engage in small group activity with fallacies analyzing political advertisements together through the LMS wiki feature.

4. *How will students synchronously interact and engage with the assessment activity?* Students will present their analyses in the classroom. Meanwhile, both instructor and classmates will identify strengths and problem areas. We then engage in a discussion of overlooked or underdeveloped areas.

5. *What portion of this assessment activity will require "reflective time" for interaction and communication?* The group online activity, assessment of debates, peer review of the final paper will allow reflective and interaction time.

6. *What tools could be used to help organize, facilitate, and direct these assessment activities?* The LMS provides a date and time stamp for online work. The instructor should provide suggested and actual deadlines for the assignments. For example, for group work, I might make recommendations about how the quality and frequency or work will be measured. In addition, the instructor could use the quiz option to assess students' understanding of the course material. As noted in earlier sections, the instructor might want to use the discussion board and/or the wiki features to facilitate group interaction and activity work. This module would also benefit from providing links to helpful Internet resources including www.americanrhetoric.com for samples for both the discussion board and wiki activity and the classroom analysis. Finally, the instructor will use recording equipment to record the student presentations in the classroom for ease of review and discussion with the student during the assessment process.

While inside of their groups, faculty members will be able to add information, tweak each other's work, and comment on their group's progress. The training facilitator should avoid entering the groups but rather observe online to monitor growth and movement.

In both Snart's and Paull's experience conducting hybrid workshops, they have seen workshop participants fall victim to the unfortunate group dynamic in which members do not participate fully in the collaborative work, leaving other group members to carry the weight of the group. This is a situation that faculty probably note in their own teaching, too. While potentially frustrating for workshop attendees, this unit serves as a warning and a moment of enlightenment for instructors. Group work can be challenging. Who will pick up the slack of group members who do not interact in the group? What work will each group member need to complete to be considered a successful group member? Will there be a group leader? Will the group set up smaller deadlines for portions of the project to allow for review/ edits from other group members?

As a final step to the active learning projects, it may be useful to ask each group member to assess each group member, including him or herself, and to provide an overall reflection on the experience as a student and as an instructor. What lessons did they take away about how to construct a successful active learning project and how did being a student within one allow for unique insights into the benefits and challenges therein?

Workshop facilitators may find it useful to begin the following class meeting by sharing some of the reflections and commenting on what the faculty pulled from the experience as a whole.

Training: Instructional Design

Instructional design decisions are crucial when offering any learning opportunity online, whether materials and activities are part of a fully online, a hybrid, or a fully f2f course. Designers (both individual faculty and technology specialists) should provide ample orientation resources for student users, since even what the designer might presume to be a transparent and straightforward course layout might not appear so from the student perspective.

We surmise that a great deal of student confusion actually does *not* stem from ineffective course design, but from students moving too quickly into online work without enough attention to content. Regardless, though, the result is a student who feels lost and frustrated. A course walk-through video can be very useful for introducing students to the basic layout of a given course, for example, especially when that video can remind students to be sure to work through content before jumping to an activity. This is, as we often tell students, the equivalent of not attending any class meetings but then showing up for the test. One cannot realistically expect great results with that strategy. But the sooner students feel oriented and comfortable in a course layout, aware of where the course policies and due dates are, and not just where the assignments to be completed are housed, the sooner they can turn their attention to course content. For workshop purposes, strategies to develop orientation resources can be usefully bundled with review of and practice with effective design principles themselves.

In a similar vein, when developing a hybrid course, it is vital to make sure students are moving as seamlessly as possible from the online environment to the classroom environment. We need to make sure that students understand that in taking a hybrid course they are indeed taking one, single class, rather than feeling like they are involved in two, barely related enterprises: the time they spend in a classroom and the time they spend online. Effective learning modality integration of this kind can be achieved in fairly direct ways. For example, if students have completed an online discussion board assignment, the next class meeting might begin with the instructor's invitation to individual students to expand on comments from the online environment. Effective integration in the hybrid format can also unfold in more structured ways as well, as when online and f2f activities can be scaffolded toward a major project so that students are working toward a common goal by completing tasks both online and in the classroom. One important design consideration, too, is whether grading points are awarded for both online and classroom work. If a course grade is deriving too heavily, or indeed exclusively, from either online or f2f work, then students will naturally assume they are to privilege one mode or the other. They may stop coming to class regularly if classroom attendance seems unnecessary for completing online work. Alternately, students can easily stop completing online tasks when they are not connected to what is happening in the classroom and there are no points attached to online activities.

The workshop unit we talk about here will ask participants to think about effective course design so that students will feel that they are part of one, unified learning experience, in which their participation in both online and f2f environments is necessary to their success in the course.

To situate this unit, it can be useful to have participants respond to the design of the workshop series. In what ways is the workshop online structure contributing toward and enhancing their learning? What aspects of the course make them clear about what to do, when to do it, and where to do it?

For appropriate contextualization, facilitators should discuss the formal group assessment approaches (see our earlier section in Chapter 2 about the role of formal group assessment tools in assessing quality hybrid courses). Having a solid course shell designed for a blended course is just as vital as it is for an entirely online course. Using these standards sets the foundation for the participants' understanding of the instructional design components of a strong hybrid course.

Navigational components are integral structural elements of instructional design. What elements of design make a course easy to navigate? Students need to be able to navigate through the online course shell and accurately pull away what needs to be done online and in the classroom each week. Their course experiences should not be confusing or stressful. If students cannot find the information when they need it, they are likely to not complete the assignments, disappear from class, or fill the instructor's inbox with panicked questions. None of these are the results we seek as instructors. Instead, spend time ensuring that instructors are careful about how they name buttons, guide students through how the course is structured, and limit chunks of text, so they do not overwhelm students. Can they find out where they can get their questions answered on campus about their computer problems, about their LMS issues, and about the course specifically? Can they also find additional help with other support services on campus?

One interesting activity for workshop participants, which can be presented either in an informal real-time discussion or as a more formal online discussion assignment, or a combination of both, is to have them consider activities they already do online and whether those tend to be relatively easy or difficult, stress free or stress inducing. Ideally we can think beyond education-related activities. Many people, for example, book travel online, or bank online, or undertake any number of daily life chores by using the Internet. Reflecting on these activities, we might ask what, as precisely as possible, makes these interactions go well or poorly. In other words, are there lessons to learn from our non-education-related Web use that can inform how we build our courses in an LMS? One benefit to this exercise is that it has those in a hybrid learning workshop thinking broadly about Web design, even if they have no formal Web design training. That is, we often know more than we think we know about effective design, thanks to our experience using the Web. This can be an empowering realization, especially for those feeling tentative about teaching, or working as an evaluator, in the hybrid setting, since it is often those folks who believe they are behind the learning curve and less tech-savvy than their peers, when that is not necessarily the case.

Here is one version of the activity as Snart uses it in his hybrids workshop, set up as an online discussion board assignment. The unit title is "The World of/is Online":

> Based on our in-person discussion and our readings for this unit (assigned and available at the end of Unit 2) please post about an "online experience" that has been particularly important for you or for somebody you know very well.
>
> Try to focus on an experience that does *not* involve teaching or taking a class online. Recall that we do MANY things online, some easy and some not so easy.
>
> Choose one of these experiences (ideally from your own personal history) that stands out for you—good or bad. You may also try to think of contrasting online experiences (one good and one bad) and reflect on how one was pleasant while the other was not.
>
> Explain what you were doing online, what went right or wrong, and how things ended up.
>
> Please also reflect on how your personal experience might be related to or has had an influence on your teaching in the hybrid/online mode (even if the experience itself was not directly teaching related). (Snart, "Learning Hybrid: Hybrid Learning")

This discussion is productively complicated by considering the limits imposed by an LMS, not to mention the considerable resources that a company like Amazon, often cited as providing a stress-free online experience, applies to making its Web interface easy to use. Further interesting can be discussion of the degree to which so-called easy user experiences often depend on making that experience individualized, and thus dependent on collecting a lot of individual user data. What are the implications for student privacy here? And how best might an institution balance the need for student privacy against the benefits of a more tailored user experience that depends for its individuation on user data? These questions in the context of the LMS can be challenging enough, but what about a data drive registration system that (like Amazon, for example) could make proactive course suggestions to students based on their past coursework and success?

After considering what workshop participants might already know from their experiences, good and bad, of completing tasks online, and once navigation has been established for their blended course shells, facilitators should move into a discussion about the ways by which instructors are going to meet the course objectives, outcomes, and predictors for student success. We review the importance of articulating the learning objectives that the instructors want their students to reach for each week, the activities or tasks to be done in each of the two environments to help them reach those outcomes, and how those activities or tasks will be assessed.

To have a successful hybrid course, instructors must be able to make it clear what will go in each environment and how both pieces support each other. Students should never get the impression that either environment is more important than the other but rather they feed into one another, working on a learning arc from start to finish.

Content structure will vary from course to course and discipline to discipline, but all instructors should be asked a series of questions to help them construct the structure of their weekly course content: What activities will be completed in each environment? Which environment most effectively lends itself to that kind of activity? More reflective, time-consuming critical thinking often flourishes online, for example, because it allows the time for students to work through that material. The classroom sessions lend themselves toward applying the concepts and working through the reading material students read outside of the classroom on their own prior to entering the classroom.

Aligning their course outcomes with specific activities and assessment techniques is often the aspect of hybrid/blended course development that instructors find most challenging, as most of us realize what the content will be and what our list of outcomes is for that course; however, we are not frequently asked to so openly articulate these ties between ideas. However, instructors will find that these exercises are incredibly helpful and, once completed, help them improve as teachers. Often instructors will find that they don't actually know why they have students engaging in a particular activity and, as a result, refine their course content to more closely align with their course outcomes.

To help them think through their instructional design for the hybrid course, instructors should review helpful resources before applying those resources to their activity for the module. For example, workshop participants might read Kaleta et al.'s "Hybrid Courses: Obstacles and Solutions for Faculty and Students," which warns teachers of the tendency to create the "course and a half" by adding online work to their existing face-to-face class structures instead of rethinking their face-to-face courses to translate some of it to the online portion of their new hybrid course, and reminds them to maintain a fluidity between the two environments rather than constructing one class in the classroom and an entirely different classroom online (2–3). Having participants read these warnings from an experienced instructor of hybrid courses can aid in their preparation for the new hybrid course and, hopefully, improve the likelihood of a positive first experience teaching in the hybrid format.

In addition to instructional design articles and resources, workshop facilitators may consider providing some helpful links to free or cheaper media sources where instructors might begin translating some course materials to AV materials for the online component of their course. For example, while Camtasia can do some amazing things, the editing and buffering times can be overwhelming and frustrating for newer online instructors and its cost can scare off some schools struggling with technology financial support. Nudging them toward easier, free systems like Screencast-O-Matic, Jing, or recorded Google Hangouts can settle nervous digital stomachs and lighten the pressure on the wallets.

Facilitators should invite inquiry and discussion about the content of the workshop training as well. To what extent has the workshop been clear and overt about its objectives and rationale for various assignments to this point? Having criticism of the workshop training can open up a level of comfort and camaraderie between the facilitators and participants. In addition to considerations of the course outcomes in the more holistic sense, the workshop training should also address issues of the Americans with Disabilities Act (ADA) and the role of universal design in the course environment as a whole.

At the center of many current debates, there are some polarizing views about the extent to which teachers must create online courses that adhere to the absolute letter of ADA law when it comes to potential students with disabilities. According to the Department of Education's statement on accessibility,

> The U.S. Department of Education is committed to making its electronic and information technologies accessible to individuals with disabilities by meeting or exceeding the requirements of Section 508 of the Rehabilitation Act (29 U.S.C. 794d), as amended in 1998. Section 508 is a federal law that requires agencies to provide individuals with disabilities equal access to electronic information and data comparable to those who do not have disabilities, unless an undue burden would be imposed on the agency. (US Department of Education)

In some ways, then, this indicates that there is some flexibility in deciding how to approach accessibility in the classroom. Whose responsibility is it to adhere to the ADA laws? Does your school have a policy in place to assure that each faculty member adheres to certain expectations? Consider the questions faculty need to ask and the actions they need to take while preparing their courses. This holds true not just for hybrid curricula, of course, but for this text's sake, we will focus on the accommodations for those types of courses. Bastedo et al.'s "Programmatic Accessibility" article provides many options, such as student surveys for the accommodations center to give to students to determine if the courses require adjustments to be made to meet the student's need (97–98) and a flowchart starting with when the faculty get their notices from the accommodations center regarding documented disabilities of their incoming students (101). These are not the only options, clearly, but they are a wonderful starting point for institutional discussions about policies regarding accommodations. Having these in place early in the development of a hybrid curriculum could help assure a standard for all of the courses.

Despite the understandable impact that attention to accessibility will have on student success, many heated debates continue to ask why the online course environment should be held to a higher standard than most face-to-face courses. Some face-to-face instructors only modify their classroom instruction when they are given notice that a student has a particular need in that class section, for example. We do not have a sign language interpreter in every f2f class for students who might be hearing impaired. But of course if a student needs that accommodation it should be—it legally *must* be—provided. In most cases, though, f2f courses are taught per the instructor's delivery choices. However, online instructors can often feel greater pressure to design and provide for all possible disabilities—from physical challenges to information processing disorders—that students in a course may have. Unlike a f2f class, many disabilities go unnoticed or unknown. As noted by McCarthy, "Once students with disabilities move on to post-secondary education it is the students' responsibility to obtain documentation for accommodations relating to disability and activating these accommodations; however, not all students with disabilities realize this and struggle early in their college career" (qtd. in Massengale and Vasquez 72). The issue becomes more than just faculty awareness of necessary accessibility by anticipating potential student needs that the students are not asking for or do not recognize they are able to request. Yes, some f2f students face this same struggle, but if accessibility for the hybrid student can be made and potentially positively impact their level of success, isn't that what everyone wants?

While time consuming and often unused, however, universal accessibility strategies are helpful not only for those with disabilities but also for those with different learning styles. Universal design approaches can include creating transcripts for otherwise unscripted, informal videos, or adding audio descriptions of visual aids, or having ASL signers sign presentations in a Web camera setup. Therefore, they are useful in a myriad of ways beyond the immediate, more obvious scope. In the hybrid structure, instructors have a clearer sense of many of these disabilities and learning styles and can accommodate and adjust the teaching approach to help all of their students learn as much as possible.

By the end of this instructional design unit, then, faculty participants should have a direction for where they wish to take their course shells. Understandably so, many faculty, especially those new to online teaching as a whole, will likely find all of these moving parts overwhelming initially. Facilitators should pace the workshop as slowly as possible through this sequence of discussions, possibly covering these over the course of two weeks of instruction, stopping periodically to have their faculty participants apply the concepts to their course shells. For example, participants might be asked to design one course module for the hybrid course that they are currently building. In the module, instructors should be responsible for the following components:

- Learning outcomes that will be covered during that particular week

- Reading and writing materials to be completed prior to entering the physical classroom

- Assignments and activities planned for the physical classroom

- Assignments and activities planned for the online portion of the course

- Forms of assessing that the students have reached each of the learning objectives

- Instructions and/or links to the technology necessary to complete the assignments

After each faculty member has completed a module, the facilitator may find it helpful to have them share their module with the rest of the participants, articulating not only *what* they constructed but also how they kept in mind the elements of instructional design while designing it. Ultimately, discussions will form out of these presentations that will bring to light aspects of instructional design that they found helpful and pivotal to changes in their hybrid pedagogy, while also bringing to light the greatest challenges they faced and getting the other participants and facilitator to start helping them work through their struggles to find some potential solutions.

We should also point out that since we encourage nonteaching staff, including campus support personnel as well as administrators, to take advantage of this kind of hybrid workshop opportunity, there need to be options available for those who would not ever need to design a hybrid learning instructional module for a course. The more flexible the workshop can remain in terms of having participants produce meaningful projects, reflective of their actual roles on campus, the more comprehensive the workshop can become and the more attractive it will be to a diversity of groups on campus.

Those workshops with a greater hands-on component may find it more useful to have the participants create pieces of their course shell in smaller chunks along the way (e.g., maybe a daily homework project if the training is being done in the summer in a more condensed structure).

Training: Formative and Summative Assessment

A fourth unit that should be addressed in a hybrid/blended training workshop series is assessment in the hybrid environment. For any course, faculty should provide formative and summative assessment, though some more traditionally structured courses or particularly large courses often find themselves relying on summative assessment and sidestepping formative assessments throughout the semester. Students also misperceive the role of assessment in many cases. Chin-Wei, Kooi-Guan, and Ai-Ping write that "[t]o the student, assessment is perceived as formal, judgmental and usually initiated, conducted and interpreted by those in power (namely teachers and the college)." If assessment is used exclusively in these end-game approaches, it is limited for both the teacher and the students. Rather than seeing assessment as something that can occur throughout the course, and in smaller, low stakes situations, students often perceive assessment only as something that occurs at the ends of units or courses, actions that mark the end of learning, not the growth and development of learners.

Therefore, the workshop series should address ways to approach summative and formative assessments in the hybrid environment to encourage increased learning and learner awareness in the classroom. By discussing some techniques that are not all consuming on the time front, instructors may find themselves more apt to integrate formative assessments throughout the hybrid courses they design.

Since assessment is an aspect with which all instructors will feel comfortable and familiar, it might be best to begin with an open discussion prompt asking the participants to share an assessment strategy that they use in their classrooms right now. What kind of assessment is it and how has it been written and possibly revised over the years? Facilitators might also find it helpful to ask open-ended questions in the discussion forum about what aspects of assessment they find most challenging and why.

Effective hybrid courses will likely be those including both formative and summative assessment opportunities, and that include assessment in the online as well as the classroom environments. If assessment tends to occur in just one of the two delivery modes, either online or face-to-face, students will almost inevitably see one mode as "more important" than the other and, as a result, may not show as much diligence in the medium in which they are less frequently assessed. We have noticed that it can happen that assessment in the hybrid format can favor the online environment, especially if the activities that instructors develop for the online portion of a blended class rely too heavily on basic rote testing (the lure of automated grading). Even when students are working more interactively with one another online via discussion boards, though, the grading points for a hybrid course can easily migrate almost entirely online. Perhaps this happens because tools we might use online, housed in the LMS, are directly connected to the gradebook. It seems only natural to favor those systems that make grading more streamlined. But this may be sending the wrong, even if unintentional, message to students.

One strategy that instructors might find effective to make classroom time meaningful for students, or at least tie it directly to assessment and the points they are earning for class, but which still preserves the efficiency that working with tools in the LMS can offer, is to consciously scaffold assessment that happens in the LMS *from* work that has begun in the classroom. This is fundamentally good design practice anyway: to integrate online and face-to-face time so students do not end up feeling that they are in two separate courses—the online and face-to-face portions of one class—with little coherence between the two. It also saves instructors from having to assign points in the face-to-face setting for such basic things as students showing up. But if students *must* show up, because the online work will depend on their having learned or done something face-to-face, then they will hopefully have the sense that both learning modes are equally valued and that even if the points for the class derive from an online assignment, they cannot simply skip the face-to-face meetings.

Now, for why summative and formative assessment is important. If students are only assessed in a summative fashion, some students may find themselves feeling overly confident that they are comprehending the information when they are not or, on the other hand, they may think they are confused when, in fact, they are right on target. Formative assessments in both modes allow instructors to encourage their students and/or nudge them in the right direction if they are off track.

Specifically, in the instructional series, facilitators will likely want to begin by defining the two terms. Formative assessment occurs throughout the course to assess student progress in order to aid in the students' continued learning wherein the instructors provide feedback about that progress and ways that the students might improve their understanding of that content. This is known as assessment *for* learning. Teachers benefit from this type of assessment, too, because it provides insights into how effectively they are conveying information and, as a result of formative assessment, teachers are better able to adjust their pedagogy to improve understanding. For hybrid instruction, teachers could integrate reflection and responses to the discussion posts students share, which are informal pieces of writing that express their applications of course concepts. Formative assessment is also incredibly helpful during the students' processes of completing projects, such as writing essays or preparing presentations. When students are provided feedback prior to earning formal, final grades on assignments, they are able to learn and grow as writers, readers, and thinkers. Meanwhile, summative assessments are judgmental, final assessments of how well students understood a main unit or chunk of information of some sort. Summative assessments often come in the form of quizzes and exams. This type of assessment is known as assessment *of* learning.

Once the differences between these types of assessments have been provided, the workshop facilitators should provide the opportunity for those enrolled in the workshop to engage in both kinds of assessments from the point of view of a student. For example, during the course of the workshop, facilitators might set up a sequence of discussion forums wherein enrollees post their comments to given prompts and are then given some formative assessments of their responses, including personal feedback and feedback in the discussion forum itself, to aid in overall course members' understanding of the material. Further, facilitators should offer formative assessments of the active learning activity done in Unit 2 as well as the individual project completed in Unit 3. By offering those kinds of assessments earlier in the workshop, when this unit begins, participants can reflect on the value of that formative assessment, which will fold in nicely into the more formal discussion of its role for both instructors and students in the hybrid course.

While formative assessment occurs throughout the workshop, few instructional training series provide summative assessment for their participants, probably because training is not commonly formally graded. Instead, the workshops/training provide a learning environment for instructors to grow and develop their hybrid course structures. Therefore, when summative assessment is addressed in this unit, the participants won't likely be summatively assessed by the facilitators; however, the participants are more than familiar with this kind of assessment and will likely not need much instruction on that end. The workshop should cover methods for summative assessment that can be done online as well as in the classroom.

By combining these kinds of assessments for participants, they will see how each contributes toward the learning experience for students. For example, the facilitators might discuss how an assignment is introduced in the classroom meeting, discussed, and then students might work on beginning pieces of that assignment online, during which the instructor provides formative assessments to the individuals and/or group members. The students can then revise that work online and bring drafts to the class meeting during which they can get formative assessment from their fellow classmates, nudging them with revision ideas. Finally, when the project is complete, the students can then get summative assessment from their instructor in the online course structure.

To wrap up this final unit of the workshop series, participants could return to the module they created in the third unit to actually develop assessment rubrics for those assignments. This will help them see how each unit folds into the next and to have fruitful discussions about rubric-building. While not all instructors necessarily use rubrics, some means for assessing their students' assignments should be provided in their modules, so having the participant engage in an assessment project for their courses (which may include revising a current assessment tool or perhaps defending their continued use of one they already have) will further develop or solidify a thoughtful assessment approach for their instruction.

Continuing Support/Education/Development beyond the Workshop

Both of us have experienced directly—and hear anecdotally—that often professional development at institutions is boiled down to a lowest common denominator. In other words, what drives the creation and delivery of professional development opportunities is the question of what might serve the most people most efficiently. Not most effectively, necessarily, but most efficiently. So the kind of hybrid learning and teaching workshop we advocate for here is robust, demanding, rigorous, and, relatively speaking, time-intensive. Such a workshop should be worth credit. It will occupy weeks in a semester, not a single afternoon. It will involve academic readings in the field. And it will have participants produce a meaningful project. As we've outlined it above, the hybrid workshop is meant to be a deep learning experience.

Therefore, after the workshop series has concluded, facilitators should mark the occasion. But what takeaway might be provided to workshop participants beyond the knowledge they have gained? Specifically, how might participants be able to document that they have completed the training for things like tenure portfolios, posttenure reviews, or future employment? Facilitators may find it helpful to provide participants with a letter that outlines the work done in the training series and which components of that training each participant completed. Those who complete all units, both online and in the classroom, should earn a more formal mark, such as a certificate of completion.

At the close of the "Going Hybrid" eight-week workshop series, all participants earn a physical certificate with the college seal and president's signature, and a detailed congratulatory letter from the workshop facilitators to include in their tenure portfolios or to submit with job applications. For those who participate as adjunct professors, the workshop series qualifies as one of their continuing education credits. At the close of the "Learning Hybrid: Hybrid Learning" workshop, participants receive a digital badge in Blackboard and another through Credly (discussed in greater detail in the next section). At the close of both workshops, though, participants leave with a portable professional credential, recognition of their hard work.

In addition to the more immediate marking of the completion of the workshop series, facilitators should set up a communication plan with participants to assure that they maintain a means for ongoing support as they work on developing their hybrid courses. For example, they might consider keeping the workshop course shell open for interaction among class members in the discussion forums and to continue to allow access to course materials, which they may find particularly helpful as they build their hybrid courses. Maintaining an open line of communication will foster community across disciplines.

Some facilitators may wish to set up an advanced training series to follow up after this introductory training series in which the participants break up into smaller discipline-specific cohorts. During these additional training meetings, faculty of specific disciplines could discuss successful strategies from seasoned hybrid instructors and listen to some challenges they faced that might be discipline-specific too. For example, a composition specialist might introduce other composition instructors to the alignments between the Quality Matters rubric standards and the Conference on College Composition and Communication's Effective Practices for Online Writing Instruction. Effective practices are fairly common throughout the online teaching community and, therefore, should be considered during development as guideposts. Refraining from referring to them as directives can prove incredibly helpful when asking instructors to revise courses. Composition instructors, or those teaching writing-intensive courses, have unique challenges when designing online and blended courses in that they are already dealing with writing-intensive curricula, but now fused with additional writing assignments through the online component of the structure. New blended learning faculty would find it helpful to have a sounding board for addressing how to handle that paperload so as not to feel overwhelmed as an instructor, and to work through the possibility of hybrid students working harder than the f2f students (what is sometimes called the "course and a half" syndrome).

Science instructors like those teaching biology often find themselves faced with the challenge of translating their lecture-based courses into the online component, without having to record, upload, and transcribe two-hour lectures. Having a veteran hybrid biology instructor leading a biology cohort could be incredibly helpful for new hybrid course instructors. What strategies might prove helpful in breaking down the longer lectures into smaller, digestible chunks? How can the lectures become more of an active learning experience? What software tool works most effectively to prepare those lectures, so that students are learning that material well? Instructors may discuss methods for making their videos more interactive like SlideShark quiz slides, simply asking students to pause the video and reflect on something, or doing a little freewriting about something to assess their knowledge or to see if they can answer a question you pose in the video about the content up to that point. Little moments of formative assessment embedded in the multimedia can encourage students' participation, engagement, and comprehension.

After the participants begin teaching their hybrid courses, they will likely find themselves having new questions about adjusting their course shells or searching for strategies for responding to concerns they have in their classes that they hadn't considered upon entering the course. To really foster this growing community, try having those participants who completed the training course become mentors for the participants of the next training series. They can offer advice and guidance along the way and help the facilitators continue to build a foundation of learners in this community. Further, these graduates from the training workshop will be able to come back to share their course shells and become a sounding board for the newer participants. In addition to aiding in the workshop series' ongoing sessions, participants who complete the course could also build panels to offer to inhouse discussions over brown bag lunches and the like, so that those faculty who had interest in the workshop series but weren't sure if it was for them could attend and have some questions answered. Moreover, administration could be brought back into the discussions by visiting these sessions, listening to what happened in the training workshop series and, as a result, potentially continue to fund or even increase funding for the training.

Fit Though Few? Acknowledging Workshop Participation

Fit though few. That is how John Milton envisioned the readership for his epic poem *Paradise Lost*. We wonder if that isn't also a useful mindset when we think about those who might be involved in designing, teaching, and supporting hybrids, especially in their early period at an institution. We understand how off-putting that might sound, though. Fit though few is hardly the language of equality and democratization we generally like to hear in the world of education. And it may sound counter-intuitive, given our enthusiasm for blended learning generally. But we have also seen how advocacy for robust professional development of the kind we describe earlier—a full workshop that requires multiple meetings over the semester and demands considerable work from its participants—runs the risk of getting boiled down to an online lecture, a single afternoon drop-in session, or some other less-than-demanding variant. So to guard against this potential flattening of otherwise immersive and extensive teacher training, we will address the topic directly here.

We are working from the very practical premise that in most cases some constituent group within the larger institution will have to be the voice that says teaching hybrids is not for everyone. Or, more precisely, that just because a faculty member has sat through an afternoon workshop on "teaching hybrids," does not mean he or she is fully qualified to design and teach in the hybrid mode. That teacher might be well on his or her way to a deeper level of expertise. The single afternoon workshop could be the beginning, but not the beginning *and the end*, of the professional development journey. A deeper level of professional development might require a more elaborate framework in which to unfold.

Any kind of one-off workshop most certainly has its place in the professional support and development structure of an institution, to be sure. Faculty could be invited to learn about Twitter, or iClickers, or Animoto, or SnagIt, or how to use the LMS gradebook more effectively. But we see these as relatively discrete, technical competencies. Yes, one's facility with them gets better with deeper immersion and practice. So it's not that one gains mastery in a couple of hours even with any of these technical tools. But none are quite the same as learning to work in an entirely new instructional delivery mode, an endeavor that might involve some of those discrete technical proficiencies but will also invite broad, philosophical considerations having to do with pedagogy, course design, and institutional infrastructure.

Let's also be clear: we've advocated previously for wide input in the development and offering of hybrid classes. So an institution will want to know, not just what instructors think about hybrids or what IT support has in mind, but also what students think, what *potential* students think, how the library feels, what does marketing know. That's a wide swathe of constituents.

And we'd also be thrilled to hear that on any given campus there is a groundswell of interest in and energy for developing and teaching hybrids. So not fit though few, but fit and far reaching (or some better phrase that preserves Milton's alliteration). We aren't trying to be exclusionary so much as realistic here.

Our sense is that in the majority of cases, there will ultimately be a relatively limited number of those on campus who are willing to devote the time and energy into hybrid curricular work that it will take to produce a truly knowledgeable and experienced cohort. This reality does not preclude early, inclusive fact-finding as an important stage in the development of an institutionally supported and sustainable hybrid curriculum. But we are also not suggesting that in an effort to make everybody a hybrid learning "expert" an institution should artificially certify any and all comers in hopes of producing overwhelming interest in hybrids and, perhaps magically, after a couple of hours in a teaching and learning center, great hybrid courses that produce amazing student and teacher satisfaction.

So if an institution is forced to choose between having many people, instructors and administrators alike, all with just a little interest in hybrids and a relatively novice working knowledge of what they are but not much more, or a smaller number of folks who have deep knowledge and experience, we'd probably opt for the latter. The fit though few, at least as an institution lays the groundwork for what we hope will be a viable and flourishing hybrid learning program.

In an ideal world, the situation we present here is a false dichotomy. Institutions wouldn't have to choose one or the other situation. They'd enjoy and benefit from lots of interest in hybrids and many people willing to invest significant time in professional development. But we have every reason to believe that that ideal situation will present itself in relatively few instances. Realistically, standard teaching loads for most instructors are such that there is little time for more than a short professional development workshop or training session here or there. Part-time faculty often face the additional challenge of teaching at multiple campuses, for different institutions, and they may not have access to any institutional office or work space that is truly their own. Time invested in professional development is not necessarily directly compensated either for contingent workers.

We understand the motivation to offer professional development that is accessible and reasonable for those with busy schedules or those not actually compensated directly from their investment of time or energy in learning something new. But we are equally concerned at how often we've seen institutions deem an instructor as qualified to teach in a new learning mode, be it fully online or hybrid, just by virtue of attending an afternoon workshop. Realistically, how much deep knowledge can one gain in such a short period? We are not trying to devalue those short professional development opportunities, by any means. They are a mainstay at many institutions and certainly faculty depend on them for continued professional growth. But will an institution truly benefit from having a large number of faculty designing and teaching hybrids when the extent of training has been an afternoon spent in a teaching and learning center? We think not.

We believe that successful completion of inhouse professional development opportunities can be used by participants to earn credit that is directly relevant to tenure, promotion, renewed teaching assignments, and the like. In other words, the institution recognizes in an immediate way when instructors, administrators, and staff invest time and energy in pursuing professional development opportunities.

This means that professional development needs to be, for lack of a better word, rigorous, a fact we hope we have reflected in the preceding discussion. Just as we know when it comes to teaching students, mere seat-time does not equate to real engagement or learning. So showing up to a one-off "workshop" on a Tuesday afternoon should not necessarily, in and of itself, confer upon the participant proof of mastery or ample evidence for movement on the salary scale. But where participants have invested real time and effort, where they have been challenged to read relevant literature and produce meaningful work of their own, institutions need to make sure that a system is in place to acknowledge such efforts.

In addition to the immediate benefits of inhouse credentialing, we'd like to suggest the use of digital badges to recognize participation in professional development opportunities.

Digital Badges

An Educause Learning Initiative article, from its 7 Things You Should Know About series, describes digital badges as "digital tokens that appear as icons or logos on a web page or other online venue. Awarded by institutions, organizations, groups, or individuals, badges signify accomplishments such as completion of a project, mastery of a skill, or marks of experience" ("7 Things You Should Know about . . . Badges"). We like the focus here on project completion, even mastery (however tricky that term might be in practice), rather than simple acknowledgement of seat-time. In one higher education initiative, Coastal Carolina College linked its first-year composition course outcomes to digital badges. Reid and Paster, both professors at Coastal Carolina, report that using a digital badging system has provided a "programmatic framework for teaching and assessing academic literacy skills central to students' development and success." The use of badges has made, report Reid and Paster, learning outcomes "more visible" to faculty and students alike. Both the programmatic framework within which digital badges can be earned and awarded, along with the high level of visibility, are what seem appealing about digital badges as a credentialing system applicable to the work of professional development.

A typical digital badge will involve a grantor and issuer and of course a recipient. In the case of badges connected to a hybrid learning workshop, the grantor will ideally be, not just the workshop leader or facilitator, but the institution itself. Issuing badges can be managed using providers like Mozilla's Open Badge Infrastructure (OBI) or Credly. Digital badges are created with these or similar systems. Each badge can be associated with a particular learning objective, or set of objectives, and a description of the criteria used to evaluate whether participants have met those objectives. A digital badge is more than just an image; it provides a method by which those who have earned badges can display their accomplishment *and* provide evidence of what they have done to earn the badge.

Digital badges can be embedded into e-portfolios, for example, or linked to professional networking sites like LinkedIn. This allows for digital badges to be meaningful beyond a single institution. In some ways, a digital badge is akin to those photocopied or mass-printed "certificates" that many of us might have received for everything from participating in a blood drive to completing institutional training of some kind. Unlike those printed certificates, however, the digital badge is much more portable, and can be made public in a variety of Web-based venues. And more importantly, the digital badge (when properly created through Credly, Mozilla's badge program, or the like) will provide access to the evidence for having earned the badge, which of

FIGURE 18. *Some of Jason Snart's BlendKit2014 digital badges in Credly.*

course that printed certificate could never do. For example, Figure 18 shows what badges look like in Credly. These were earned by Jason Snart for his work in the Educause/University of Central Florida's hybrid learning MOOC, BlendKit.

The BlendKit resource divided material into various units and each featured a different series of badges. Thus, participants

FIGURE 19. *Final "Blended Learning Designer" badge in the BlendKit series.*

could complete just pieces of the course and still earn badges, without necessarily having to finish all the material to earn just one single badge. The BlendKit MOOC did involve a final, capstone project, though. Completion of this project, along with previous assignments, would earn the participant a final badge, pictured in Figure 19.

Participants who earn the badge can link it to their Facebook, Twitter, or LinkedIn accounts in addition to presenting it in e-portfolios.

The badge link will take you to further information, the really useful part, that explains what the badge is for, who the issuer is, and what evidence was evaluated before awarding the badge. Figure 20 shows what the badge looks like on a Facebook page. The badge is visually appealing, but it is unlikely to mean much to a potential employer or academic administrator with no prior knowledge of the BlendKit course to which the badge is connected. But following the link that is provided in this social media post, we can discover more about what the badge is and how the owner has earned it.

This Blended Learning Designer badge description reads: "This badge recognizes those who have demonstrated blended learning design competencies through a rigorous, peer-reviewed portfolio submission following the completion of the five-week MOOC BlendKit2014: Becoming a Blended Learning Designer sponsored by the University of Central Florida (UCF) and EDU-CAUSE" ("Becoming a Blended Learning Designer"). The criteria explain that "[i]ndividuals earn this badge by submitting a successfully peer-reviewed portfolio demonstrating competence in designing a blended learning course." If badges are designed to do so, they can provide any viewer with access to the work that was submitted to earn it.

It is this last piece—access to actual evidence of participation or mastery or proficiency—that still confounds the world of digital

FIGURE 20. *Final "Blended Learning Designer" badge on Facebook.*

badging. Ultimately, as open systems, digital badges can be created and awarded by more or less anyone. We could create one and award it to you for reading this book. Or pretending to read it. Or reading a few words in it. How valuable would that badge be?

As the "7 Things You Should Know About . . . Badges" article indicates, "Many details remain for badges to be broadly accepted as legitimate indicators of education, skill, or experience. . . . Acceptance depends, at least in part, on the level of quality control for these awards." We agree that "ongoing work will be done to validate badges to ensure those who earned, issued, and endorsed them are who they claim to be" but badging still seems to be an important way to honor participation in professional development programs, especially where those programs are time-intensive and involve the completion of significant project-based work.

Recognizing time and energy invested in professional development through a badging system might be especially important for those adjunct faculty who are not otherwise compensated for their time and for whom limited, inhouse credentialing only serves them at that single institution. Since many adjuncts teach at multiple institutions, having a portable credential like a digital badge can be especially important. Not only can that credential be displayed across institutional boundaries, but it can also be used outside of academia entirely. Many adjuncts teach in addition to working in their given field, and often employers and professional associates are interested to see evidence of ongoing professional development. As Matthew Pittinsky, former CEO of Blackboard, notes, "Credentials matter in a knowledge economy." We think digital badges, as both meaningful and portable credentials, can constitute a valuable piece of hybrid learning professional development.

CHAPTER FOUR

Hybrids Across the Curriculum

Here we would like to provide a series of snapshots: various hybrid courses from across a typical college curriculum. We are not so much interested in offering these as ideals or perfected models of design. Certainly each of these courses has clear strengths, and some could surely function as truly exemplary courses. But we are more concerned with suggesting what hybrids might look like in a number of different academic areas.

And we are especially interested in looking at the reality of hybrids, not the hype. We approached a number of colleagues who teach hybrid courses and wanted to hear from those faculty about what works and what doesn't. We wanted to know about how it felt to offer a hybrid course within the context of a curricular area. What is the relationship between a teaching faculty member and an immediate supervisor, for example? What support existed in the development phase of the course–if any? What support continues to exist as the course is being offered—if any? And how accepted is the hybrid course by colleagues in a disciplinary area? Is it welcomed? Have others embraced the idea? Or is it ignored? Maybe the hybrid is, on the face of it, just "tolerated," maybe as a necessary nod to so-called innovation, when the truth for some might be the sense that the hybrid model is just one more step along the path to the dissolution of higher education as we know it.

In each of the snapshots that follow, then, we try to give a sense of some particulars, like how face-to-face and online learning time are divided. We'll look at what kinds of activities occur in a typical course unit, module, or week. And we'll suggest, with a few screenshots, what the course looks like, both as it exists in an LMS but also how it lays out in a syllabus.

We'll also examine some of the background, the history, that led to each hybrid course's creation and the faculty member's participation in that history. Again, we are especially interested to understand how hybrids develop. Do things begin with individual instructor interest? With a core group of teachers? Does the mandate come from an administrator or area coordinator that curriculum *must* be moved into the hybrid mode?

And last but certainly not least we asked teachers to share their successes and their challenges in teaching hybrids. What, if anything, does the hybrid mode allow them to do better or more efficiently than their face-to-face or online teaching? And what problems have teachers encountered?

In our discussion with various members who have designed and taught a hybrid course, we asked about the following:

- Course description, background and context: we were interested to know about the course itself and how it came to be. Was the hybrid course created out of initial faculty interest, was it motivated by suggestion or request from administration, or did it emerge from a combination of factors? We were further interested to know about what we called "context": In other words, how did the hybrid course exist, if at all, in relation to other offerings in the discipline or department? Was it viewed as an integral part of a program or set of curricular options for students, or was it either implicitly or explicitly a kind of outlier, maybe even the result of otherwise singular, and maybe siloed, faculty effort?

- LMS course menu screenshot: We were interested in how a course "looked" in an LMS at the top level, or what we called the course menu. We wanted to know, more or less, what students first arrived to when they accessed the course online. We wondered if that top-level menu gave any sense of what activities students might be doing online and/or if the course's existence in the LMS, at that topmost level, suggested ways in which the online component was a coequal piece with its face-to-face counterpart.

- Syllabus screenshot and/or sample unit screenshot: Here again we wondered about ways that faculty could suggest to students that the hybrid course was partly online and partly face-to-face, and that, ideally, those two modes exist as equally important and appear and feel as integrated to students. Might a course syllabus and sample unit or module suggest a kind of dialogue between the learning modes that make up the hybrid?

♦ Successes: We were certainly interested in what seemed to be going right, both in terms of student *and* faculty satisfaction. In fact, we hoped to tease out this latter piece, since the experience of the instructor is often overlooked when it comes to assessment (formal or informal, qualitative or quantitative) of the teaching and learning experience. Higher education is rightly concerned with the student experience, but we wondered what the teaching experience was like too.

♦ Challenges: We know that the hybrid model is not perfect nor is it some magical panacea. We don't pretend that any degree of curricular or instructional redesign is going to have all students engaged and learning at the deepest, most meaningful level that we ideally strive for. So we wanted to know about challenges too. Were there hurdles to be overcome in the earliest stages of course design or even proposal? Was there resistance to the very idea of the hybrid format? And if so, where did that resistance seem to come from? Was it overt? Implicit? Or both? Or maybe challenges emerged in the actual delivery of the course. Were students registering but ultimately not aware that they had signed up for a delivery mode that depended on both face-to-face and online engagement? Were there administrative roadblocks, maybe in the form of scheduling or accountability for the seat-time that had been "traded" for online work in the hybrid format? It is often by assessing the challenges that hybrids present—that is, by identifying what went *wrong*—that we can most successfully grow the learning model.

Perhaps due to the nature of our fairly open-ended questions, our various interviewees responded to each question we asked quite differently. It was our hope that the various faculty members that we talked to would discuss their hybrids freely with us, rather than feeling like they needed to complete a kind of homework project that we had assigned. What we found is that while some focused on course design strategies, other respondents focused on challenges or successes. Further, some of our faculty interviewees answered at great length while others were more abbreviated. And in some cases we were talking with faculty with whom we had collegial ties. In these cases, beyond what we gleaned from our interview questions, we were also able to understand a lot of their hybrid design and teaching insights from informal conversations.

So what we have tried to do is to synthesize for each instructor the various responses we received. In doing so, however, we have also tried to preserve the voice and unique perspective for each. All quotations in the course examples below that are attributed to individual instructors come from emails we have exchanged with them and from in-person conversations.

Here is what we found.

Fundamentals of Speech Communication—Stephen Thompson

Fundamentals of Speech Communication is a general education requirement at the College of DuPage. As such, many sections are offered in any given term and students arrive to class—or show up online—with widely varying degrees of enthusiasm, focus, and preparedness. The course is, as Thompson notes, "an introduction-level course" that focuses on the theory and practice of the communication process. Students are required to prepare and deliver to an audience a series of speeches throughout the term. Thompson notes that per departmental and Illinois state requirements "fifty percent of the course" must focus on "public speaking." What this means is that a large part of the instructor's challenge is to help students overcome basic public-speaking anxieties.

Thompson indicates that the hybrid form of the course developed somewhat haphazardly, with no particular or intentional departmental planning. A faculty member filled out the requisite "form" and the course came into existence. Students, Thompson reports, "were not informed they enrolled in a hybrid course until they showed up on the first day."

What followed some years after this initial, somewhat ungrounded course development phase was a more targeted request from the department administrator, herself a champion of the hybrid format, to (re)develop the hybrid Speech class and to make sure it was flagged in the registration system as such in an effort to alert students early on about the hybrid nature of the course.

Unfortunately, as Thompson indicates, while there are usually a couple of sections of Fundamentals of Speech Communication in the hybrid format offered each term, growth of the hybrid offering "has stalled out." Thompson speculates that this has resulted from lack of better institutional support for, and advertising of, the hybrid mode. So despite those redesign attempts that helped to flag the hybrid class *as a hybrid* in the registration system (the course code included an HYB tag), students were still not aware of exactly what that meant. Students might be seeing the HYB label in the registration system, but if the implications of that label were not clear, it seemed likely that students were not choosing to register for those sections. So despite predictably high enrollment in face-to-face and online offerings of the course, the few hybrids offered each semester were not necessarily going to run. They were more likely to be cancelled due to low enrollment.

What Thompson suggests is that no broader faculty interest developed in the hybrid mode, or in requests to teach that particular class, precisely because faculty were never sure that the course would run and that they would have a full teaching load. When classes are cancelled for low enrollment at the last minute, the faculty member is left scrambling to pick up a new class, not to mention the students who *had* registered are left to rebuild a semester's schedule just days before a term begins.

We'd like to pause here to emphasize how incentivizing faculty to design and teach hybrids can be so tightly connected to those broader institutional questions we have been asking throughout this book—like how do hybrids exist in the registration system. Local, departmental efforts to develop hybrid courses are apt to die on the vine when such efforts seem to exist in a larger institutional vacuum.

Thompson's Fundamentals of Speech Communication course divides learning evenly between online and face-to-face instruction. That division occurs (by college mandate) on a weekly basis: one day in the classroom each week and then an online component each week. The main course menu affords access to basic class material, like the syllabus, but also a series of unit/module areas, labeled by each week in the given term (see Figure 21).

The course schedule, provided as part of the syllabus (see Figure 22), is similarly divided into weeks, each listing in-class activities as well as "out of class" assignments, available in the LMS. Figure 23, the sample unit, or "week," from Thompson's Fundamentals of Speech Communication course in the LMS,

Getting Started
Announcements
Syllabus & Schedule
E-Book
Week 1
Week 2
Week 3
Week 4
Week 5
Week 6
Week 7
Week 8
Presentations
Self Assessments
Discussion Board

FIGURE 21. *Fundamentals of Speech Communication— course menu in Blackboard.*

provides a sense of the variety of activities that students are doing online. There are readings, quizzes, or other assessments, and links to publisher-provided content.

The course divides online and face-to-face learning 50/50 and on a weekly basis (as mandated by the college). What Thompson indicates, though, is that this mandated weekly division does not necessarily serve the best interests of the students. The fairly formulaic way in which his institution handles the scheduling of hybrid classes is what Thompson identifies as his most significant challenge.

It is hard, he reports, to develop a sense of flow or continuity, especially when students are giving speeches (an activity best suited to the face-to-face environment). So if the class is delivering persuasive speeches, it would make more curricular sense, according to Thompson, to be able to meet in consecutive face-to-face sessions until all speeches are complete,

Course Schedule – Summer 2014 **Schedule may change. Notice will be given in class or posted within Blackboard.	
Description of Events, Topic of Discussion	Out of Class Assignments & Other Material *To be completed on your own
Week 1 (June 10)	
Tuesday Student Scavenger Hunt Class Introductions: Professor & Student Introductions Syllabus Introduction Chapter 1: Communicating for Life (time permitting) Introduction to the Communication Field Activities & Discussion	For Friday, 6/13: Student Questionnaire Complete PRCA Assessment (in BB) Complete PRPSA Assessment (in BB) Read Ch. 1 Ch. 1 Module Read Ch. 12 (20 pages) Chapter 12 Module (10 minutes) For Tuesday, 6/17: Chapter 1 Quiz Chapter 12 Quiz

FIGURE 22. *Fundamentals of Speech Communication—syllabus excerpt.*

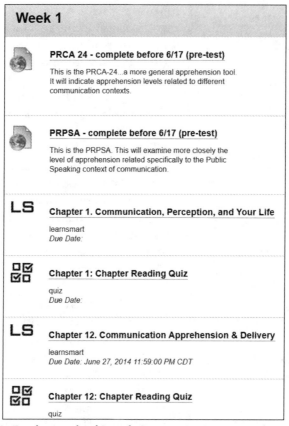

FIGURE 23. *Fundamentals of Speech Communication—typical "week" in Blackboard.*

rather than meeting once per week, completing a few speeches, then going online, then coming back the next week to resume speeches, etc. But that more flexible division of learning time is not, at present, possible.

A related challenge that Thompson notes is lack of professional development opportunities related to hybrid pedagogy. While his institution offers any number of focused "how to use the LMS" kinds of training opportunities, there is not much chance to have meaningful conversation with other faculty about hybrids, conversation that Thompson describes as "deeper pedagogical discussion or theoretical discussion about the place of hybrid learning in higher education."

Introduction to Biochemistry—William (Gary) Roby

Gary Roby's biochemistry course is a one-semester introductory course that, as Roby says, "introduces students to the major areas of biochemistry." In its fully onsite (sixteen-week) format, the course involves a two-hour lecture and four-hour lab each week.

Roby notes that this course in particular seemed to invite instructional redesign because the lecture time was "targeted at conveying introductory information and knowledge." It seemed to Roby that much of this material could be presented online more effectively for students than having it delivered face-to-face. Not only could students view and review material more easily online, but the very practical matter of freeing up what would otherwise be that two-hour lecture block—which was already in addition to four hours of lab time every week—made the hybrid format especially appealing. The students would, as Roby notes, "only need to come to lab [on campus]," rather than making two separate trips.

Roby's biochem course is perhaps a good example of how many lab-based science classes could work in the hybrid format: online learning works to prepare students for the hands-on work they will be expected to complete in the lab. He describes this online work as involving a combination of lecture (offered via video embedded in the LMS) along with interactive material offered from the textbook publisher (delivered via McGraw-Hill's Learnsmart/Smartbook but still tied to and accessible from the LMS). The face-to-face lab time then offers students the chance to ask questions about material they have worked through online before starting the lab work.

Roby provides his students with a syllabus (see Figure 24) that lists face-to-face and online assignments, organized by week. Each week, students can see what topics and activities they will be covering, in addition to assignment information (which points

Week	Date	Tentative Topic & Activities	Assignment (due at start of class)
1	Due 8/28	Ch 16 - Carbohydrates: *Types, Monosaccharides, Stereochemistry, Biologically Important Mono-,Di, and Polysaccharides*	
	8/26	Review syllabus and course policies Check in, Safety video Introduction to *Connect* software	(Fri, 8/28) Ch. **16** *-Log into Connect* *-LearnSmart Ch16*
2	Due 9/4	Ch 17a - Lipids & Their Functions in Biochemical Systems: *Biological Functions of Lipids, Fatty Acids & Their Chemical Reactions, Eicosanoids, Glycerides (Neutral and Phosphoglycerides)*	Ch. **17.1-17.3** *(9/6) LearnSmart Ch17a*
	9/2	Quiz – Ch 16 Experiment 26, Part A: *The Characterization of Known Carbohydrates* (pp.29 – 44)	Expt 26 Preliminary Exercises [PE] (p.39) & Lab Prework for ENTIRE lab (Parts A & B)
3	Due 9/11	Ch 17b - Lipids & Their Functions in Biochemical Systems: *Nonglyceride Lipids (Sphingolipids, Steroids, and Waxes), Complex Lipids, The Structure of Biological Membranes*	Ch. **17.4-17.6** *(9/13) LearnSmart Ch17b*
	9/9	Quiz – Ch 17a Experiment 26, Part B: *The Characterization of an Unknown Carbohydrate* (pp.29 – 44)	

FIGURE 24. *Introduction to Biochemistry—syllabus excerpt.*

them to material that is either housed in or accessible through the LMS). Additionally, Roby provides a calendar view in the syllabus as shown in Figure 25. The calendar shows students what material will be covered each week in addition to what online materials they need to access and assignments they need to complete. Figure 26 depicts what Roby's course menu looks

		FALL Semester 2015 Chem 2213-HYB01			Instructor: Gary Roby			
Week	SUN	MON	TUE	WED	THUR	FRI	SAT	Weeks Left
1	-August-	Fall Semester starts		Check-in, Safety video Syllabus & Course Policies *Intro to Connect*	View Ch16 Lectures	Log into Connect LearnSmart Ch16		17
	23	24	25	26	27	28	29	
2			-September-	Quiz Ch 16 Expt 26, Part A Carbohydrates		View Ch17a Lectures		16
	30	3	1	2	3	4	5	
3	LearnSmart Ch 17a	Legal Holiday No Classes		Quiz Ch 17a Expt 26, Part B		View Ch17b Lectures		15
	6	7	8	9	10	11	12	

FIGURE 25. *Introduction to Biochemistry—syllabus calendar.*

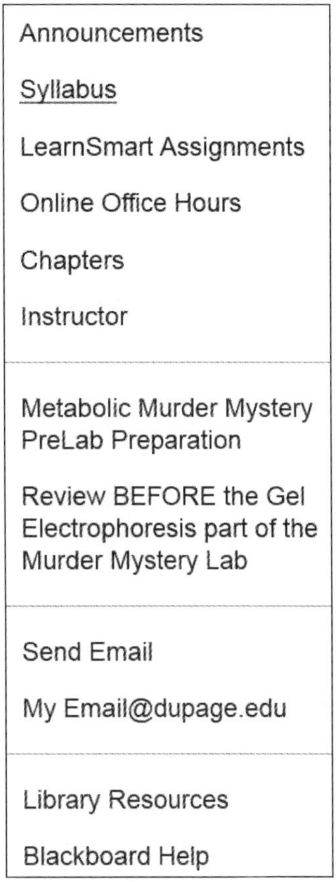

Announcements
Syllabus
LearnSmart Assignments
Online Office Hours
Chapters
Instructor
Metabolic Murder Mystery PreLab Preparation
Review BEFORE the Gel Electrophoresis part of the Murder Mystery Lab
Send Email
My Email@dupage.edu
Library Resources
Blackboard Help

FIGURE 26. *Introduction to Biochemistry—course menu in Blackboard.*

like in the LMS. A sample unit or chapter might include, as pictured in Figure 27, a review of that unit's learning objectives along with a video lecture in which Roby walks students through a particular concept. Additionally, Roby provides access to publisher content via the LMS as well (organized by textbook chapter), as pictured in Figure 28.

Roby notes that he was personally motivated to investigate the hybrid design idea for this lab-based class, in large measure because the class as a whole required so many face-to-face hours on a weekly basis: the two lecture hours plus the four lab hours. And yet what was happening in the lecture hours did not always seem to require a fully face-to-face presence in the way that hands-on lab work might. On the contrary, those two hours just made for scheduling difficulties for students as they were trying to schedule other classes around the six hours required of the Introduction to Biochemistry course, not to mention trips to campus (not always easy for the commuting student) to engage with material that could just as easily, if not even more effectively, be presented online. The course seemed, as Roby says, "the perfect candidate" for the hybrid model. So unlike many situations we encounter in which faculty are more or less arbitrarily assigned to teach a hybrid course, in this case it was Roby's own initiative that got the ball rolling. Hybrids starting from faculty initiative

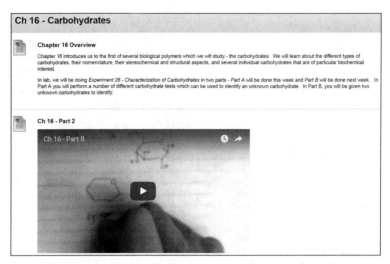

FIGURE 27. *Introduction to Biochemistry—sample unit with reading assignment and video lecture.*

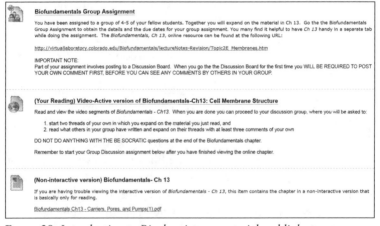

FIGURE 28. *Introduction to Biochemistry—material and links to resources.*

and interest is, as we have stressed throughout, a preferable situation relative to those instances where faculty are simply told they will be teaching a hybrid course.

Roby reports being supported by his associate dean in his curricular design efforts, and he has actively sought out professional development opportunities ranging from the hybrid learning workshop offered on campus to various software-based training modules (specifically geared to lecture capture and video editing so that he could provide students with a robust experience online in the new "lecture" portion of the course). He even reports—happily—that his associate dean strongly encouraged that Roby pursue this range of professional development, despite him already having a degree of expertise teaching online thanks to previous employment, before venturing too far. This reflects, to Roby, that "the college is recognizing the need for instructor preparation." Roby also benefits from collegial support; he notes that "one of my peers has done her own hybrid class and was very willing to . . . help in any way she could."

Responding to our question about successes, Roby makes a particularly noteworthy observation: in designing his hybrid course and in prepping materials for it, he has also reflected on ways to improve his teaching by bringing concepts to life for students and by creating more opportunities for peer to peer interaction. He started, for example, to build online components into his fully face-to-face courses, like interactive homework, discussion boards, and blogs. He has learned "a lot about managing groups online" and what he calls the "peculiarities of different online tools." The students, he reports, "seem to enjoy" the online work. In short, though, Roby's efforts to design his Introduction to Biochemistry class for the hybrid format has provided him with the opportunity to rethink all of his teaching. This might sound daunting, but Roby seems to have made very thoughtful choices about what to change and how best to change it when it comes to how he delivers content to students and how he asks them to engage with that content.

When it comes to challenges, or perceived challenges, Roby is acutely aware of the technology aspect of teaching online and in the hybrid mode: "Anyone who has had a computer or projector or other tool fail in the middle of a class knows what I am talking about," he says. So while he would like to use non-LMS tools, like Skype for example, to stay virtually connected with his students, he remains particularly sensitive to what dependence on those technological affordances mean. They may not work perfectly; and they may not work equally well for all students.

Paralegal Studies: Personal Injury, Tort, and Insurance Law—Capper Grant

This course is offered as part of the Paralegal Studies program and covers personal injury, tort, and insurance law, in addition to elements of medical records review and analysis. It is a three-credit (or three hours per week, in the sixteen-week format) class that divides time evenly in the hybrid format between face-to-face and online learning. The particular offering shown in the screenshots that follow occurred in an eight-week summer term. Delivering a three-credit class in that compressed format would normally mean class meetings twice per week that each lasted three hours (for a total of six in-class, onsite hours every week). That is a lot of time in the fully face-to-face mode, and often challenging for teacher and student alike (not just in paralegal studies but in most disciplines).

So in some cases not only might a particular course lend itself to the hybrid model (as when a good deal of lecture material can be more usefully provided online), but the delivery term, like a compressed summer term, might also suggest the opportunity for beneficial redesign into the hybrid format.

Grant chose to move a number of different activities online for his paralegal course. As Figure 29 indicates, students have access to the class syllabus and schedule via the LMS. Students have access to relatively static content, like study guides, but in addition they will find more dynamic pieces of the course, including discussion board assignments, simulations, and exams, as pictured in Figure 30. The course schedule, excerpted in Figure 31, reflects the weekly division of learning time between face-to-face classroom meetings (the "Tuesday Class" column on the left) and online or other out-of-class work (indicated in the "Lessons, Hybrid work and Projects" column at right).

In Grant's case it was largely administrative mandates that moved the otherwise primarily face-to-face curriculum into the hybrid format. Grant was assigned to teach one of these courses in the hybrid format and thus had to undertake the course design and professional development to accommodate administration's

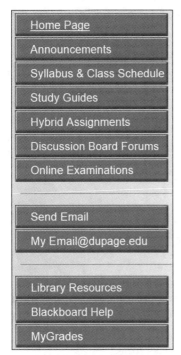

FIGURE **29.** *Paralegal Studies—course menu in Blackboard.*

requests, not necessarily because he was personally motivated to move into the hybrid format. He talks now about embracing the challenge of learning to teach in the hybrid format, but it is not something he actively sought out either for personal interest or because it suited his pedagogical beliefs or strengths.

He has found some value, though, in certain online activities, particularly discussion boards, which he now incorporates into many classes, although not always within an overarching hybrid course format. So online discussions now often make a useful addition to Professor Grant's courses, he reports, but not necessarily "as a substitute for class

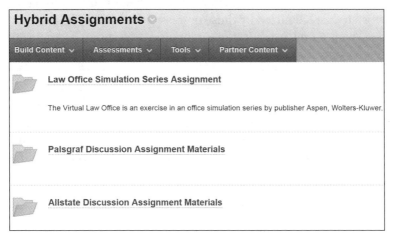

FIGURE 30. *Paralegal Studies—online assignments page.*

Tuesday Class Dates	Week	Thursday Online Due Dates	Lessons, Hybrid work and Projects
June 10	1		Course Introduction
			Introduction to Legal Files Project
			Introduction to Law Office Simulation Series
			Chapter 1. Introduction to Tort Law
		June 12	**Law Office Simulation Series, Assignment 1**
June 17	2		Chapter 2. Intentional Torts
			Chapter 3. Defenses to Intentional Torts
			Legal Files 1
		June 19	**Law Office Simulation Series, Assignment 2**
June 24	3		Chapter 4. Introduction to Negligence
			Chapter 5. Duty
			Legal Files 2
		June 26	*Palsgraf v. Long Island Railroad*, Online Discussion

FIGURE 31. *Paralegal Studies—course schedule excerpt.*

time." He is also careful, he says, to keep discussion quite focused: students are tasked to answer specific questions so that, as Grant says, "the chats are not free form." Grant further indicates that while his students "enjoyed the [hybrid] course" and "got high grades," they ultimately "preferred class time."

One interesting aspect to the disciplinary area that Professor Grant teaches in—Paralegal Studies—is that it, like many professional and career programs, can choose to reflect curricular requirements from nonacademic professional organizations if they wish to be recognized by those professional bodies. The program in which Grant teaches, for example, is advertised as American Bar Association (ABA) approved. However, the ABA "prefers student face time," as Grant says. That is, in Grant's view, why few of the paralegal studies courses in his program are offered in the fully online format, and thus perhaps why the hybrid format seemed like a viable delivery option: potentially an easier sell to the professional certifying body, the ABA. As of this writing, the American Bar Association website on paralegal studies course certification—for what they term "Alternative Delivery"—is in the process of being updated (the site was marked as last updated "02/24/2015" as we write in July of 2016). The ABA's "Alternative Delivery Information" page begins with: "The information on this page is not current. We are in the process of updating this information" (ABA). Apparently under way is a project called the "Joint Task Force on Alternative Delivery," which will at some point provide updated guidelines and/or procedures for programs wishing to offer paralegal studies courses in formats other than the fully face-to-face model, like hybrid or fully online.

What this "Alternative Delivery" website currently provides, among various other materials, is a lengthy document entitled "Compilation Guideline-Specific Information Relating to Alternative Delivery Course Requirements." This somewhat daunting twenty-page PDF provides guidelines about (re)designing existing paralegal courses into different, "alternative," formats. Much of this is good course-design advice, like "[c]ourses must be designed to promote active and effective learning" (ABA).

But the document also outlines methods by which the professional organization might review newly designed courses to evaluate continuing compliance with its certifying standards. Among the methods named in the document are potential site visits: "The team may view the online course sites from both the student and faculty perspective. The team may also meet with faculty, instructional design staff and technology staff to verify that faculty were provided with support during the process of developing online courses and while teaching online courses" (ABA).

It will be interesting to see if the ongoing task force efforts to revise these materials result in significant changes to the approval-granting process for paralegal courses delivered in the hybrid or online formats. The standards as they exist right now are rigorous; in truth, they reflect what should be common practice in higher education generally, even if such practice is not so common in reality: faculty should be supported in their professional development work related to online and hybrid teaching, courses should be thoughtfully designed to engage students and have them interacting regularly with each other, and a screening process should be in place so that students can make good choices about which course delivery formats are best suited to their learning needs and basic technology skills and access.

Biomedical Terminology—Judy Vierke

This Biomedical Terminology course provides an introduction to medical terms for each body system and for specialty medical fields. It is a four-credit course, which is relatively time intensive even in the sixteen-week format, let alone the eight- or twelve-week versions, and is also, as Professor Vierke and others who teach it explain, very content heavy. There are, quite simply, a lot of medical terms to learn and memorize in the Biomedical Terminology course.

Vierke believes that the hybrid format developed after a history of the department offering the course both fully online and fully face-to-face (in addition to early independent study versions of the course). There came what Vierke describes as a "divisional management" decision to move the course into the hybrid format, which preserved the face-to-face time that seemed beneficial to students, but that reduced the weekly four-hours-in-class time commitment, which was taxing for student and teacher alike. Discussion of the course as a potential hybrid also might have involved "staff curriculum development committees," but as Vierke points out, those are "mainly comprised of full-time faculty." Vierke, as a part-time faculty member, did not have much, if any, input on offering the course in the hybrid format.

She does, however, have the opportunity to at least request teaching assignments that include fully face-to-face, online, and hybrid formats (though those requests are not always granted). Further, now that the course is being offered as a hybrid, and now that Vierke is teaching it, she reports having "a lot of individual faculty freedom" in terms of design. The course time is divided evenly between face-to-face and online learning on a weekly basis, but Vierke has a good degree of latitude in deciding what students will do each week in the various learning modes that the hybrid affords.

To support this freedom, though, Vierke reports feeling that her campus provides "a lot of resources which have been helpful," which, for Vierke who has sought them out, have included in-depth professional development workshops, for-credit courses,

FIGURE 32. *Biomedical Terminology—course menu in Blackboard.*

and teaching-and-learning training sessions that focus on effective use of technology.

Vierke's Biomedical Terminology course menu, pictured in Figure 32, provides links to basic course material, like the syllabus and course handouts, in addition to online publisher material and online course assignments. Her syllabus makes clear the weekly division of time, both outlining weekly homework assignments and also identifying online work students will be responsible for. As we see in the Figure 33 screenshot, students are made aware of regularly recurring due dates and also point values attached to various coursework they will be doing. Vierke also lays out a course schedule (see Figure 34) for students that shows how face-to-face and online learning time will occur each week.

Homework Assignments:
- **Weekly Homework Activity (10pts / week X 15)**
  - Each week there will be an activity / assignment you have to submit or post. This may include watching a brief video and then completing the specified activity / assignment or quiz. **Due prior to class each week.**

- **Online Quick Quiz Homework (10pts / chapter with the exception of skipping chapter 6)**

  - Students will be expected to complete **one** "quick quiz"online for each chapter and email the results to ▓▓▓▓▓▓▓▓▓ Please include course number and section after your name when emailing report.

  - Each quiz is worth 10 points, maximum of 10 pts. / chapter. If a quiz is submitted with less than 100% **no** credit will be issued. Students may repeat an exercise as needed to obtain a score of 100% prior to emailing results to the instructor from the **Elsevier website**.

  - **Due night prior to class each week at 11:59pm.**

FIGURE 33. *Biomedical Terminology—syllabus excerpt.*

Session # / Attendance	Date	Chapter Preparation **Prior** to Class	Online Homework **Due** __By Tuesday 11:59 pm prior__ to class	In Class Exams
1	January 14	Chapter 1 - Basic Word Structure Chapter 2 - Terms pertaining to the Body as a Whole	Quick Quiz: Ch. 1 & 2 (preferably by Jan. 14 but definitely by Jan. 17)	
2	January 21	Chapter 3 – Suffixes Chapter 4 – Prefixes	Quick Quiz: Ch. 3 & 4 HW Activity #1: Syllabus Quiz Sign up for Homework Options in Blackboard	
3	January 28	Chapter 5 – Digestive System (note can skip chapter 6)	Quick Quiz: Chapter 5 HW Activity #2: Discussion Board - Introduction Initial Post by Saturday Jan 24 & Response by Tuesday Jan 27	Exam # 1 Chapters 1-4
4	February 4	Chapter 7 – Urinary System	Quick Quiz: Chapter 7 HW Activity #3: Wiki	

FIGURE 34. *Biomedical Terminology—course schedule excerpt.*

Vierke reports that her students seem to do well in the hybrid format and that it does not take long for them to understand "the material and the technologies." Vierke benefits from previous experience teaching fully online and has also made a conscious effort to build her own how-to videos that walk students through various aspects of the course, like using discussion boards, accessing the publisher website, and submitting homework. She is also in the habit of responding to student technical-help requests by recording brief video screencaptures (using software called SnagIt). In these screencaptures she can visually *show* students what or where to click, rather than trying to explain it all in text.

Vierke also recognizes that her curricular design efforts are part of an ongoing process. So she notes, for example, that she already has changes in mind for the next time she offers the course. She remains interested in developing an experience for students that is less lecture-based and more, as she says, "high end," but the biomedical terminology course does invariably involve a lot of vocabulary memorization.

Principles of Sociology—Traci Sullivan

This course is described in the course catalog at Lakeland Community College in the following way:

This course provides an introduction to the theoretical perspectives and research methods used by sociologists to understand and interpret our social world. Major components of the course include a sociological analysis of culture, social institutions, stratification, and social change within society. (3 contact hours). (289)

More specifically, though, Sullivan specifies that "[a]s a hybrid course students are expected to attend and participate in classroom assignments, lectures, presentations, and discussions, and complete all online work such as discussions, quizzes, and exams." As noted earlier in our book, there is a need to emphasize the importance of being present in both aspects of the hybrid course.

When Sullivan first arrived at Lakeland Community College four years ago, she taught this course in the online and the face-to-face platforms. However, there was no hybrid course offering. When asked about her decision to create a hybrid offering, Sullivan had this to say:

I decided to develop a hybrid section of our Principles of Sociology course for two reasons. First, I wanted to provide a unique opportunity for students who are not quite comfortable with the independence of online courses but feel they do not need the thorough explanations offered in traditional face-to-face classrooms. Secondly, I wanted to create a classroom format that would require students to be more accountable for their learning by completing online assignments and quizzes, and allow me to interact with them face-to-face in a way that differed from traditional lecture.

When designing the course (see Figure 35), Sullivan paid careful attention to developing assignment arcs wherein students would prepare themselves for the face-to-face discussions and unpacking of the course material. Sullivan wrote in her interview that

I have structured my hybrid courses to require students to show up to class prepared for chapter discussions. The assumption is that they have already read the materials and completed all online assignments related to the chapter materials before we even meet in class. If students did not understand a particular theory or concept they can use class time to ask for clarity. I also

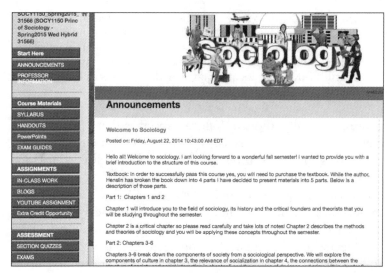

FIGURE 35. *Principles of Sociology—LMS welcome page.*

provide students the opportunity to email me their questions and I will address them during our face-to-face classroom time. The activities and assignments completed in class support the chapter materials and online writing assignments (blogs) already completed. As a professor I thoroughly enjoy arriving to class knowing that the majority of them have already reviewed the materials that we will be discussing that day. We have some amazing discussions when students are already engaged in the materials.

As a result of this development, Sullivan notes that she is passionate about this hybrid construction of the course and that "I prefer hybrid over online or face-to-face because of the creativity it affords me and the increase in student accountability."

By reviewing the course schedule (see Figure 36), readers can identify the assignment arcs a bit more clearly. It indicates what is assigned and how those online materials serve as precursors to meetings in the physical classroom.

Further, Sullivan has provided a copy of one of the blog assignments (see Figure 37), which allows her to review each student's level of understanding of that assigned material. In the classroom, she will pull up the blogs that illustrate particular strengths in critical thinking or use what she has read to identify

SCHEDULE

All quizzes are due by class time on Wednesdays.

***All blogs are due on Mondays by 11PM
****All Exams are due on Tuesdays by 11PM

WEEK	Date	In-class Wednesday	Read	Assignments
1	1/14	Review: Blackboard classroom and syllabus.	Read: CHPT 1 and Citations Handout	Explore Blackboard
2	1/21	Q&A: Chapter 1	Read: CHPT 2	Blog: Chapter 2 Science Due Monday, 1/26
3	1/28	Q&A: Chapter 2 Science Units 2.1 - 2.5	Read: CHPT 2 and Sociological Theory Handout on Blackboard	Blog: Chapter 2 Theory Due Monday, 2/02 Section Quiz 1: Chpts. 1 & 2 Due Wednesday, 2/04 11am
4	2/04	Q&A: Chapter 2 Theory Units 2.6 - 2.8	Read: Chapter 3	
5	2/11	Q&A: Chapter 3	Read: Chapter 4	
6	2/18	Q&A: Chapter 4	Read: Chapter 5	Section Quiz 2: Chpts 3-5 Due Wednesday, 2/25 11am
7	2/25	Q&A: Chapter 5	Read: Chapter 6	Blog: Deviance Due Monday, 3/02 Section Quiz 3: Chpt 6 Due Wednesday, 3/04 11am
8	3/04	Q&A: Chapter 6	Read: Chapter 7	

FIGURE 36. *Principles of Sociology—course schedule excerpt.*

trends in misunderstandings of concepts, allowing her to spend time further explaining those ideas to students, sending them back online after the class with increased comprehension and confidence about those concepts.

As a result of her approach toward the hybrid course construction, Sullivan finds that

> the most rewarding success is student engagement. They know the topics and have participated in the blogs before we even begin to discuss the materials in class. Class time reinforces what they have learned and allows me to address ideas that need clarification. I get to be creative with my face-to-face interactions. If students are expected to know the terms and theories I have the opportunity to use classroom time for activities that bring to life the terms and theories learned. This is often a struggle in

face-to-face classes where students depend upon the professor to feed them the information they need to know rather than work ahead to be prepared.

While Sullivan has had some strong successes with her course, she has, like any teacher, also encountered challenges with the hybrid course. For example, she noted in her interview that

> students either participate or they don't. Every semester I have students who just won't log in and complete the online tasks, or they complete all the online tasks but never show up to class. Either way they will fail. No matter how strongly I emphasize this point to them there is always a handful that will not commit.

In addition to many not participating, Sullivan also noted that

> unfortunately class sizes are smaller than traditional classes and this is a concern as we continue to see enrollments shrink across the campus. I had hoped enrollments would increase as they have in my online sections. I don't really know why the hybrid courses are not as popular but I fear we will eventually do away with them if improvements are not made.

With lower enrollments and limited engagement (something we have addressed earlier in the book with regards to the struggles with development of hybrid curricula), hybrid courses can sometimes be challenging to get off the ground and demonstrate retention and completion rates as high as the face-to-face, though the retention rates are often as low as seen in many online sections of courses.

In response to her struggles, instead of giving in, Sullivan adjusted her approach toward reminders for her students to complete course tasks by this technological innovation:

> This past year I started using remind.com to send text message reminders to students regarding assignments due dates and times. Participation is voluntary and students have to have cell phones but the feedback I have received this semester has been positive. We shall see what the outcomes are at the end of the semester.

Create a research hypothesis by selecting an independent and a dependent variable from the list below. Answer the following 5 questions. I suggest reviewing the rubric to see how I grade posts.

1. Clearly state your hypothesis.

2. Identify the independent (IV) and dependent variables (DV).

3. Identify which research method you would use to test your hypothesis and <u>explain why</u>?

      **Incorporate a page citation as you explain which research method you would use to test your hypothesis.

4. Will the results of this study produce qualitative or quantitative data? (See the handout located under HANDOUTS)

5. Does your research result in objective or subjective data? (See the handout located under HANDOUTS)

VARIABLES:
Gender   Age   Marital Satisfaction   Race   Job Satisfaction   Occupation   Income   Political Party   Family Goals   Education Level   Hours of sleep per night   Religious Affiliation   Volunteering   Pet Ownership   Transportation   Residency   Dollars spent on groceries   # of TV's in home   Physical Activities   Overall Happiness   Computer Ownership   Marital Status   # of Children   Support System   Length of Marriage   # of Marriages   # of hours worked per week   Health Insurance   Stress   Have fun   Travel   Sexual Orientation   Child Care   Grades (GPA)
Okay...... that should be plenty of variables, have fun with this assignment but please be thorough!

FIGURE 37. *Principles of Sociology—blog assignment.*

The use of this unique technology is a great way to encourage students to marry the everyday technology of their smartphones with the online aspects of their academic lives, which they may not check every day like they do their phones.

Just like any course, there are students who enjoy the hybrid environment and those who struggle. One of Sullivan's students who enjoyed the experience commented that

> I really liked having the ability to work at my own pace at home but be able to ask questions in class. I have taken online classes before and I hated not being able to ask questions or hear the instructor answer other students' questions. I know I could have emailed my questions in the online class but I never did.

This student clearly identifies the strengths of having that face-to-face, synchronous component as unique from an exclusively online course. On the other hand, other students struggled to manage the balance between the roles of each component of that hybrid course and found the course confusing or challenging. For example, one of Sullivan's students wrote, "I might as well have taken the online class since I learned what I needed from doing the assignments online. The class time just reviewed what I had already learned."

The Writing-Intensive Hybrid

We'll devote time here specifically to writing-intensive courses, English composition and technical writing in particular, with emphasis on how the hybrid format might be ideally suited to courses that have students producing a lot of their own writing and interacting with classmates about that writing. One good argument for why and how the hybrid format lends itself to writing-intensive courses is that in writing-intensive courses we often find that instructional time needs to account for students working on relatively individual writing projects. Many writing instructors we've talked to who teach in the hybrid format have noted that before going hybrid, they often found themselves sitting with their classes, face-to-face, not knowing exactly what more to do for yet another fifty-minute session. Of course, as good instructors we fill that time, but the elephant in the room is that, rather than talking as a group about yet another rhetorical approach or yet another course reading, everyone would be better served with greater one-to-one attention and time to develop an individual project.

In short, instructional time in the traditional face-to-face model—we all meet from 9:00 to 9:50 on Monday, Wednesday, and Friday morning—just wasn't always that effective. Ever had students complain of "busy work"? Ever knew, deep down, that what you were assigning *was* "busy work"? That's the nature of the writing-intensive course that does not provide for, well, enough writing time.

Of course, classroom time works well when a class is learning something as a whole, whether through instructor lecture or demonstration, or through group activities that involve discussion and immediate interaction. But there comes a point for many writing instructors when what their students need is time to write, time to receive and process written feedback from peers, and time to talk about *their* writing with the professor—not to see another generic example projected in class. The hybrid format does not lose the dynamic energy of the classroom setting, which so many students and teachers find valuable and rewarding, but it also does not lock learners into just that one educational setting. Instead, it provides the opportunity to move the class online, a setting that lends itself to the iterative work of writing-intensive courses: drafting, writing, and revising.

This is not to say, however, that the writing-intensive course in the hybrid model becomes a disjunctive split between face-to-face group interaction and solitary online work. Quite the contrary. The online writing environment can be an engaging and dynamic space. It is simply not one that has been commandeered by the clock.

In this section, then, we provide a sequence of writing-intensive hybrid course examples, highlighting some unique characteristics as well as some navigational consistencies that help create that cohesive structure needed for a hybrid course.

English Composition 2—Joanna N. Paull

The English 2 course description is as follows:

> This course analyzes argumentative strategies, models, and texts. Students will focus on the research process: identifying sources through electronic and print-based research strategies, evaluating research materials, and integrating and synthesizing research material. The course culminates in the production of a fully documented argumentative paper. (Lakeland Community College, *Course Catalog* 226)

This course as a whole is a follow-up to a prerequisite English 1 course and provides students with the foundational characteristics of a strong critical thinker, reader, and writer (see Figures 38 and 39).

In 2008 the English department decided to offer two sections of hybrid English 1 and two sections of English 2, to be held in the same classroom, one day each (see Figures 38 and 39). The other 50 percent of the courses were each held online, adhering to the institution-wide definition of hybrid as a 50-50 balance of the workload. More specifically, Figure 40 lists the assignments as they are given for one specific week's plan. Notice that the assignments are broken down for students to clarify which need to be done prior to the class meeting (the start of the week) and which are to be done online.

This English hybrid course has been offered each semester since the fall of 2008 and usually fills with initially enthusiastic students. The hybrid course provides students with a solid anchor of course discussions and question-and-answer sessions regarding assigned reading material, which students value in a writing course. To support this in-class work, the online portion allows

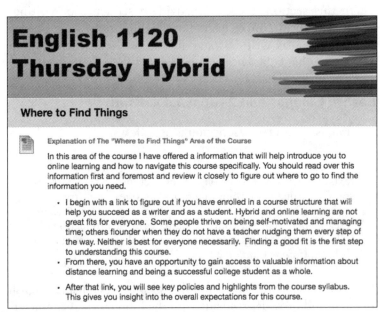

FIGURE 38. *English Composition 2—LMS welcome page.*

Weekly Plans

Explanation of The Weekly Plans Section of the Course

In this section, I will reveal a folder for each week of the semester, one at a time. Again, this is not a self-paced course. We will work through the course material together as a class. The course syllabus lists the assigned reading and assignment due dates, which will help you read ahead and/or view ahead, if you like. However, in this section, each week you will see a folder for that particular week. I will reveal each week's plan three days before that week opens. Remember that there are weekly deadlines, so get used to the pace of the course and be prepared to submit things on their designated due dates. Inside each week I offer a bunch of really helpful information:

1. The course objectives that will be addressed during that week.
2. Questions you should be able to answer by the end of that week
3. Assignments you need to complete PRIOR to our classroom meeting. This will include links to quizzes and reading beyond the textbooks given to you.
4. Overarching plans for what we will do in the classroom that week.
5. Once our class meeting is over, I will add in any materials students got during that class meeting. Please note, though, that if you miss class you will have to come see me in my office hours or chat with a classmate to get caught up. I will not spend class time catching you up or send you all of my notes. You will gain access to the PowerPoint slides or handouts but not anything beyond that.
6. Assignments you will complete online for that week. In addition to just listing what to do online, I will also include links to quizzes and reading beyond the textbooks given to you, if there is anything beyond our books assigned for that week.
7. My approaches toward assessing how you met those objectives for the week (i.e., how I will determine if you are able to answer the questions I have posed).

You will gain access to each weekly plan at midnight at the start of our week. You will continue to have access to that information for the remainder of the semester. HOWEVER, you will only be able to take the quizzes during their designated assigned week. Once the week ends, the quiz links disappear. That means that if you miss a quiz for a week, you will also not see the link to the assigned discussion forum for that week either.

FIGURE 39. *English Composition 2—weekly plan introduction/explanation.*

Prior to our classroom meeting, you will:
- Read Chapter 1 of Reynolds & Rice's s *Portfolio* book.
- Prepare your e-portfolio shell by following the first two videos in your syllabus' portfolio folder:
  ○ Develop the shell by heading to "Syllabus," into the "Building the E-Portfolio" folder, and watching/listening to videos 1 & 2. Submit that website address in the "E-portfolio web address" slot linked below.
  ○ Upload a response to the "Taking Stock" prompt on page 7 of the portfolio book.
  ○ Use video #5 to help you set your privacy settings. I suggest not making it a public portfolio but rather making it private and inviting people using their gmail addresses. Mine is drjoannapaull@gmail.com. Invite me in!
- Copy and paste your e-portfolio's website address in the "E-Portfolio Address" slot posted below.
- Take the online quiz on R & R's Chapter 1.

During our classroom meeting, we will:
- Get an introduction to your first major writing assignment, the argument analysis.
- Begin our discussion about what a portfolio is, why we do it, and how you will use it in this course.
- Engage in face-to-face activities that apply the thinking process to your initial thoughts about building a portfolio.

For the online portion of our course, we will:
- By Friday:
  ○ Read Ruggiero's Chapter 1 (*The Art of Thinking*).
  ○ Read the Argument Analysis assignment sheet and corresponding documents in the "Argument Analysis" folder inside your Bb "Assignments" area.
  ○ Read the "Building Quote Sandwiches" handout to inform and inspire your online discussion posts this week.
- By Saturday
  ○ Take the quizzes about all of this assigned reading. Don't forget that you have to take the week's quizzes in order to get access to the online discussion forum. Don't forget!!
  ○ Post your thread to the online discussion forum.
- By Monday, post your classmate responses to the online discussion forum.

FIGURE 40. *English Composition 2—one week's plan.*

students the time necessary to work on their writing, sharing with their classmates, and tweaking in small groups prior to bringing more polished writing to the classroom itself.

One of the key components of a successful hybrid is creating a feeling of an ongoing course from classroom to online and back again. For this course, Paull provides the opportunity for students to work on individualized projects. But she makes particular efforts to keep students connected to one another, despite not being physically present together all the time.

As part of Paull's technology use in her hybrid courses, in addition to the LMS, she takes advantage of some useful Google applications. In 2013, Lakeland Community College moved all student emails to Gmail, thereby giving all students a Gmail account and thus access to other Google tools, including Drive, Docs, and Hangouts. Paull familiarizes students with the features of these tools as part of their introduction and orientation to her hybrid courses.

Students are able to create a fluid community of learning by interacting in these venues. By having students engage in peer review workshops using the Google Docs tool by sharing their essays with each other, Paull allows students to write essays outside of the classroom, discuss them in the classroom in small groups, and then continue those discussions in the online environment by using the Google Doc's commenting feature without having to worry about compatibility with programs. By having all of the comments running on a single copy of the essay, students see patterns in strengths and weaknesses that they might have missed had they needed to aggregate the comments from separate hard copies of the essays. Once students responded to the comments, they were able to click the "Resolve" option to have that comment disappear from the margin, allowing them to focus solely on those comments that they had not yet addressed.

With students having their essays shared, they are also able to work in small, live groups via the Google Hangouts feature, inviting Paull to the chat if they choose to do so. This interactivity promotes writing communities, and as many instructors have experienced, community building of any kind, in any sort of classroom, can increase retention and student success.

Aside from the required use of Google Docs for peer review, students do not have to use any of the other tools. Instead, Paull instructs them briefly on each of the Google features, giving screencapture instructions online, references to the Google Help section of textual instructions, and encourages them to work with the tools they find most helpful.

One semester, Paull experimented by using the Google Calendar feature for listing all requirements and setting up push notifications and email notifications in an attempt to increase student completion rates. Unfortunately, Paull did not find any noticeable increase in submission rates. Many students at Lakeland Community College (as elsewhere) do not actively check their student email accounts. In fact, only about 25 percent of students regularly check their school email accounts at Lakeland, so email-based notifications were not especially helpful and other students never set up the push notification options for their phones. As is so often the case, instructors are left to decide between devoting time to course content and devoting time to basic technology instruction and demonstration (and, potentially, troubleshooting). As we've advocated for elsewhere, when basic technology instruction cannot be meaningfully folded into course content, it may behoove the institution as a whole to build basic how-to materials for students, showing them how to have student email push to their smartphones, for example.

While there have been some successes with the course, Paull has run into what appears to be the most common struggle of the hybrid courses: retention. Many students initially believe that the course meets only once a week for seventy-five minutes and that's it, so they are drawn to it. Once they find out there is an online component, something mentioned in the online schedule but often overlooked by students, there is an initial drop of students, usually from twenty-five to fifteen or so. Once students are in the course and realize what the hybrid course consists of, they do embrace the experience, though many embrace only one of the two platforms, making there an online constituency and another in the classroom, often impacting the fluidity of the learning community. Teachers must make a concerted effort to bring these groups of students together, sending many reminders and announcements and assigning many points to the assignments in both platforms in order to ensure that students succeed in the hybrid writing course. This is likely due, at least in part, to the students being either first- or second-semester college students, with little practice with self-motivation and time management.

Business Writing and Correspondence—Michael W. Gos

The course catalog entry for Gos's course reads: "Business Report Writing and Correspondence Theory and applications for technical reports and correspondence in business." Specifically, Gos, the director of Technical Communications Programs at Lee College, notes that the course as a whole

> was designed for technical students pursuing an AAS degree to replace the traditional ENGL 1301: Freshman Composition. All assignments are workplace-related. They include letters, memos, proposals, recommendation reports, progress reports, instructions and resumes [see Figure 41]. We developed this course for two reasons. First, the technical students had a dismal success rate in the traditional Freshman Comp course (57%). Second, most of our first year comp professors used literature, essays and other reading-based methods and relied heavily on MLA formatting, etc., things these students would never see again. We tried steering these students into our existing Technical Writing course, but it was extremely rigorous. It is a sophomore-level course but because it has a reputation for rigor, it transfers as a replacement for the junior-level Technical Writing course at most Texas universities. Also many of the students enrolled in the online version of the course are currently university students. As a result, this was not a viable option for students in Welding, Process Technology, Instrumentation, etc.: hence, the birth of this class.

Unlike other typical course development, Gos's English course actually started out as a hybrid course. In fact, he notes that

> [a]ll of my online courses are first offered as hybrid classes. This gives me the opportunity to meet with students in class to straighten out any misunderstandings and for me to get a better sense of what is working and what isn't so I can make revisions before going fully online. In this particular course, after week 10, students were asked to decide as a class whether they want to finish the semester entirely online or continue to have class meetings. In only one semester did they choose to continue meeting in class, but every semester the vote was close. Students clearly valued the face time in this course, so we never offered it fully online (for 6 years now). We don't offer it in the traditional face-to-face format because more than 90% of

Source 2152-1583 | Examination 2152-5582 is Complete. To access the detailed log, click here

Course Content

Build Content ▼ Assessments ▼ Tasks ▼ Partner Content ▼

Start Your Course Here
Read each of the items in this module. Be sure to study each one in the order it is presented. Do not skip ahead. You can always go back and re-read previously viewed files.
Click on the heading above ("Start Your Course Here"), to open this module and begin your journey through ENGL 1301T.

Audience, Tone and Purpose
In this module we will examine the readers of documents in the workplace and discuss how we accomplish our goals in writing.

Visuals in the Workplace
In this module we will study the proper use of visuals in the workplace. You will have two graded assignments along the way.

Writing Memos and Reports
This module begins with a second look at Chapter 2. Read it again and study it carefully, paying particular attention to the discussion of memos and the memo checklist presented. Along the way, you will be doing two exercises in your textbook. The module then culminates in your creation of two memo reports, one of which is a progress report. These reports will make up two thirds of the course portfolio you submit at the end of this semester so they will make up a large part of your grade.

Instructions
In this module we will tackle one of the most difficult forms of writing in business and industry, instructions.

Summaries
In this module you will learn how to create the most common types of summaries used in the workplace.

Resumes
In this module we will examine written documents in the job-hunting process. Your chapter will cover job application forms, cover letters, resumes, interviews and follow-up documents. All are important parts of the job-hunting process.

FIGURE 41. *Business Writing and Communication—sample course content page.*

these students come to class after a full day working in the oil refineries and chemical plants in the area. They are worn out by the time they get to class. Reducing the number of class sessions encourages them to enroll and then stay with it.

Clearly, Gos's experience highlights the impact that socioeconomic profiles can have on course construction, revision, and manipulation. If student success is on the front burner, colleges need to ask themselves which platform is most likely to help their students succeed. In Gos's case, that meant the hybrid platform.

Having had six years of instructing and tweaking this course, Gos noted something about his courses that seems to align with some of the research regarding higher retention rates in hybrid courses than in straight online courses: "Completion rates for this course in the last four years are 97% with an average GPA of 2.0 (Compared to 57% completion in Freshman Composition)."

Despite the success he has had in the classroom with interactions and student success, Gos has identified one unanticipated challenge, but it isn't inside of his classrooms. It's with the faculty. Gos remarked that

> [r]eally, the biggest challenge has been convincing the faculty on the Tech side that their students should be taking this course instead of traditional freshman comp. Many were concerned that employers would be looking for English 1301 on a transcript. To address this, we have just changed the course number to ENGL 1301T. This change goes into effect this fall. The dean of the tech programs assures me the course will now be heavily populated.

As a whole, this seems like a minor concern, though, further emphasizing how successful hybrid courses can be.

Technical Writing—Sara Jameson

Jameson notes that prior to creating this ten-week hybrid course she took an online workshop at Chemeketa Community College, in Salem, Oregon, on designing and teaching hybrid courses. From there, she participated in a hybrid faculty learning cohort at Oregon State University.

The technical writing course itself was a 50-50 hybrid, meeting once a week in the classroom and doing the rest of their work online each week of the ten-week standard session (see Figure 42). Having taught this course in both the face-to-face and purely online environments, Jameson writes that "[t]he transition was easy enough because I already had the recorded lectures and other resources from an online version of the same course I had already built. It was just a matter of deciding what parts should be f2f."

While Jameson's department at Oregon State University—the School of Writing, Literature, and Film—hasn't had much faculty interest in hybrid instruction, three have tried it. Jameson is the only one to continue teaching hybrid courses. As for the other two instructors' rationale for no longer having interest in teaching hybrid courses, Jameson writes that "[f]or one person, the reason I think was doing all the work online. For the other person, the reason I think was that it was not her version of WR 327 (instructors have their own) but mine and she did not know my version."

Not only has Jameson continued teaching hybrid courses, but she also writes that when she teaches this technical writing course she prefers to teach it in the hybrid format, despite students' selection of the course generally being tied to their only having to meet face-to-face once a week. Interestingly enough, though, she remarks that in "winter 2015 my WR 214 Writing in Business course was about 75% campus students and only 25% true distance students, which was a surprise. The local students said that the online course was a better fit for their schedules." Despite the students being considered "campus students," they chose the hybrid format to avoid coming to campus. Who are these students, then, we must ask ourselves? Is there a new, unique student profile that needs to be targeted with hybrid courses?

Ultimately, Jameson feels that writing courses are ideal for a hybrid platform because "the success is that this is a writing class and there is not much need for lecture or discussion, in my opinion. I explain the concepts, answer questions, and guide students in creating the documents." In this arrangement, then, the work is done predominantly outside of the classroom by having students go online, while the classroom meetings are set up to allow for students to work through that assigned material and examine their writing with the instructor present (see Figure 43).

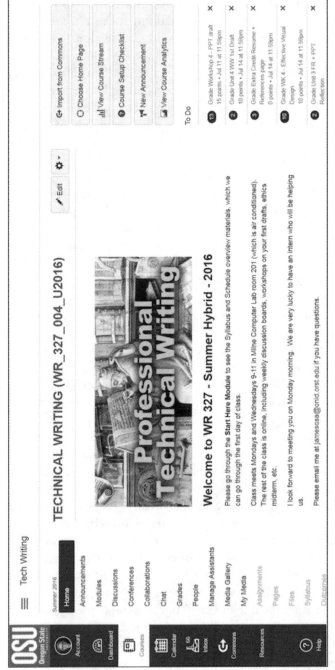

FIGURE 42. *Technical Writing—screenshot of navigational panel and announcements page.*

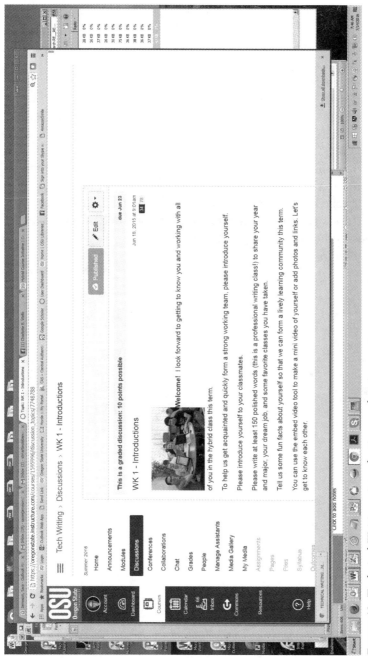

FIGURE 43. *Technical Writing—introductions and assignments.*

While her courses have had their share of successes, Jameson has also faced challenges. For example, Jameson's students are unaware of what a hybrid course really is and are, therefore, not prepared or expecting to do the level of online work they are assigned each week. Specifically, as a result, she finds that "some need more hand-holding." This challenge is not entirely on the shoulders of the students, though, because Jameson notes that the university scheduling system does not have a way to make it "obvious" that students are enrolling in a hybrid section. This further emphasizes our earlier suggestions for institutions to ensure that if they are going to introduce a hybrid curriculum, their scheduling system should provide differentiation between platforms so students are as aware as possible of what sort of courses they are adding to their schedules.

CHAPTER FIVE

Hybrids and the Question
of Technology

As we move toward our conclusion, we'd like to expand the discussion in this penultimate chapter to broader consider-ations, beyond what we hope to have been the relatively focused, instrumental, and actionable topics from early chapters. Certainly topics we cover here might reflect back to earlier discussions about developing and sustaining an institutional framework for hybrid curricular and professional development. But what follows is a little less tethered to the purely institutional concerns that have dominated our work to this point.

First, we would like to think about how certain emerging trends and technologies might be productively mapped onto the hybrid format. We are especially interested in the possibili-ties of mobile learning within the hybrid format. Not that one necessitates the other, by any means. But since the nature of the hybrid format, in its combination of fully face-to-face with online distance learning, opens a space for developing effective online learning experiences for students, the blended format seems ideal for incorporating promising new educational technologies.

This will lead us to the topic that follows our consideration of mobile learning as an interesting possibility in the hybrid framework: "technology." We've just used the term above, and throughout the book in fact, in its most common sense: to de-note a particular physical artifact or to suggest a virtual tool or platform delivered by some physical device. So, in a formulation likely recognizable to those in higher education, we are said to "teach with technology." We use a learning management system, we ask students to build a wiki, we ask students to use a device that they are either required to own or that might be provided by the institution; whatever the case, technology is everything *but* the user.

Below, we will reframe the term "technology," not in some vain attempt to unseat its more common usage (again, one we've defaulted to throughout this book), but rather to invite some new ways of thinking about what it means to teach with technology, especially when it comes to what we ask of students and what we ask of instructors.

But first, a suggestion of what might be on the near horizon for hybrid learning and emerging educational technology.

Hybrids and Mobile Learning

Here we explore why the hybrid format might be usefully integrated with emerging directions in higher education around mobile, or what is sometimes called ubiquitous, learning. We use the terms *mobile learning* and *ubiquitous learning* more or less interchangeably, since both suggest the scenario in which learning can take place outside of the classroom. The term *mobile learning* does, however, carry with it the idea that learning opportunities are mediated by a mobile device of some kind, be it smartphone, tablet, netbook, or something similar. Our focus is primarily on this kind of ubiquitous learning, the kind that involves a mobile device, not simply learning that occurs outside of the classroom walls.

We should make clear, though, our contention is not that mobile or ubiquitous learning can *only* thrive as part of a hybrid learning model. Nor do we suggest that all hybrid courses must, or even should, integrate mobile learning opportunities for students. The use of mobile learning within the hybrid context just seems like a mutually beneficial arrangement, and might be most productive if early curricular planning in one area is informed by the other. Because of the way that the hybrid format, by definition, balances in-class seat-time with out-of-class, non-seat-time, it seems to afford the ideal opportunity for those interested in mobile learning to infuse the curriculum with dynamic, out-of-class learning experiences. The sheer computing power of mobile devices, not to mention the degree of connectivity most people enjoy via their mobile device, or devices, makes mobile learning within the context of the hybrid format more realizable than ever. Further, thanks to that computing power and connectivity, mobile learning truly seems to offer meaningful learning opportunities, ones not laden with likely technical challenges and/or requiring of the instructor an inordinate investment in technology training or troubleshooting.

First, the basic idea of ubiquitous learning has a long tradition in education, though it now often connotes relatively newer technologies, like tablets and smartphones. (Thus our preference for the term *mobile learning,* with its connotation of the network-capable mobile device as part of the equation.) As with many transformative possibilities that are labeled, at some point, "emerging," ubiquitous learning has a long history, stretching at least back to the progressive educational theory of John Dewey. In his 1915 *The School and Society,* Dewey was already outlining what he saw as the problematic separation between in-class and out-of-class learning, between knowledge delivered by an authority to passive recipients and hands-on, experiential learning as an apprentice might receive, learning by actually practicing his or her chosen trade. Dewey, and many after him, have argued for a smoother integration of theory (the decontextualized knowledge of the lecture hall) and lived experience (the real practice of everyday life).

We can here see the outlines of what would eventually become identified as ubiquitous learning, whereby the acquisition—and the creation—of knowledge are not discretely time- or place-bound phenomena. Rather, students could be encouraged to create, gather, and practice knowledge beyond the classroom space and outside of classroom time. And perhaps just as important, the reflective and intellectual habits of the classroom could travel beyond those brick-and-mortar walls to influence, and hopefully improve, the daily life of citizens. Here we feel echoes of the aphorism ascribed to Socrates: "the unexamined life is not worth living." Dewey's sense of learning as ubiquitous (not a term he used, necessarily, but a basic framework he advocated for) was as much about making what happened in the classroom happen outside of the classroom as well, not just inviting the lived experience of everyday life into the classroom.

In short, though, ubiquitous learning is an emerging trend in higher education, as evidenced by the degree to which learning management system providers are working to make their systems available on mobile devices, either through dedicated apps or by designing websites so that they will display properly on small, mobile-device screens. Certainly most major LMS providers, like Blackboard, Canvas, and Desire2Learn, seem eager to tout their systems' integration with mobile devices. During a recent Canvas demonstration at Snart's home institution, a sales representative from Canvas asserted that he had recently completed an entire course "on this": he held up his mobile phone (Canvas by Instructure Demonstration Recording). A 2012 Educause Center for Applied Research bulletin, "The Future of Mobile Learning," notes more generally that "established e-learning systems have evolved to offer mobile components, fostering anytime, anywhere access to coursework" (Oller 2).

So mobile learning, understood in its broadest terms, beyond learning that happens via a modern smartphone, has a long history worth acknowledging. It may truly go as far back as the ancient Greeks but certainly found a voice in turn-of-the-century progressives like Dewey. And where it now provides a so-called emerging trend for LMS vendors to hang their hats, we are most interested in recontextualizing it within a broader learning framework, specifically here the hybrid model.

So ubiquitous learning, as unmediated by a digital technology, has informed educational theory for decades and is a foundational practice for disciplines that depend on hands-on learning, as many career and technical programs do.

What has made such learning seem like a new, promising, and thus "emerging" trend is of course the way in which portable, networked, and multifunctional devices have become so much a commonplace part of so many people's lives. Smartphones seem to get more powerful, connectible, and accessible by the day. And their presence, unwelcomed or not, in the twenty-first-century classroom is a recognizable reality for most instructors.

Undoubtedly, student use of smartphones in class to text or update social media can be disruptive. Not only are those students probably not able to pay attention to what is happening in the classroom the way they need to, but often one student's smartphone use can be distracting to others in the room. But by the same token, the sheer number of students who now have smartphones, and the myriad ways they can be used, suggest some real educational possibilities, particularly outside of the classroom (where they can otherwise be such a nuisance, turning otherwise easygoing teachers into device cops).

So what might mobile learning look like in the hybrid framework? We offer the following example from one of the coauthors' courses: Jason Snart's Honors Composition II course, the second course in the first-year composition sequence.

The problem that Snart identified, and that some kind of mobile activity afforded a potential solution to, was that his hybrid course had students going online on a weekly basis, but much of that work seemed somewhat static. Students were being asked to interact via discussion boards and collaborate on wikis, but all of that work still seemed overly stationary, with students having to sit at a computer to complete the work. What he wanted was a little variety, and something, ideally, much more kinesthetic.

In addition to mobile learning providing a nice change of pace, the activity described in the following section helped Snart to realize one of the basic course objectives he felt was particularly important, especially in the context of the Honors class, which was designed not simply to demand more work from students, but rather to provide greater degrees of creativity and self-direction. That objective has to do with what Snart describes to students as "synthetic" thinking: in other words, the habit of mind that forms connections, not just between elements from within a class, but between what is "in" a class and what is "outside" the class, in both literal and metaphorical terms. Snart challenges his Honors students to synthesize course material, other academic material they are engaged with, and extracurricular material as well, whether in popular culture writ large or from students' individual lives.

This idea of cultivating in his students a greater capacity for synthetic thinking seemed to be hampered at points by always having students work either literally in the class or online yet still constrained to the LMS. Via mobile learning, though, Snart could ask—or require—his students to think critically and creatively outside of both the physical classroom and whatever time each student might spend sitting stationary with the LMS. That online time often seemed much like classroom time, in that students were tethered to a particular place. It seemed hard to think not just outside of the classroom but outside of the class, when students had to otherwise remain so immersed in the course when they completed work: they were either literally in class or sitting at a computer. They were not out in the world, thinking synthetically about how class connected to it, or it connected to class.

Mobile learning afforded the opportunity not just to sit at a computer and reflect on one's lived experience and the ways it might connect to course content, but to actually *live* that experience and connect it to coursework.

For this particular assignment Snart uses a digital tool called Padlet (find it at Padlet.com). Padlet allows a user (like the instructor) to create the equivalent of a virtual corkboard. Each padlet (or corkboard) is assigned a unique URL (which can be manipulated by the creator to some degree). The padlet creator can then provide that unique URL to other users, and anyone with the URL can post material to the corkboard: text, links, audio, video, and still images. A particularly nice feature of Padlet is that multimedia, like images, can be added in more or less real time if the user is on a mobile device with picture-taking capabilities. Padlet seemed an ideal tool for enabling students to capture moments from their own lives that reflected course content and to share them with others from the class. (Padlet also embeds easily into the LMS and updates in real time.)

For one particular unit in his Honors composition course, Snart had students read Susan Glaspell's short play, *Trifles*. This work relates the story of a woman who has apparently murdered her husband. A group comes to investigate the crime, including the sheriff, a neighbor, and the county attorney. The sheriff's wife, Mrs. Hale, and the neighbor's wife, Mrs. Peters are also present. There seems to be little doubt that a local farmer, John Wright, has been murdered by his wife, Mrs. Wright. The play turns, though, on how the male characters, in their efforts to find evidence of the motive for the murder, completely overlook what is so obvious to the female characters: the so-called "trifles" that clearly indicate what a repressed and constricted life Mrs. Wright had to endure.

Students generally understand the basic themes of the play. And even if they do not right away, they can do a little research to find them out. But that is precisely the information-age limitation that Snart's invitation to think synthetically looks to overcome. We have such ready access to information that knowing a particular thing is in many cases of limited value. How can we contextualize what we know and what we learn into some broader, more meaningful array? Snart's "Trifles We Have Found" mobile activity asks students to do just this. The assignment invites students to take a picture using a mobile device from somewhere, some moment, in their real, everyday lives that revealed a similar dichotomy to what was happening in the play. Their pictures would suggest the so-called important thing, the thing we were "supposed" to look at, but evident, if you looked for it, was something we were not supposed to see, something that was, in truth, important, but that might not be generally, culturally valued as such.

The example Snart provides is an image taken from inside a restaurant. The foreground of the image shows what the restaurant would like us to see: white linens, soft candlelight, the ambiance of fine dining. But what Snart happened to capture was the kitchen door swung open to reveal the actual work going on behind the scenes, the so-called trifles we weren't really supposed to notice but without which the restaurant couldn't function. Of course, the example does not map perfectly on to the play. Gender was noticeably replaced by ethnicity, for example. And the "trifle" of the kitchen was not really in plain sight, as are the trifles in the play (to the women at least).

Most students embraced the assignment, though, and many contributed more than one image to the padlet. Inasmuch as students are actively thinking about coursework, but outside the confines of either the physical classroom or the stationary LMS, the assignment seems successful in encouraging the synthetic thinking that Snart is interested in. The hybrid format provides the ideal instructional mode to have students in class for initial close-reading discussion of the play, in addition to a review of how Padlet works. With that foundation in place, though, it makes sense to be able to trade further classroom meeting time for more flexible learning time, which is what the blended model affords.

When students returned to class the following week, they were invited to talk about their posts and explain how, synthetically, they connected back to the play and to the basic idea of "trifles" and, as the play invites us to ask, who gets to decide what counts as a trifle and what does not. Figure 44 shows the Padlet page from the Fall 2014 version of this assignment.

Other mobile learning opportunities might involve augmented reality (AR), which was identified as an important emerging trend in higher education by the New Media Consortium in its 2011 *Horizon Report* (5). The 2015 *Horizon Report* wiki notes that AR "has shifted from what was once seen as a gimmick to a tool with tremendous potential" ("What Is Augmented Reality?").

Augmented reality can be defined in relatively broad terms: "the fusion of digital information with either live streaming video

FIGURE 44. *Mobile learning example using Padlet.*

or the viewer's real environment" (Hamilton). An Educause research brief describes augmented reality as "technology that merges visual perception of real-world environments and objects with virtual, computer-generated content" (Oller 3).

For example, students could be asked to visit particular physical locations, but then use their smartphones to access computer-generated images and information that is layered over the physical environment. Smartphone apps like CultureClic (developed by the French company youARhere and available on the French version of the iPhone app store) allow users to point their smartphone at a landmark in Paris and have basic information like distance to that landmark displayed (see Figure 45). Further, users can click items on the smartphone display to discover deeper information about those landmarks ("CultureClic: An Augmented Reality").

Tools like Aurasma let users view otherwise static images on a smartphone and view what Aurasma describes as an "augmented reality experience" that has been assigned to the image. An example featured on the Aurasma website, part of an advertising campaign for Dewar's scotch, involves a portrait of the Scottish poet Robert Burns. When this portrait is viewed through the Aurasma app, the figure comes to life, takes a drink of scotch, and recites "Now simmer blinks on flowery braes" ("Robert Burns"). Another example involves viewing a dollar bill through a smartphone, using the Aurasma app, and then watching as the static image of the dollar bill morphs into a short animated video ("Dollar Bill"). Snart has experimented with augmented reality for how students might visit a course webpage in the LMS that provides textbook information and by using their smartphones, pointed at the image of the textbook cover, be directed to bookseller websites. This also works such that students can be shown a physical copy of a course textbook and, using augmented reality technology, have their phone (or camera-equipped smart device) load up the bookstore webpage.

Proponents of mobile learning see it as an almost inevitable future, especially as smartphone use continues to increase. As the computing power and connectivity of mobile devices improves as well, the learning opportunities seem promising. We have not even touched here on how wearable technology might figure as an important mobile learning tool. As with many emerging trends,

FIGURE 45. *CultureClic: An augmented reality mobile application.*

however, optimism for its role in education can seem a little too fanciful, as here: "Imagine living in the magical world of Harry Potter, where the school hallways are lined with paintings that are alive and interactive"; or, "There are endless ideas and possibilities for using AR" (Minock).

Talking portraits or maps on the wall that you could interact with using your phone sound fun, to be sure, but we'd want to balance enthusiasm for the possibilities with some grounded discussion about exactly how this all might happen. What kinds of institutional investment might be needed to promote AR, or mobile learning generally, as possible tools in the hybrid framework? And to get practical, who will have the time to learn to use these tools effectively and not just as shiny new gadgets that are, in truth, as likely to frustrate students as they are to afford them a deep learning experience? As we've advocated throughout, pedagogy—basic learning goals—need to drive technology use, not the other way around.

Consider a tool like Aurasma: instructors could face a potentially daunting professional development challenge if the aim is to make this AR tool a recurring piece of any curriculum (not just a "let's use this once" digital aside). Using the Aurasma app to view "auras" that have been created by the Aurasma company's designers is relatively straightforward, but creating one's own involves learning to use the Aurasma studio software. Even our earlier example, the one involving the Padlet tool, will, for many instructors involve learning a new tool. And not just its features but also how it behaves relative to an LMS. Learning basic features is only the beginning. The real question will be how this new digital tool allows the instructor to do something better than before or how this application solves an existing pedagogical problem. Who will have the time, and will this learning be entirely self-directed, or will some institutional framework exist to support such efforts?

The considerable investment of faculty energy is yet another reason why mobile learning might map so productively onto the hybrid format, since in that mode the faculty member is no longer having to account for all of the traditional seat-hours attached to a course (and plan activities to fill those hours). Non-seat-time in the hybrid format is not about routine homework (like out-of-class reading) but can now be devoted to more engaging and dynamic activities, though ones that might require much more prep work on the faculty member's part. In fact, as Snart has argued, the hybrid format—by the very nature of its radically different configuration of traditional learning time—invites robust curricular change (Snart, *Hybrid Learning* 73).

We know that good hybrid design does not equate to moving static, text-based material online and retaining whatever classroom activities still fit into half the allotted time in the hopes that great student (or instructor) experiences will emerge. Or, as some faculty might experience, instead of cutting away classroom activities for which there is just no seat-time, we feel obliged to do everything we used to do in the traditional, fully face-to-face environment but in half the time, rushing, condensing, skimming as best we can. Then we add an online component. We are teaching, and students are taking, what Aycock et al., among others, have identified as "a course and a half": we "take everything from the face-to-face course and add online work on top" (30). Equally true, though, is that good hybrid design does not just mean adding technology to what we already do. As virtual learning advocate Andrew Miller has asserted: "Blended learning is not simple technology integration!"

Good hybrid design means, in many cases, building a course from the ground up, including re-seeing old practices in new ways, and developing entirely new strategies for both online and classroom environments. As Snart has argued, "even where basic pedagogies can be applied across instructional settings, they invariably will need to be adapted to suit the new context" (Snart, "Hybrid and Fully Online OWI" 97).

As is suggested in the chapter on design and delivery in the *Blended Learning Toolkit*, offered by the University of Central Florida, "Universally, successful blended faculty cite redesign of their course as the key element to creating integration between the face-to-face classroom and online components" ("Design and Delivery Principles"). Design efforts that look for this deep integration of learning modes take time. Building a hybrid class that feels, to students, like one, unified learning experience, rather than two separate (and not always equal) experiences, may, in fact, be one of the most challenging aspects of teaching in the hybrid format. As Jay Caulfield recognizes in her book, *How to Design and Teach a Hybrid Course*: "For me, integrating the in-class and out-of-class teaching and learning activities . . . was the toughest to learn. Sometimes I still don't get it right, yet I know it is an essential component of effective hybrid teaching" (62).

So the hybrid format might invite opportunities for using emerging instructional technology, like mobile learning, simply because it provides—at least to a greater degree than fully face-to-face instruction might—the literal and metaphorical space to accommodate such technologies. But if redesigning, or simply designing, as we'd prefer, hybrid courses will be a significant undertaking, how can we think productively about technology without it becoming either burdensome or just a shiny new thing, the latest fad whose miracle cure has shown up in our inbox?

This leads to one of our final discussions: exactly what is the role of "technology"—that ubiquitous catchall that seems to mean everything and nothing at the same time—relative to the hybrid format?

"Technology": The Everything and the Nothing

Writing in *Scientific American* in 1991, Mark Weiser asserted that "[t]he most profound technologies are those that disappear. They weave themselves into the fabric of everyday life until they are indistinguishable from it." Subsequent thinking has deepened this idea, positing, for example, that the computer, as a stand-alone machine, will ultimately dissolve its capacities into our everyday environment such that noncomputer objects will be capable of wireless networking and communication. In their 2007 collection, *The Disappearing Computer,* Streitz et al. predicted "a new generation of technologies, which will move the computing power off the desktop and ultimately integrate it with real world objects and everyday environments" (v).

Their point, as perhaps Weiser's was at least in part, is that individuals would be in data- and communication-rich environments potentially all of the time: computing would be "ambient," as Streitz et al. have suggested (v), rather than localized to one, particular machine, like the desktop computer.

As we write, for example, the number of items that make up what has been called the "Internet of things" continues to grow. A wirelessly networked refrigerator might, for example, provide you with access to the Internet (to stream music or connect to a virtual calendar which will display on the fridge's touchscreen). Some manufacturers are offering full lines of networked appliances. Jeff St. John, writing in 2013 for *GreenTechMedia*, describes an appliance line from LG that includes "a refrigerator, a dishwasher and a washer/dryer unit equipped with . . . technology, which allows each appliance to be turned on, link up to a household Wi-Fi network, and show up on customer smartphones, tablets and PCs." Appliance manufacturer Whirlpool offers its own line of networked machines, and, yes, there's an app for that. "My Smart Appliances" is available through iTunes for those who would like to activate appliance features remotely or be reminded on their iPhone that the fridge door has been left open: "This ground-breaking app allows you to easily interact with your Wifi connected Smart appliances" ("My Smart Appliances").

It might seem, then, that in this communication-rich environment technology would be everywhere, indeed hard to escape. The notion of the disappearing computer seems hardly about fewer devices and rather about more and more devices. The prediction, though, is that as cross-device communication becomes an everyday reality, and not either a new marketing angle or the latest sparkle to attract the techno-futurist's attention, we will cease to be surprised by or even aware of the ubiquity of devices or appliances that talk to each other and to us.

We like this spin on the notion of the disappearing computer: "technology" might be usefully defined, not as a physical *thing*, be it smartphone or dishwasher, but rather as the individual's awareness of having to actively *use* that thing to accomplish a task.

Why do we think this definition is helpful? And why particularly for discussion of technology in the context of higher education and hybrid learning?

First, it makes technology less about the thing and more about the user, which in the context of our discussion will generally be a student, a teacher, an administrator, or support staff. This helps to steer conversation surrounding educational technology—or edtech—toward education. As Kunal Chawla notes in his series of *EdSurge* articles on effective online course design, we might too often "focus on 'tech'—the new apps, data systems, assessments and other technologies" when it fact it is primarily the "ed" in edtech that needs our attention.

And when it comes to hybrid learning, once all is said and done, it is really the student experience that is paramount. So we sometimes need to re-ground ourselves in the fact that a technology, like a smartphone or tablet, does not exist in some absolute space outside of how we hope to use it. What follows is that the physical thing does not exist equally for all users. Being "easy to use" or "complicated" is not intrinsic to the device or digital tool itself (no matter how many, or how few, buttons or virtual features it has). Rather, if we imagine that technology is defined as the user's awareness of manipulating a physical device, then what constitutes "technology" for one student might not for another. Or what might be an "easy" or "simple" technology for one user is actually quite difficult to use and complex for another.

Consider the ramifications for that fairly common phrase we mentioned earlier: teaching with technology. If every student in a class is well versed in producing shared documents using Google Docs or Office 365, do we still say that course uses technology? Or, if we do, why is that assertion useful? Does it differentiate that course from other courses? We're not sure we see how the designation is especially helpful in this case. If those students are not particularly aware of having to figure out the document sharing software—i.e., what buttons to click to accomplish certain tasks—then the technology (the virtual tool) has faded into the background. Users concentrate on learning about writing as a collaborative process (no easy task, by the way); they do not concentrate on learning the tech tool.

Now consider the opposite scenario: same course objective of having students learn about and practice collaborative writing, but none of the students has great familiarity yet with the virtual tool that will enable that collaboration. The instructor—and the institution as a whole—will need to be much more responsible for introducing students to the "technology." So perhaps counterintuitively, the least tech savvy class is the one that will be most about "teaching with technology," because those users' awareness of the digital tools will be far greater than in a class where students are already familiar with the tools at hand.

The very practical implication, as we just noted, is that the individual instructor—like it or not—will inevitably become the point person for IT support and troubleshooting. This is not ideal, by any means, but students are more likely to reach out to an instructor first with technical questions rather than seeking out a student help desk or other similar institutional support resource. Thus, if technology is more about the user experience than some objective measure of any given device or tool, teachers will be well served to gauge early on just how savvy students are with whatever digital tool or device will figure into a course. So one would not assume, for example, that mobile learning will be easy because smartphones are a common, and thus an easy-to-use technology. Such an assumption trades on the notion of technology as the device, the physical thing, itself. We want to know about the user of that device.

Another seemingly counter-intuitive irony that many instructors face is that students who are otherwise frequent social media users are not always necessarily tech savvy. They are just frequent social media users. As Snart has pointed out in *Hybrid Learning*, "we should be especially careful not to assume that students who are immersed in technologies of one kind will necessarily have an immediate facility with technologies of another kind or even with familiar technology when it is deployed in a new way" (19–20). We are firm believers in frequent informal surveys in classes to help instructors find out what their students currently do online and on what devices, and to assess how much orientation it will take for students to feel comfortable using the digital tools that will figure in any given hybrid class. We realize too, of course, that what most instructors face is not a class in which all students are familiar with a piece of software or no student is familiar with that software. We almost always face a wide range of abilities. But this again is reason to reframe our use of the term "technology" to point to the user experience—as diverse as this may often be—rather than a physical or virtual thing itself. This latter formulation just tells us so little of what we actually need to care about in the educational setting: the individual student and his or her awareness of having to learn about a digital tool as a condition of using it to accomplish a course task.

Thinking about technology not as a series of physical things or virtual tools but rather as premised on individual user awareness of that thing or tool ultimately helps to refocus our attention away from the hardware or software and onto the user. As

Michelle Wiese, a senior research fellow at the Clayton Christensen Institute for Disruptive Innovation, has noted, "There is this tendency for pundits, policymakers and institutional leaders to take any kind of technological advancement, call it a 'disruptive innovation,' cram it into the classroom experience and then hope that somehow efficiencies are going to magically appear" (qtd. in Waters). Wiese recognizes how easy it can be to adopt a technology—a thing—and push its use across campus, touting it as somehow intrinsically, or magically, as Wiese says, able to generate change. There is no small monetary investment in this magic, either. The 2011 Center for Digital Education's *Converge Yearbook*, for example, reports that the "IT spend" for higher education for 2010/11 "was approximately $19.7 billion—$9.4 billion for K–12 and $10.3 billion for higher education" (4).

What matters, though, as we argue here, is how and why those technologies are used, not just *that* they are used. How do those billions spent address an identified need or set of needs? One of the most common barriers to technology adoption that we have noted is not the presumed intransigence of teaching faculty or the unwillingness of higher education to change, but rather how poorly new technologies are presented within a framework of user experience (this latter being precisely the revised definition for "technology" we prefer).

Another practical implication to consider is that "technology" workshops, in whatever form they might take, can be usefully situated not just in terms of what buttons to push, but rather how a digital tool can actually be used in the context of teaching. So "technology" is, again, less about the hardware and software involved, and much more about users. Faculty will benefit from understanding how, pedagogically, a digital tool might serve their needs, without assumptions about that tool being either "easy" or "hard."

We also like how our version of "technology"—as a measure of user awareness, rather than an absolute existential category applied to some physical item—dovetails with emergent thinking about perhaps the most prevalent technology for those teaching online and in the hybrid mode: the learning management system. An April 2015 report from the Educause Learning Initiative, entitled "The Next Generation Digital Learning Environment," describes a new future for how learning management systems mediate teaching and learning (Brown et al.). The report looks at "gaps between current learning management tools and a digital learning environment that could meet the changing needs of higher education" (1). What the authors note is that while conventional learning management systems have been relatively effective when it comes to "enabling the *administration* of learning," they have proven much less useful at fostering learning itself (2). The distinction here is between the LMS as a lively, collaborative digital space (the preferable option) and the LMS as little more than a convenient repository where students can access grades, download a PDF, or watch a video, for example. These latter are useful tools to help with the administration—or management—of a course. What the Educause report authors found problematic, though, was how the traditional LMS seemed overly instructor-centric and rather more a one-size-fits-all approach to learning in the twenty-first century, which is otherwise becoming increasingly characterized by anything *but* the monolithic architecture that a typical LMS provides.

To put our spin on it, the LMS has become the technology, the thing, that needs to be taught to faculty, and then from faculty to students. At risk of oversimplifying, we learn to use the LMS, rather than it responding to our needs. But if we invert this formula, we insert the user as the driver of technology use, we arrive at a place not too far removed from where Brown et al. are at in "The Next Generation Digital Learning Environment": they advocate for a next generation of digital learning that might "include a traditional LMS as a component [but] it will not itself be a single application like the current LMS" (3). Rather, a next generation digital learning environment (or NGDLE) will embrace a mash-up, or "Lego," approach, in which various kinds of digital tools are brought together to reflect the needs of a given group of students and teachers. So instead of the "uniformity and centrality" that characterize current learning management systems (and how they are deployed on most campuses), next generation digital learning environments will "need to support personalization as an option at all levels of the institution. The NGDLE will not be exactly the same for any two learners, instructors, or institutions" (3).

It is hard to imagine what this might actually look like or how current information and learning technology offices would handle such diversity and individuation. Nonetheless, we agree that digital learning tools, which will likely figure so prominently for blended learners in particular, need to be flexible and should reflect the needs of the users. Perhaps a basic starting point for IT and LT offices looking to reimagine how they support teaching and learning in an increasingly multifaceted digital landscape will be to reframe how they offer services. For example, we like the idea, as wishful as it may sound, that instead of an instructor arriving to a learning technology office at an appointed day and time to learn how to use the discussion board features in the LMS, that faculty member will instead walk in asking what options are available to help students interact virtually, after they have had class meetings for the week, in a platform that is mobile, enables multimedia collaboration, and is of course accessible. This pedagogically grounded question will provide the generative moment for LT staff to introduce the instructor to a variety of potential digital tools that might address his or her need.

We realize that this hypothetical might require a significant revisioning of how information technology and learning technology offices are charged to support teaching and learning. Rather than rolling out tech sessions that are otherwise decontextualized from individual pedagogical needs, technology offices will need to adapt to more individualized and open support. But if an institution believes in the mission of enhancing how teachers use technology in all delivery modes, not just online or in the blended format, investment in flexible support must be recognized as a concomitant reality. In our example, we've put the user first, bringing the digital tool to bear on an existing pedagogical need, expressed by the individual. We do not find ourselves, as is so often the case, looking for reasons to use features housed exclusively in the LMS or, perhaps even worse, reining in our innovative energies because what we'd like to have students doing in the digital environment is not something the LMS can handle or that a tech office is charged to support.

Conclusion

A s part of our discussion about hybrid learning, we have al-
luded to the fact that, for many institutions, basic elements of
curricular quality control and adequate professional development
and training in the area of *online learning* might be happening
retroactively. Many schools already have an online presence and
deliver online courses as a component of their curricular offerings. Online courses might exist in many disciplines and many
faculty might be involved in designing and teaching them. But
not quite so many institutions have the robust infrastructure to
support online teaching, whether in the form of a professional
development office, dedicated IT support, or library resources
available fully online. What should have been part of early online
curriculum planning efforts is now happening relatively late in
the game, if happening at all, and it is often costing institutions
considerable resources and energy.

But hybrid learning, as it exists at many institutions, is likely
not as far along in its lifecycle. Thinking about hybrid learning
from the ground up, early in its institutional existence, sets the
stage for informed and meaningful curricular development. This
development will involve discussion of basics, like how hybrids
are defined and what flexibility instructors will have in managing
the online and f2f components of a blended class.

Equally important will be the establishment of campus resources to facilitate professional training and ongoing development so that hybrid courses are well designed and implemented
from the start. Administrators who will be tasked with managing
academic or support areas in which hybrid classes are housed
should feel equally part of planning and development conversations, and they should feel supported by an institutional environment in which policies surrounding hybrids are clear and applied
equally and thoughtfully across an institution.

Further, part of a campus infrastructure for successful hybrids will be the creation of communication and sharing networks that can unite faculty who teach and design hybrids across different departments. Of vital importance, too, is not just initial professional development support for those looking to propose, design, and teach a hybrid for the first time, but also that broader institutional framework and set of mechanisms to enable continued communication among those teaching, advertising, and sustaining the hybrid curriculum.

In a 2013 address at the Florida Leaders Summit, Florida House Speaker Will Weatherford declared that he wanted Florida to be a leader in online education. He went on to assert that he'd like other states to look at Florida and say, "it looks like they figured out this online learning thing" (qtd. in Call).

We'd like to address here, by way of concluding, the notion that online, hybrid, or whatever new modes of learning will emerge in the future, are to be somehow definitively "figured out." Studied? Yes. Improved upon? Yes. Better tomorrow than yesterday? Sure. But the sense of finally figuring out something like online or hybrid learning suggests that at some point we will reach an end, a stopping place in our efforts to engage students and prepare them for a rapidly changing twenty-first-century world. It would be as though we finally decided that we no longer needed to be challenging ourselves or our students to invent and reinvent the work of teaching and learning in higher education.

On the contrary, we have tried to make the point throughout this book that getting better at educating students is an ongoing process. Support for teachers, students, administrators—all the constituent groups involved—needs to be continuous. On a very practical level, if an institution develops a hybrid teaching workshop, as outlined earlier, that workshop should not remain static, simply rolled over every fall or spring to be offered on the same day at the same time. It will need to be kept alive, updated with new information and activities for workshop participants.

At the institutional level, too, we hope that the sense is not to "figure out" hybrid learning only so as to move on to some other project, some new flavor of the month. The hybrid learning community needs to be kept vital and relevant, which means continuing support and investment on the part of the institution.

We hope that what we have provided here—the questions, the challenges, the advocacy for sometimes disruptive institutional change—can help to position your institution for the development of a meaningful and sustaining hybrid curriculum: one that serves students well, serves teachers well, and can become a recognized mark of excellence at your school.

We believe that *Making Hybrids Work*, our book title, suggests a useful double meaning. We want to make hybrids work so that they are effective. That has hopefully emerged throughout the preceding pages. But hybrids will also take work to develop and offer well. Even with motivated and energetic people behind it, the project to design and teach hybrids across a variety of disciplines, within the framework of a shared vision for what hybrids are and how they fit into a larger institutional picture, is unlikely to be easy, or happen on its own, and it certainly won't happen overnight. Yes, that project is, we hope, ultimately rewarding, but it will take real effort, real work, to think and act at the campuswide level to develop, design, and deliver great hybrid courses, across the curriculum.

So we have not intended to suggest that with a semester or two of trading vague ideas or anecdotes about what happens in one or two classes, or that with the formation of a committee or two, or that by virtue of the good graces and unpaid labor of a few staff and teachers, we will reach an endpoint for hybrid curricular development. We've gone through the motions so now we declare that hybrid learning has been figured out.

Our hope is rather that such figuring out becomes an ongoing aspect, a living part, of your institution's culture.

WORKS CITED

Adams, Susan. "The College Degrees and Skills Employers Most Want in 2015." *Forbes*, 15 Apr. 2015. Web. 2 June 2015.

AFC Franchise Corporation. "Hybrid Sushi." *AFC Franchise Corp*, 2015. Web. 3 June 2015. <http://www.afcsushi.com/index.php?main_page=concept>.

Allen, I. Elaine, and Jeff Seaman. *Changing Course: Ten Years of Tracking Online Education in the United States*. Babson Survey Research Group, 2013. Web. 1 Apr. 2015. <http://www.onlinelearningsurvey.com/reports/changingcourse.pdf>.

American Bar Association (ABA). "Alternative Delivery Information." *American Bar Association*, 24 Feb. 2015. Web. 31 Mar. 2015.

————. "Compilation Guideline-Specific Information Relating to Alternative Delivery Course Requirements." *American Bar Association*, 24 Feb. 2015. Web. 31 Mar. 2015. <http://apps.americanbar.org/legalservices/paralegals/downloads/Compilation_Joint_Task_Force_Information.pdf>.

Anonymous. Email correspondence. 29 Oct. 2012.

Autry, Meagan Kittle. "WPA's Guide to the Hybrid Writing Classroom." *WPA Guide to the Hybrid Writing Classroom*, 13 June 2011. Web. 15 Dec. 2014. <https://wpahybridguide.wordpress.com/>.

Aycock, Alan, et al. *Sloan-C Certificate Program: Faculty Development for Blended Teaching and Learning*. Sloan-C and Learning Technology Center and University of Wisconsin-Milwaukee, 2008. Web. 15 Oct. 2014.

Bastedo, Kathleen, et al. "Programmatic, Systematic, Automatic: An Online Course Accessibility Support Model." *Journal of Asynchronous Learning Networks* 17.3 (2013): 87–102. Web. 5 Apr. 2015.

"Becoming a Blended Learning Designer." *UCF/Educause BlendKit2014*. Credly Digital Badge. Web. 10 May 2015.

"Blended Learning Toolkit." *University of Central Florida*, 2015. Web. 15 Oct. 2014.

Brown, Malcolm, et al. "The Next Generation Digital Learning Environment: A Report on Research." *Educause Learning Initiative*. EDUCAUSE, Apr. 2015. Web. 21 May 2015. <http://net.educause.edu/ir/library/pdf/eli3035.pdf>.

"Browse Course Catalog." *University of Central Florida*. Web. 16 July 2015.

Call, James. "Weatherford Wants State Tops in Online Classes." *Florida Current*, 9 Sept. 2013. Web. 18 Dec. 2013. <http://www.thefloridacurrent.com/article.cfm?id=34448967>.

Canvas by Instructure Demonstration Recording. *College of DuPage*. Web. 20 Feb. 2015.

"Capitalize on New Skills More Quickly with New Programs in Online Education." *JobJournal.com*, 22 Sept. 2013. Web. 22 Oct. 2014. <http://www.cajobjournal.com/articles/capitalize-on-new-skills-more-quickly-with-newprograms-in-online-education>.

Carrington, Allan. "The Padagogy Wheel V4.0 . . . the Next Generation." *The Padagogy Wheelhouse*, 7 Mar. 2015. Web. 15 July 2016.

Caulfield, Jay. *How to Design and Teach a Hybrid Course: Achieving Student-Centered Learning through Blended Classroom, Online, and Experiential Activities*. Sterling: Stylus, 2011. Print.

Center for Distributed Learning. *Types of Courses at UCF*. University of Central Florida. Web. 15 July 2016. <https://online.ucf.edu/online-programs/types-of-courses-at-ucf/>.

Center for Teaching and Learning. *Hybrid Course Initiative*. Oregon State University, 2016. Web. 15 July 2016.

Chafin, Chris. "When Your Dream School Accepts You (but Only Online)." *Fast Company*, 20 Apr. 2016. Web. 2 May 2016. <http://www.fastcompany.com/3057949/when-your-dream-school-accepts-you-but-onlyonline>.

Chawla, Kunal. "6 Essential Tips for Planning an Effective Online Course." *EdSurge*, 11 June 2015. Web. 24 June 2015. <https://www.edsurge.com/news/2015-06-11-6-essential-tips-for-planning-an-effectiveonline-course>.

Chin-Wei, Bong, Cheah Kooi-Guan, and Teoh Ai-Ping. "A Progressive Hybrid Assessment Model in Open Distance Learning." Proceedings of the 20th Annual Conference of the Asian Association of Open Universities. Yunnan Radio & TV University, Yunnan, China. 2006. Web. 15 July 2016.

College of DuPage. "Hybrid Courses." *College of DuPage*, 2015. Web. 12 Feb. 2015. <http://www.cod.edu/academics/hybrid.aspx>.

"Converge Yearbook—2011 Overview and Highlights." *Center for Digital Education*, 2011. Web. 22 Apr. 2015. <http://www.center digitaled.com/Converge-Yearbook-2011Overview-Highlights-11-1-11html>.

Corbett, Amanda, and Abbie Brown. "The Roles That Librarians and Libraries Play in Distance Education Settings." *Online Journal of Distance Learning Administration* 18.2 (2015). Web. <http://www.westga.edu/~distance/ojdla/summer182/corbett_brown182.html>.

"CultureClic: An Augmented Reality Mobile Application." *CultureClic*. iTunes App store, 2014. Web. 8 Apr. 2015.

"Definitions of Online, Hybrid, and Supplemental Courses." *Aiken Technical College*, 2014. Web. 12 Nov. 2014. <http://www.atc.edu/catalog/handbook/S4.aspx>.

"Design and Delivery Principles." *Blended Learning Toolkit*. University of Central Florida and the American Association of State Colleges and Universities, 2015. Web. 8 Apr. 2015. <https://blended.online.ucf.edu/effective-practices/design-delivery-principles/>.

Dewey, John. *The School and Society*. Rev. ed. Chicago: U of Chicago P, 1943. Print.

"Dollar Bill." *Aurasma*, 2015. Web. 7 Apr. 2015.

Educational Technology and Mobile Learning. "Don't Miss This Awesome Bloom's Taxonomy Wheel." *Educational Technology and Mobile Learning*, April 2013. Web. 15 July 2016.

Finley, Sharriette, and Jeanna Chapman. "Actively Including Online Students in the College Experience." *Academic Advising Today* 34.2 (2011). Web. 10 May 2015. <http://www.nacada.ksu.edu/Resources/Academic-Advising-Today/View-Articles/Actively-Including-Online-Students-in-the-College-Experience.aspx>.

Freire, Paulo. *Pedagogy of the Oppressed*. 30th Anniv. ed. Trans. Myra Bergman Ramos. New York: Continuum, 2005. Print.

Furnham, Adrian. "Insight: Passion Takes a Teacher from Being Merely Good to Great." *Telegraph*, 1 Jan. 2001. Web. 1 Dec. 2014. <http://www.telegraph.co.uk/finance/2906525/Insight-Passion-takes-a-teacher-from-being-merely-good-to-great.html>.

Garrison, D. Randy, and Norman D. Vaughan. *Blended Learning in Higher Education: Framework, Principles, and Guidelines.* San Francisco: Jossey-Bass, 2008. Print.

Gos, Michael W. Email correspondence. 18 Feb. 2015.

Grajek, Susan, et al. "Top 10 IT Issues, 2015: Inflection Point." *Educause Review Online,* 12 Jan. 2015. Web. 13 Apr. 2015. <http://er.educause.edu/~/media/files/article-downloads/erm1511.pdf>.

Grant, Capper. Email correspondence and interviews. June 2014 to July 2016.

Hamilton, Kathy. "Defining Augmented Reality." *Augmented Reality in Education*, 2015. Web. 8 Apr. 2015. <https://augmented-reality-in-education.wikispaces.com/>.

Hewett, Beth, and Kevin DePew, eds. *Foundational Practices of Online Writing Instruction*. Parlor Press and WAC Clearinghouse, 2015. Web. 15 Apr. 2015. <http://wac.colostate.edu/books/owi/>.

Horn, Michael. "Moving Beyond the 'Does Blended Learning Work?' Question." *EdSurge*, 20 May 2015. Web. 3 June 2015. <https://www.edsurge.com/news/2015-05-20-movingbeyond-the-does-blended-learning-work-question>.

Jaggars, Shanna Smith. "What the Research Tells Us about Online Higher Education." *Community College Research Center*. Columbia University, 18 May 2013. Web. 15 Dec. 2014. <http://ccrc.tc.columbia.edu/presentation/what-the-research-tells-us.html>.

Jameson, Sara. Email correspondence. 16 Mar. 2015.

"Job Outlook 2015." *National Association of Colleges and Employers.* Bethlehem: NACE, 2014. Web. 14 May 2015. <http://www.naceweb.org/surveys/job-outlook.aspx>.

Kaleta, Robert, et al. "Hybrid Courses: Obstacles and Solutions for Faculty and Students." 19th Annual Conference on Distance Teaching and Learning. Board of Regents of the University of Wisconsin System, 2005. Web. 15 June 2015. <http://www.uwex.edu/disted/conference/resource_library/proceedings/03_72.pdf>.

Keen Footwear. "Hybrid.ology." *Keen*, 2015. Web. 3 June 2015. <http://www.keenfootwear.com/hybridology.aspx>.

Lakeland Community College. *Course Catalog. Lakeland Community College*, 2016. Web. 15 July 2016. <http://www.lakelandcc.edu/c/document_library/get_file?uuid=8cf156d9-76e8-48c5-9edd-eb1939be7d6a&groupId=347086>.

———. "Distance Learning." *Lakeland Community College*, 2015. Web. 20 May 2016. <http://www.lakelandcc.edu/web/about/distance-learning>.

Learning Technology Center. *Hybrid Courses*. University of Wisconsin-Milwaukee. Web. 15 Jul. 2016. <http://www4.uwm.edu/ltc/hybrid/>.

Massengale, Lindsey R., and Eleanzar Vasquez III. "Assessing Accessibility: How Accessible Are Online Courses for Students with Disabilities?" *Journal of the Scholarship of Teaching and Learning* 16.1 (2016): 69–79. Web. 25 May 2016.

Miller, Andrew. "Virtual Schooling: Where Are We Now? Where Are We Headed?" *Edutopia*. 6 June 2013. Web. 18 July 2016. <http://www.edutopia.org/blog/virtual-schooling-where-are-we-andrew-miller>.

Minock, Drew. "Augmented Reality Brings New Dimensions to Learning." *Edutopia*, 4 Nov. 2013. Web. 8 Apr. 2015. <http://www.edutopia.org/blog/augmented-reality-newdimensions-learning-drew-minock>.

"Most Young People Entering the U.S. Workforce Lack Critical Skills Essential for Success." *The Partnership for 21st Century Skills*, 2 Oct. 2006. Web. 2 June 2015. <http://www.p21.org/news-events/press-releases/250-most-young-people-entering-the-us-workforce-lack-critical-skills-essential-for-success>.

Murray, Seb. "Growth of Blended Online and Campus MBA Learning Gathers Pace." *Business Because*, 17 June 2015. Web. 29 June 2015. <http://www.businessbecause.com/news/mba-distance-learning/3323/blended-learning-growth-gathers-pace>.

"My Smart Appliances." *iTunes*, 7 Apr. 2015. Web. 15 May 2015.

NACADA. "Technology in Advising Commission." *National Academic Advising Association (NACADA)*, 2014. Web. 20 Apr. 2015. <http://www.nacada.ksu.edu/Community/Commission-Interest-Groups/Theory-Practice-and-Delivery-of-Advising-II/Technology-in-Advising-Commission.aspx>.

National Education Association. "NEA Policy Statement on Digital Learning." *National Education Association*, 5 July 2013. Web. 13 Oct. 2014. <http://www.nea.org/home/55434.htm>.

Naylor, Brian. "FCC Chairman Wants to Help Low-Income Americans Afford Broadband." *National Public Radio*, 28 May 2015. Web. 1 June 2015. <http://www.npr.org/sections/thetwo-way/2015/05/28/410351224/fcc-chairman-wants-to-help-low-income-americans-afford-broadband>.

NEA Education Policy and Practice Department. "Blended Learning: A Policy Brief." *NEA Policy Brief*, 2012. Web. 10 Sep. 2014. <https://www.nea.org/assets/docs/PB36A_Blended_Learning_Policy_Brief2-final.pdf>.

The NMC *Horizon Report*: 2011 Edition. *New Media Consortium*, 2011. Web. 8 Apr. 2015. <http://www.nmc.org/pdf/2011-Horizon-Report.pdf>.

The NMC *Horizon Report*: 2013 Higher Education Edition. *New Media Consortium*, 2013. Web. 10 Nov. 2014. <https://www.nmc.org/pdf/2013-horizon-report-HE.pdf>.

Oller, Rick. "The Future of Mobile Learning." *EDUCAUSE Center for Analysis and Research*, 1 May 2012. Web. 7 Apr. 2015. <https://library.educause.edu/resources/2012/5/the-future-of-mobile-learning>.

"Oracle and Nirvanix." *Oracle*, 4 Dec. 2013. Web. 3 June 2015. <http://www.oracle.com/us/corporate/acquisitions/nirvanix/index.html>.

OWI Open Resource. "Effective Practice in Online Writing Instruction Committee." *Conference on College Composition and Communication*. National Council of Teachers of English, 2015. Web. 12 Jan. 2015. <http://www.ncte.org/cccc/owi-open-resource>.

Parry, Marc. "Online-Course Enrollments Grow, but at a Slower Pace. Is a Plateau Approaching?" *Chronicle of Higher Education*, 9 Nov. 2011. Web. 9 Aug. 2014. <http://chronicle.com/blogs/wiredcampus/online-course-enrollments-grow-but-at-a-slower-pace-is-a-plateau-approaching/34150>.

Pasquini, Laura. "Implications for Use of Technology in Advising 2011 National Survey." *NACADA Clearinghouse for Academic Advising Resource*, 2014. Web. 30 Mar. 2015. <https://www.nacada.ksu.edu/Resources/Clearinghouse/View-Articles/Implications-for-use-of-technology-in-advising-2011-National-Survey.aspx>.

Pasquini, Laura, and Clay Schwenn. "Best Practices in Online Academic Advising Delivery." *Slideshare.net*, 8 June 2010. Web. 15 Nov. 2014. <http://www.slideshare.net/LauraPasquini/best-practices-in-online-academic-advising-delivery>.

Paull, Joanna. "Going Hybrid: A Faculty Workshop." Lakeland Community College Faculty Workshop Series, 2012. Web. 15 July 2016.

Paull, Joanna, and Jason Snart. "Building Hybrid Curriculum." *SurveyMonkey*, 2014. Web. 14 July 2016.

Pittinsky, Matthew. "Making Credentials Matter." *edSurge*, 31 Mar. 2014. Web. 1 Apr. 2015. <https://www.edsurge.com/news/2015-03-31-making-credentials-matter>.

"Position Statement of Principles and Effective Practices for Online Writing Instruction (OWI)." *CCCC OWI Committee for Effective Practices in Online Writing Instruction*. National Council of Teachers of English, 2013. Web. 20 Apr. 2015.

Reid, Alan J., and Denise Paster. "A Digital Badge Initiative: Two Years Later." *Campus Technology*, 6 Apr. 2016. Web. 22 Apr. 2016. <https://campustechnology.com/articles/2016/04/06/a-digital-badge-initiative-two-years.later.aspx>.

"Robert Burns." *Aurasma*, 2015. Web. 7 Apr. 2015.

Roby, William. Email correspondence and interviews. June 2014 to July 2016.

"Rubric for Online Instruction." *Technology and Learning Program*. California State University, Chico, 4 Feb. 2009. Web. 15 Jul. 2016. <https://www.csuchico.edu/tlp/resources/rubric/rubric.pdf>.

"Search for Classes." *University of Central Florida*. Web. 15 July 2016.

"Search for Credit Classes." *College of DuPage*. Web. 16 July 2016.

"7 Things You Should Know about . . . Badges." *Educause*, 11 June 2012. Web. 1 Apr. 2016. <http://net.educause.edu/ir/library/pdf/ELI7085.pdf>.

"7 Things You Should Know about . . . the HyFlex Course Model." *Educause*, 9 Nov. 2010. Web. 1 June 2015. <http://net.educause.edu/ir/library/pdf/eli7066.pdf>.

Shattuck, Kay. "Quality Matters: Collaborative Program Planning at a State Level." *Online Journal of Distance Learning Admin-*

istration 10.3 (2007). Web. 15 May 2015. <http://www.westga
.edu/~distance/ojdla/fall103/shattuck103.htm>.

Snart, Jason. "Hybrid and Fully Online OWI." *Foundational Practices
of Online Writing Instruction.* Ed. Beth L. Hewett and Kevin Eric
DePew. WAC Clearinghouse and Parlor Press, 2015. Web.

————. *Hybrid Learning: The Perils and Promise of Blending Online
and Face-to-Face Instruction in Higher Education.* Santa Barbara:
Praeger, 2010. Print.

————. "Learning Hybrid: Hybrid Learning." *Teaching and Learning
Center Workshop.* College of DuPage, 2016.

St. John, Jeff. "Whirlpool Launches the Wi-Fi Smart Appliance."
GreenTechMedia, 25 Apr. 2013. Web. 15 Apr. 2015. <http://www
.greentechmedia.com/articles/read/whirlpool-launches-the-wi-fi-
smart-appliance>.

Streitz, Norbert, et al. Preface. *The Disappearing Computer: Interaction
Design, System Infrastructures and Applications for Smart Environments.* New York: Springer, 2007. Print.

Sullivan, Traci. Email correspondence. 16 Feb. 2015.

Taylor, Loralyn, and Virginia McAleese. "Beyond Retention: Using
Targeted Analytics to Improve Student Success." *Educause Review,* 17 July 2012. Web. 5 Dec. 2014. <http://er.educause.edu/
articles/2012/7/beyond-retention-using-targeted-analytics-to-
improve-student-success>.

Teichman, Jennifer. "Psychology Exercise." *Going Hybrid: A Faculty
Workshop.* Cuyahoga Community College, 2013. Web. 16 Jul.
2016.

Thompson, Stephen. Email correspondence and interviews. June 2014
to July 2016.

Tutor.com. 2015. Web. 15 Jul. 2015.

University of Minnesota Center for Teaching and Learning. "What Is Active Learning?" University of Minnesota, 8 May 2008. Web. 17 June
2014. <http://cei.umn.edu/support-services/what-active-learning>.

"University of Wisconsin Flex Option FAQs." *University of Wisconsin,* 2015. Web. 4 Sep. 2014. <https://www.wisconsin.edu/news/
download/news_documents/2012/november_28,_2012/FAQ_
FlexOption.pdf>.

University of Wisconsin-Milwaukee. "Hybrid Courses." *University of Wisconsin-Milwaukee*, 2015. Web. 13 Feb. 2015. <http://www4. uwm.edu/ltc/hybrid/>.

———. "Hybrid Courses: Faculty Development." *University of Wisconsin, Learning Technology Center,* 2014. Web. 23 June 2014. <http://www4.uwm.edu/ltc/hybrid/faculty_development/>.

US Department of Education. "Evaluation of Evidence-Based Practices in Online Learning: A Meta-Analysis and Review of Online Learning Studies." *U.S. Department of Education Office of Planning, Evaluation, and Policy Development,* Sept. 2010. Web. 15 Feb. 2015. <http://files.eric.ed.gov/fulltext/ED505824.pdf>.

Van Duzer, Joan, et al. "Instruction Design Tips for Online Learning." *Humboldt State University.* 2002. Web. 15 July 2016. <http://www .csuchico.edu/tlp/resources/rubric/instructionalDesignTips.pdf>.

Vierke, Judy. Email correspondence and interviews. June 2014 to July 2016.

Warnock, Scott. *Teaching Writing Online: How and Why.* Urbana: NCTE, 2009. Print.

Waters, John K. "Disrupting Higher Education." *Campus Technology,* 16 Apr. 2015. Web. 22 Apr. 2015. <https://campustechnology.com/ articles/2015/04/16/disrupting-higher-education.aspx>.

Weiser, Mark. "The Computer for the Twenty-first Century." *Scientific American* 3.3 (1991): 3–11. Web. 13 Mar. 2015.

"What Is Augmented Reality?" *NMC Horizon Report: 2015 Higher Education Edition Wiki.* Horizon Project. New Media Consortium, 2015. Web. 8 Apr. 2015. <http://he-2015.wiki.nmc.org/ augmented+reality>.

Wheeler, Tom. "A Lifeline for Low-Income Americans." *FCC Official Blog,* 28 May 2015. Web. 1 June 2015. <https://www.fcc.gov/news-events/blog/2015/05/28/lifeline-low-income-americans>.

Xu, Di, and Shanna Smith Jaggars. "Online and Hybrid Course Enrollment and Performance in Washington State Community and Technical Colleges." *Community College Research Center.* Columbia University. Mar. 2011. Web. 17 Feb. 2015. <http://ccrc.tc.columbia. edu/publications/online-hybrid-courses-washington.html>.

INDEX

Academic counseling, 72–76
  access to, 75
  advisor role in hybrid design,
    72–74
  online, 74–75
  use of technology in, 74, 75–
    76
Accessibility, 34, 47, 91, 132
Active learning strategies, faculty
    training in, 119–26
Adjunct teachers, 68–69, 98
Administrators, assessment by,
    98–100
Adobe Connect, online tutoring
    via, 82
Advertising of hybrids, 40–57
  in course-level explanations,
    54–57
  marketing, 40–46
  publicity fliers, 49, 50
  in registration system, 46–54
Advising, 72–76
Ai-Ping, T., 135
American Bar Association (ABA),
    164–65
Americans with Disabilities Act
    (ADA), considering in
    course design, 132
Assessment, 87–100, 135, 136–
    37, 161
  by administrators, 98–100
  challenges of, 161
  of continuous improvement,
    94
  course design checklist, 93–97
  faculty training in, 135–39

importance of, 137
learning objective measured in,
    85–86
  by peers, 97–100
  role of formal assessment
    groups in, 87–93
  scaffolding of, 136–37
  student misperceptions of, 135
Augmented reality (AR), 194–97
Aurasma, 195, 197
Autry, M. K., 35
Aycock, A., 198

Bastedo, K., 132
Biochemistry, hybrid course in,
    157–61
  calendar view of, 158
  course menu for, 159
  materials and resources for,
    160
  sample unit of, 160
  successes of, 161
  syllabus for, 157–58
Biomedical terminology, hybrid
    course in, 166–68
  course menu for, 167
  course schedule for, 167
  syllabus for, 167
Blackboard Collaborate, 103,
    140, 148
Blended learning, growth of, 2–3
BlendKit workshop (University
    of Central Florida), 7,
    147–48
Bloom's taxonomy, 120
Brown, A., 76, 77

Burns, R., 195
Business writing, hybrid course
  in, 180–82
  challenges of, 182
  course description of, 180

California State University,
  Chico, Center for
  Excellence in Learning and
  Teaching, 96–97
Call, J., 207
Campus management, 53
Camtasia, 131
Canvas, 190
Carrington, A., 120
Cates, S., 2
Caulfield, J., 5, 198
Chafin, J., 2
Chapman, J., 74, 75
Chawla, K., 200
Chin-wei, B., 135
City University of New York
  (CUNY), 109
Clarity, in definition of hybrid
  courses, 27–29
Clayton Christensen Institute for
  Disruptive Innovation, 85,
  203
Coastal Carolina College, 146
College of DuPage, 44, 153
Conference on College
  Composition and
  Communication,
  Committee for Effective
  Practice in Online Writing
  Instruction (OWI), 64, 89,
  91, 92, 93, 141
Corbett, A., 76, 77
Counseling, academic, 72–76
Course design checklist, 93–97
Course evaluations, 86–87
Course explanations, advertising
  of hybrids in, 54–57
Credit, 1–2, 139, 142–49
  for faculty training workshop,
  139, 142–49

instructional delivery mode
  and, 1–2
Credly, 140, 146, 147
Critical thinking, 86
CultureClic, 195, 196

Daly, U., 20, 21
DePew, K., 93
Desire2Learn, 190
Dewey, J., 189
Digital badges, 7, 69, 145–49
  definition of, 145
Dziuban, C., ix

Educause Learning Initiative,
  145, 149, 190, 195, 203–4
Efficiency model of hybrid
  courses, 34–36
Ellucian, 53
Embedded librarians, 77–81
English composition, hybrid
  course in, 175–79
  challenges of, 179
  course description of, 175
  LMS welcome page of, 176
  retention in, 179
  weekly plans for, 177
Enrollment, pressure to grow,
  17–18

Facebook, 148
Face-to-face (f2f) instruction, 1,
  27–38
  balancing in hybrid courses,
  27–38
Fact-finding, in institutional
  planning, 36
Faculty, 5, 7, 12, 27, 37–38,
  61–62, 63, 66–67, 83–84.
  See also Teachers
  autonomy of, 19–20, 63, 66–
  67
  communication among, 27
  community of support for, 67
  involvement in defining hybrid
  courses, 37–38

IT support for, 84
peer mentoring groups, 83–84
training of. *See* Teacher
training
vetting of, 61–62
virtual space for sharing
among, 84
Faculty training workshop series,
112–49
acknowledging participation
in, 142–49
active learning strategies, 119–
26
defining hybrid/blended
courses, 118–19
follow-up to, 139–42
formative and summative
assessment, 135–39
instructional design, 126–35
location for, 113
structure of, 113–17
technological components,
112–19
Field and experiential learning,
59–62
Finley, S., 74, 75
Formal assessment groups,
87–93
Formative assessment, training
in, 135–39
Freire, P., 120
Furnham, A., 66

Garrison, D. R., 5
Georgia Perimeter College-
Online (GPC), 74
Glaspell, S., 192
Global Community for Academic
Advising (NACADA),
75–76
"Going Hybrid: A Faculty
Workshop Series," 112,
114, 115–16, 118, 119,
122–23, 124–25
active learning assignment in,
124–25

course menu for, 114
defining hybrids in, 119
structure for, 115–16
Google Calendar, 179
Google Docs, 178, 201
Google Drive, 178
Google Hangouts, 82, 84, 131,
178
online tutoring via, 82
Gos, M. W., business writing
course of, 180–82
Graham, C., ix
Grajek, S., 70, 71, 72
Grant, C., paralegal studies
course of, 162–65

Hamilton, K., 195
Hess, K., 20, 21
Hewett, B., 93
Horn, M., 85
Hybrid, definition of, 25, 26
Hybrid courses, 5–8, 25, 27–38,
46–48, 54–55, 77–81,
91, 93–97, 131, 153–86,
187–205
access considerations for, 34,
47, 91, 132
balancing face-to-face and
online instruction in,
27–38
in biochemistry, 157–61
in biomedical terminology,
166–68
challenges of, 152, 156–57,
161, 172, 179, 182, 186
across curriculum, 150–86
definition of, 25, 27–29, 119
design checklist for, 93–97
design of, 5–8, 93–97, 126–35
efficiency approach to, 34–36
embedded librarians in, 77–81
incentivizing faculty to offer,
154
Internet access requirement
for, 47–48
labels for, in registration

system, 46–47, 153–74
mobile learning and, 188–99
in paralegal studies, 162–65
pedagogical basis for, 36–38
retention in, 179
scheduling considerations for,
    33
in sociology, 168–74
in speech communication,
    153–57
successes of, 152, 161, 171–72
syllabi for, 54–55
technological support for, 34,
    187–205
technology and, 187–205. *See
    also* Technology
in writing-intensive courses,
    174–86
Hybrid curricula, 19–20, 59–
    100, 101–3, 106–7
assessment of, 85–100
development of, 63–69
early adopters of, 106–7
essentials of, 58–59
faculty vetting for, 61–62
feasibility of, 62
field and experiential learning
    and, 59–63
scheduling concerns in, 61
support for, 69–85, 101–3
teacher autonomy in, 19–20,
    63, 66–67
teacher training for, 63. *See
    also* Faculty training
    workshop series
Hybrid learning, viii–ix, 1–23,
    25, 27–38, 40–57, 59, 63,
    188–99
advertising of, 40–57
challenges of, vii–viii, 9–14
constituents in, 56–57
course design for, 5–8
defining, 25, 27–38
early investment in, 10
field and experiential learning
    as, 59–62

framework for, 16–23, 27
growth of interest in, 3
HyFlex, 3
impact on higher education, 5
institutional history of, 39–40
institutional sustainability of,
    5, 8, 17, 20–23
lifecycle of, 9–15
literature on, 5
long-range view of, 18
marketing of, 16, 40
mobile technologies and, 1,
    188–99
network of support for, ix, 3
opportunities provided by,
    3–4, 16–23
overview of, 1–9
pioneers of, viii–ix
planning for, 15, 18–23
reform of, ix–x
roadmap for, 20–23
technological support for, 34
Hybrid moment, 26–27
HyFlex hybrid courses, 3, 8

Illinois Online Network's Quality
    Online Course Initiative
    (ION's QOC), 88–89
Immersive learning, 59
Independent study courses, 1
Institutional change, process for,
    20–23
Instructional design, faculty
    training in, 126–35
ADA considerations in, 132
content structure in, 130
integration of online and
    classroom environments
    in, 126–27
navigational components in,
    128
resources for, 131
Instructional time, management
    of, in hybrid courses,
    27–38
Internet access requirement for

hybrid courses, 47–48

Jaggars, S. S., 13
Jameson, S., technical writing
  course of, 182–86
Jing, 131
JobJournal.com, 42
JoinMe, 84

Kaleta, R., 131
Kirkwood College (Iowa), 20
Kooi-Guan, C., 135

Lab-based science classes, 157
Lakeland Community College,
  45, 48–49, 53–54, 168,
  169, 175, 178, 179
registration system of, 53–54
"Learning Hybrid: Hybrid
  Learning" faculty
  workshop series, 112, 115,
  116, 117–18, 119, 123
components of, 116, 117–18
course menu for, 115
defining hybrid courses in, 119
hands-on component of, 123
Learning management system
  (LMS), ix, 55, 64, 65, 66,
  73–74, 82, 83, 84, 92, 97,
  103–4, 115, 118, 124–25,
  128, 129–30, 136–37,
  151, 154, 156, 162, 170,
  176, 190, 191–92, 193,
  204–5
advising support for, 73–74
course menu screenshots, 151
course welcome pages, 170,
  176
integration with mobile
  devices, 190
Learning strategies, active,
  119–26
Learnsmart/Smartbook, 157
Lee College, 180
Libraries, campus, support for
  hybrid curricula from,

76–81
embedded librarians, 77–81
online support sessions, 76
LinkedIn, 146

Macardi, A., 2
Marketing, 16, 40–46
Massengale, L. R., 133
McAleese, V., 71
Miller, A., 198
Milton, J., 142, 143
Minock, D., 196
Mobile learning, 1, 188–99
activities for, 191–93
augmented reality
  opportunities for, 194–97
LMS integration with, 190
MOOCs (massive open online
  courses), 7
Murray, S., 2
My Smart Appliances, 200

NACADA. *See* Global
  Community for Academic
  Advising
National Association of Colleges
  and Employers (NACE),
  86
National Education Association
  (NEA) Education Policy
  and Practice Department,
  4, 108
Needs assessment, 20–21, 36
New Media Consortium (NMC),
  4, 194
Next generation digital learning
  environments (NGDLE),
  204–5

Office 365, 201
Oller, R., 190, 195
Online advising, 74–76, 82
Online learning, 1, 9–14, 27–38,
  42–43, 63–64, 206
balancing in hybrid courses,
  27–38

historical trajectory of, 9–14
impact of, 1
pedagogy workshops for, 63
perceived ease of, 42–43
problems with, 12–14
retention rates for, 13–14
role in developing hybrid
  curricula, 63–64
Online Learning Commission
  (OLC), 89
Online tutoring, 82
Online writing instruction
  (OWI), 91–93
Open Badge Infrastructure, 146
Open Education Consortium, 20
Oregon State University (OSU),
  7–8, 182, 183
Hybrid Initiative of, 7–8
OWI. See Conference on
  College Composition
  and Communication,
  Committee for Effective
  Practice in Online Writing
  Instruction

Padagogy Wheel 4.0
  (Carrington's), 120
Padlet, 192, 193, 194, 197
Paralegal studies, hybrid course
  in, 162–65
administrative mandate for,
  162
course menu for, 163
online activities for, 162–63
schedule for, 164
Partnership for 21st Century
  Learning, 86
Pasquini, L., 75
Paster, D., 146
Paull, J., 11, 45, 46, 47, 49, 55,
  77, 112, 175–79
English composition course of,
  175–79
Paul Smith's College, 71, 72
Pedagogy, hybrid course
  grounding in, 36–38

Peer evaluation, 97–100, 178
Peer mentoring community,
  83–84
Picciano, A., ix
Pittinsky, M., 149
Professional development, 5, 7,
  27, 68–69, 82, 103–10,
  206. See also Teacher
  training
for adjuncts, 68–69
finding leaders for, 103–8
inhouse, 82–83, 108–10

Quality Matters (QM), 88–89,
  91, 111

Registration system, advertising
  of hybrids in, 46–54, 153
Reid, A. J., 146
Research, support for, in hybrid
  curricula, 76–82
Retention, 13–14, 179
Roby, W., biochemistry course
  of, 157–61

Sacred Heart University
  (Connecticut), 2
Scalability, 18–19
Scheduling, 33, 61
administrative perspective on,
  61
impact on hybrid courses, 33
Schwenn, C., 75
Screencast-O-Matic, 131
Skype, online tutoring via, 82
SlideShark, 141
Sloan-C, 89
Smarthinking, 82
Smartphones, 190–91
Snart, J., 5, 11, 17, 26, 44, 46,
  53, 55, 112, 129, 147,
  191, 192, 193, 197, 198,
  202
Sociology, hybrid course in,
  168–74
blog assignment, 172–74

challenges of, 172
course catalog description of, 168–69
development of, 169–70
LMS welcome page for, 170
schedule for, 170–71
successes of, 171–72
Speech communication, hybrid course in, 153–57
challenges of, 156–57
course menu for, 155
development of, 153–54
sample week in, 156
syllabus for, 155
Steelcase LearnLab, 113
St. John, J., 199–200
Streitz, N., 199
Students, 82–85, 132–33
with disabilities, 132–33
support for, 82–85
Sullivan, T., sociology course of, 168–74
Summative assessment, training in, 135–39
Support services, 69–85
academic counseling and advising, 72–76
access to, 82
from libraries, 76–81
online, 74–75, 82
for research, 76–81
for students, 82–85
for teachers, 82–85
Syllabi, 54–55, 151, 155, 157, 158, 167, 168
calendar view of, 158, 168
screenshots of, 151, 155, 157, 167
Synthetic thinking, 191–92

Taylor, L., 71
Teachers, 68–69, 82–85. *See also* Faculty
adjunct, 68–69, 98
peer assessment among, 97–100
support for, 82–85
training of. *See* Professional development; Teacher training
Teacher training, 5, 7, 12, 63, 82–85, 101–49. *See also* Faculty training workshop series; Professional development
acknowledging, 142–49
digital badges for, 145–49
finding leaders for, 103–8
identifying topics for, 110–12
inhouse workshops for, 108–10, 142–49
ongoing, 108–10, 139–42
rationale for, 101
workshops for, 112–39, 182
Teamwork, as essential skill, 86
Technical writing, hybrid course in, 182–86
challenges of, 186
Technology, 70–72, 105–6, 107, 112–19, 187–205
administrative support for, 105, 107
developing inhouse expertise in, 105–6
emerging trends in, 187
faculty training in, 112–19
hybrids and mobile learning, 188–99
role in student support, 70–72
Thompson, S., speech communication course of, 153–57
Tutor.com, 82
Tutoring services, 82

Ubiquitous learning. *See* Mobile learning
University of Central Florida (UCF), 7, 52–53, 147–48, 198
BlendKit workshop of, 7, 52, 147–48

registration system of, 52–53
University of Florida, 2
University of Miami, 2
University of North Carolina at
Chapel Hill, 2
University of Wisconsin (UW),
Flex Option of, 2
University of Wisconsin-
Milwaukee (UW-M), 6–7,
43, 96
faculty development workshop
series at, 111
Hybrid Learning website, 6–7,
43
Learning Technology Center
website, 96
U.S. Department of Education,
132

Van Duzer, J., 96
Vasquez, E., 133
Vaughan, N. D., 5

Vierke, J., biomedical
terminology course of,
166–68

Warnock, S., 66
Waters, J. K., 203
Weatherford, W., 207
Weiser, M., 199
Wiese, M., 203
Wiley, D., vii
Workshops. *See* Faculty training
workshop series; Teacher
training
"The World of/is Online"
activity, 129
Writing-Central/WC Online,
online tutoring via, 82
Writing-intensive hybrid courses,
174–86
English composition, 175–79

Xu, D., 13

AUTHORS

Joanna N. Paull earned her master's in English from Slippery Rock University and PhD from Indiana University of Pennsylvania. She has been teaching college English since 1998 but has been a professor of English at Lakeland Community College in Kirtland, Ohio, since 2007. She edited a collection titled *From Hip-Hop to Hyperlinks: Teaching about Culture in the Composition Classroom* (2008). Her departmental interests include online and hybrid pedagogy, including developing her online film course focused around the films of Quentin Tarantino. In addition to her classroom passions, she currently serves as Lakeland's curriculum coordinator, helping colleagues to develop new or modify existing curricula to adhere to campus guidelines. She has had her American Cinema course QM-certified and is a certified Quality Matters Peer Reviewer.

Jason Allen Snart received his master's in English from the University of Alberta, in Edmonton, Alberta, Canada, and his PhD in English from the University of Florida. He is currently professor of English at the College of DuPage, in Glen Ellyn, Illinois, where he has worked since 2002. His earlier books include *The Torn Book: UnReading William Blake's Marginalia* (2006) and *Hybrid Learning: The Perils and Promise of Blending Online and Face-to-Face Instruction in Higher Education* (2010). He has worked as the editor-in-chief for the Online Writing Instruction Open Resource (OWI OR), which he developed while serving on the NCTE/CCCC Effective Practices for Online Writing Instruction Committee. He is currently editor of the *Online Literacies Open Resource (OLOR)*, which is part of the Global Society for Online Literacy Educators (gSOLE).

This book was typeset in Sabon by Barbara Frazier.
Typefaces used on the cover include Museo 300 and Galaxie Polaris
Medium Condensed.
The book was printed on 50-lb. White Offset paper
by Versa Press, Inc.